TEAMBUILDING
with INDEX CARDS

180 activities for teachers, trainers, facilitators & group leaders of all kinds that turn ordinary index and playing cards into extraordinary teaching tools.

With index cards, colorful markers and a few simple props – you can create all of the training activities, team challenges, teaching lessons, icebreakers, puzzles, games & reviewing techniques in this book.

JIM CAIN, Ph.D.

Kendall Hunt
publishing company

Author of *Teamwork & Teamplay* and *Essential Staff Training Activities*

Cover image © Shutterstock.com
All interior photos taken by Jim Cain, except photos on pg 245 taken by activity participants.

www.kendallhunt.com
Send all inquiries to:
4050 Westmark Drive
Dubuque, IA 52004-1840

Copyright © 2019 by Jim Cain

ISBN 978-1-5249-6498-6

Published in the United States of America

CONTENTS

INTRODUCTION

A Little Inspiration and a True Story   v

INDEX CARD ACTIVITIES

1. Icebreakers and Opening Activities   1
2. Team Challenges   33
3. Puzzles and Games   89
4. Reviewing, Reflection, and Closing Activities   149
5. Creative Things to Do with Playing Cards   173
6. Special Activities for Teachers, Trainers, and Facilitators   191
7. Bonus Activities   215

CREATING YOUR OWN COLLECTION OF INDEX CARD ACTIVITIES

Recommendations, Tips, Ideas, and Suggestions for Creating and
Storing Your Own Collection of Index Card Games and Activities   235

RESOURCES AND REFERENCES

Books with Card Activities   239
About Jim Cain and Teamwork & Teamplay   245
The Teamwork & Teamplay Training Cards   247
The Teambuilding with Index Cards Playlist   248
What People Are Saying about Jim Cain's New Book *Teambuilding with Index Cards*   250

INTRODUCTION

A LITTLE INSPIRATION

I love books. I love libraries and bookstores and yard sales with books. Did I mention that I love books? I love everything about them, and over the years I've managed to collect some very interesting and unique publications from around the world.

One book in particular introduced me to another book that was the spark of inspiration for this book! The book *Everything I Need to Know I Learned from a Children's Book* by author Anita Silvey is filled with dozens of powerful books that inspired some of today's most noteworthy people. *Harold and the Purple Crayon* by author Crocket Johnson inspired such legendary authors as Maurice Sendak (*Where the Wild Things Are*) and Chris Van Allsburg (*Jumonji*, *The Polar Express*, *The Mysteries of Harris Burdick*). In it, Harold draws everything he needs for his adventures. What a great concept! Whatever you need, you can create yourself. Wouldn't it be great if you could create all the things you need for any occasion?

As a teacher, trainer, facilitator and group leader, I often find myself working and playing in social and professional groups. It can be invaluable to have a collection of tools and teambuilding props available at a moment's notice. But some of those props are too big and too heavy to bring along for every event. What I wouldn't give to be able to create a collection of useful props to assist me in my teambuilding adventures. Lightweight, easy to carry, inventive, creative, inexpensive, thought-provoking, powerful and oh so useful. Now where did I put that purple crayon?

So, thank you Crocket Johnson (and Harold!) for inspiring me. In this book I have created and collected a hundred and eighty unique card activities that you can share with your next audience. In fact, with some colorful markers, a few hundred index cards and some simple props, you can create <u>all</u> the activities mentioned in this book and have fun doing it.

I hope you enjoy this collection of powerful card activities that can be both playful and professional as required. Some of the most outstanding moments I've experienced working with groups have occurred while sharing these activities.

A TRUE STORY

A few years ago, I was scheduled to facilitate a teambuilding retreat for a new corporate client. My flight was delayed several hours and when I finally arrived at my destination, all my luggage was missing. It was now 2 a.m., I still had an hour's drive ahead of me and twenty people were coming to my workshop promptly at 8 a.m. I found a 24-hour discount store and purchased two packs of index cards, a can of tennis balls, 100 feet of rope and a pack of colorful markers. The next morning, I quickly created several of the card activities mentioned in this book and proceeded to facilitate a full day of teambuilding activities for the client, using only these minimal props—with outstanding results.

The next time you find yourself without your typical collection of teambuilding props or you just want to try something new, try some of the DIY teambuilding activities in this book. You'll be amazed how many different and unique activities you can present with such a minimal amount of equipment. Index card activities are inexpensive, lightweight, convenient, thought-provoking, powerful and fun. Good Luck!

Jim Cain
Teambuilding with Index Cards

*I recollect no conversation of the next day worth preserving, except one saying of
Dr. Samuel Johnson, which will be a valuable text for many decent old dowagers and other good
company in various circles to descant upon. He said, 'I am sorry I have not learnt to play at cards.
It is very useful in life: it generates kindness and consolidates society.'*

The Journal of a Tour to the Hebrides
James Boswell, 1786

ICEBREAKERS AND OPENING ACTIVITIES

CHAPTER ONE

This first chapter is a collection of icebreakers, get-acquainted games and opening activities that can all be facilitated with index cards. Not only are they great activities to start a program, they also create wonderful teachable moments with your participants.

NO.	ACTIVITY NAME	TEACHABLE MOMENT	IDEAL GROUP SIZE
1-1	The Big Question	Open Conversation	10 or more people
1-2	Autographs	Icebreaker	10 or more people
1-3	First Impressions	Delaying Judgment	Multiple groups of 3
1-4	Who Belongs to This Card?	Name Recognition	10 or more people
1-5	Thought for the Day	Powerful Quotes	Any
1-6	Have You Ever?	An Active Icebreaker	Groups of 10–30 people
1-7	Doodles	Creativity	Any
1-8	A Personal Pyramid	Character, Values, Beliefs	Multiple groups of 3–6
1-9	Are You More Like?	Icebreaker	10 or more people
1-10	Draw Me Your Story	Creative History Giving	Multiple groups of 2–3
1-11	Best / Worst / First	Icebreaker	10 or more people
1-12	Statistical Treasure Hunt	Mathematical Icebreaker	Multiple groups of 3–6
1-13	X Marks the Spot	Opening Activity	10 or more people
1-14	Crossword Names	Opening Activity	Multiple groups of 6–8
1-15	Story Cards	Icebreaker	Multiple small groups
1-16	Believe It or Not	Icebreaker	Any
1-17	Broken Tokens	Group Formation Technique	10 or more people
1-18	The Question Box	Icebreaker	Any
1-19	The To-Do List	Encouraging Participation	Any
1-20	The Soap Box	Commitment to the Group	Any
1-21	Links of Chain	Group Formation Activity	Multiple groups of 10

1-1 THE BIG QUESTION

A get-acquainted activity with interesting questions, simple instructions and one that makes finding a partner a breeze.

Begin your preparation for this activity by writing interesting questions on index cards, one question per card. You can find a dozen great questions on the next page of this activity description, and if you need even more questions, there is an app for that. The Question of the Day app has a great collection of interesting questions. There is also a published book version of this app, by Al Katkowksy, called *Question of the Day* (ISBN 978-1-59963-292-6). For still more questions, see the publication list at the end of this activity description.

Next, invite each member of your audience to take a question card and find a partner. One person in each group of two reads the question on their card and their partner answers it. Then the other partner reads the question on their card and their partner answers it. When the conversation is complete, partners switch cards with each other (so now they each have a new question) and raise their new card high above their head (the sign for *I'm looking for a new partner*). The activity continues with partners trading questions, answers and finally cards before moving on to a new partner.

One of the things I like most about this activity is that even with large groups, the actual interactions are only between two people. I also like to choose questions that are nonthreatening, so that even complete strangers can easily discuss them.

For this activity, you can create the required number of question cards in advance or you can provide your audience with blank cards and ask them to each write an interesting question on their own card.

While facilitating The Big Question for the first day of classes at a small high school (about 180 students), I noticed one freshman boy standing quietly off to the side of the group. I looked over the crowd and suggested, "Why don't you take that guy over there as your next partner?" as I pointed to an athletic-looking senior standing nearby. "Well, that guy is the captain of our football team," he said. "I'm not really in the same league as a guy like that."

So, I temporarily stopped the activity and walked over to the football captain and asked him, "When you raise your card into the air, are you open to anyone in this room being your next partner?" "Absolutely," he said, and quickly waved over his younger classmate to join him.

A few days later, one of the teachers from the school emailed me and said there had been a shift in the behavior of the students in the school. "Tell me about it," I said. "Well," she said, "the cafeteria is different. In the past students typically grouped together with the students from their same class year. Now students are mingling and sitting everywhere. That card activity did a great job breaking down barriers between our students."

For a national conference, I was asked to present a workshop for about three hundred people. When the time came for my workshop to begin, only about eighty people were present, as more continued to slowly arrive from other locations. Rather than start an activity and have to restart and reexplain it every few minutes, I had a better plan.

I invited the eighty or so folks in the room to each take an index card and write down a question they could ask someone if they were interviewing them for a local radio talk show. Then I instructed them how to play The Big Question. Next, I stood in the doorway and as more participants joined us, I simply handed them an index card and said (as I pointed to the group in the middle of the room already engaged in the activity), "Ask them what to do."

Participants entered the room and were immediately pulled into the game, and those already playing were glad to help newcomers with their question cards and the rules of the game.

You can facilitate this activity using the Teamwork & Teamplay Training Cards, pictured here. This deck of cards includes three levels of The Big Question on each card. Level One is for groups that do not know each other. Level Two is for groups that are somewhat familiar with each other, and Level Three is for groups that know each other very well. There are fifty-two questions for each level, for a total of one hundred fifty-six wonderful questions. These cards are available from www.trainerswarehouse.com and www.training-wheels.com.

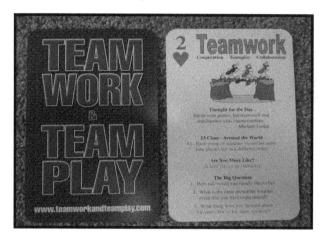

INTERESTING QUESTIONS FOR THE BIG QUESTION

If you could replace a character in any book you have ever read, what role would you play? When was the last time you were truly surprised? What is the most unusual thing you have ever eaten? Tell me about one of your family's funniest stories. Name three things you really like about yourself. Of all your life's accomplishments so far, of which one are you most proud? Which is your favorite pair of shoes and why? What makes your best friend your best friend? Describe a perfect day. You have just won two tickets to a future concert or sporting event—what event is it and who would you take with you? Name three people you admire. What is something that you will never forget? Who inspires you? Who is your most unique relative, and why? What have you done that you never thought you could? What are you waiting for? If you could change cultures, what culture would you like to experience? When was the last time you danced? What are you grateful for?

You can find sixty amazing questions for this activity in the book *Find Something To Do!* (ISBN 978-0-9882046-0-7) by Jim Cain, available from www.healthylearning.com, www.training-wheels.com and www.amazon.com. For even more sources of interesting questions, read the following:

The Book of Questions by Gregory Stock (three versions available)
Spill Your Guts! The Ultimate Conversation Game by Bob Basso & Andrews McMeel
If- Questions for the Game of Life by Evelyn McFarland and James Saywell
Think Twice—An Entertaining Collection of Choices by Bret Nicholaus and Paul Lowrie
Question of the Day by Al Katkowsky (also available as a smart phone app)
You Gotta Be Kidding! The Crazy Book of Questions by Horn, Ring & Fierz

AUTOGRAPHS

An Icebreaking Activity from Teamwork & Teamplay

Write your first name in the block to the right. Then find a partner and have them sign one block on this paper. Ask them to sign at the top of the block if they have done the activity in the block or sign at the bottom of the block if they have not done it.

HELLO, MY NAME IS:

Your first name here, in big letters.

I have done this signature

EXAMPLE: HAS GONE WATER SKIING

I have not done this signature

Knows someone famous

Has an unusual hobby

Knows how to program a DVR

Has been to Mount Rushmore

Has many siblings

Has ridden a camel or elephant

Had an unusual job

Collects something interesting

Plays a musical instrument

Can speak a foreign language

Likes their dentist

Has been to summer camp

Would bungie jump if the opportunity occurred

Has performed on stage

Works as hard as you do

Looks the most like you

1-2 AUTOGRAPHS

An inspired variation of the classic icebreaker Name Bingo.

Collecting signatures (autographs) is a classic icebreaking activity. You may have played an earlier version of this activity known as Name Bingo. On the previous page you will find my favorite variation of this classic icebreaker.

Begin by providing each participant with a copy of the Autograph activity and a pencil or pen. Then invite participants to collect signatures for the top and bottom of each block. Partners sign the top of the block if they have done this particular thing and the bottom of the block if they have not. Although the instructions for this activity are clearly printed at the upper left corner of the page, I find it helpful to present these same instructions verbally before the activity begins.

In this version of the game, every person you meet becomes important because they can either answer yes or no to any topic on the page. For example, if the topic is "plays a musical instrument," your partner will sign the top portion of the block if they play a music instrument or the bottom portion if they do not. Either way, their signature is needed.

You are welcome to photocopy the Autograph page from this activity description and then print it onto large index cards, or heavy index-grade paper. Then invite your audience to mingle and find people to sign the upper and lower portion of each block.

In my training programs, I like to use what I call the TGR model for group dynamics. TGR stands for Task, Growth and Relationships, the three ingredients that I believe make up a high performing work group or team. In the game of Autographs, participants are typically focused on gathering autographs and filling in all the blocks on their sheet of paper. Halfway through this

activity, I typically stop the group, share the TGR model, and then invite them to continue, but focus less on completing the task (filling their sheet with signatures) and more on the relationship component (hearing the story behind the signature). On the sheet for example, there is a statement that says, "has ridden a camel or elephant." For those who have, you know there must be a story behind that event. Encourage participants to listen to the stories in addition to gathering signatures.

You can find this activity and many more creative icebreakers in the book *100 Activities That Build Unity, Community & Connection* (ISBN 978-1-60679-374-9) by Jim Cain, available from www.healthylearning.com, www.training-wheels.com and www.amazon.com.

1-3 FIRST IMPRESSIONS

A Get-Acquainted Activity from Teamwork & Teamplay

Form a group of three with two other participants that you do not know very well (yet) and have a seat. Within this group, you are to guess the following traits about your partners. This is not a conversation or an interview, but a guessing game. For each trait, make your best guess and write that guess in the outer spaces below. When each of the three participants in your group has finished, begin sharing your guesses and then the true information about each trait with the other members of your group. How many traits did you guess correctly?

Person on your left side			*Person on your right side*	
Your Guess	The Truth	Traits	The Truth	Your Guess
		Where were they raised? (farm, city, suburbs, etc.)		
		What would be a perfect gift for them?		
		What is their favorite food?		
		What type of music do they listen to?		
		What talent or skill do they possess?		
		What do you have in common with this person?		

1-3 FIRST IMPRESSIONS

This activity explores the quality of our first impressions.

The ability to form instant impressions of the people we meet each day is a reality. But in some cases, our first impressions may not be accurate. This activity encourages participants to share their first impressions with two other members of the group and then explore the accuracy of these impressions.

You can conduct this activity by photocopying the information on the previous page or writing several topics on a flip chart or whiteboard and inviting your audience to write their first impressions on a large index card. This activity is most profound when partners do not know much about each other in advance of the activity. However, even long-term partners or work teammates often draw new insights from this activity, long after they thought they knew their partners.

Begin by inviting your participants to form groups of three and have a seat. Then ask each person to guess the traits shown on the previous page about each of their partners. This first part of the activity is not a conversation or an interview, but rather a guessing game.

When everyone in the group is finished writing down their guesses, players share what they have written and then find out the truth for each trait. Players keep track of how many traits they guessed correctly and incorrectly. Continue sharing until all topics have been discussed.

In addition to the traits listed on the previous page, you may consider substituting some of the following for your version of this activity:

What is their favorite toy? Sport? TV show? Vacation location? Automobile? Sports team? Beverage? What does their desk (workspace) look like? How many books do they read each year? What would they do on their day off? What motivates them? How many languages do they speak? What adventures have they had? What kinds of house do they live in? How many people are in their family? What is their occupation? What kind of education have they had? What kind of vehicle do they drive? What month is their birthday? How would they define success? Where were they born? What holidays do they celebrate? What challenges them? What do they do that makes the world a better place? What musical instrument would they play? What movie is their favorite?

You can find this activity in *Essential Staff Training Activities* (ISBN 978-0-7575-6167-2) available from www.kendallhunt.com and in the book *100 Activities That Build Unity, Community & Connection* (ISBN 978-1-60679-374-9) available from www.healthylearning.com.

1-4 WHO BELONGS TO THIS CARD?

A nametag icebreaker that will test the short-term memory of your group.

Here is a brilliant technique for learning the names of people in your group, especially when business cards or removable nametags are available.

Invite your audience to hold their business card or nametag in one hand. For the first round of the game, ask everyone to find a partner and introduce themselves. At the end of the introduction, partners switch cards or nametags.

For the next exchange (and beyond), each person introduces themselves when meeting a new partner, but then also produces the card or nametag they are holding and points out this person to their new partner as well. "Hi, I am Jim. But that person over there (pointing) is Kirk." At the end of conversation, partners again switch cards or nametags and the activity continues.

After five or six exchanges, the facilitator halts the game and invites everyone to return the business card or nametag they are holding to the original owner (introducing themselves when they do). Then play this game again and encourage your audience to meet different people in the second round of the game.

If you don't happen to have business cards or nametags available for this activity, you can still play by having everyone write their first and last name on an index card. You can also invite participants to draw a self-portrait on the index card next to their name.

I first learned a variation of this activity from Chris Cavert, which he calls That Person Over There. Chris's latest book is *Portable Teambuilding Activities—Games, Initiatives and Team Challenges for Any Space* (ISBN 978-1-9390-1914-1). For more information about this book and other great books and ideas from Chris Cavert, visit www.fundoing.com.

1-5 THOUGHT FOR THE DAY

An inspirational technique for bringing positive content into the first activity of the day.

Here is an inspirational way to begin a meeting, workshop, training event or class. Begin by preparing index cards with inspirational quotes that reflect the theme of your gathering. Then pass out these cards, one per person, and invite everyone to find a partner and share the inspiration written on their card. Encourage partners to reflect on the words of each inspiration and to explore the meaning there. Then invite partners to exchange cards and to find a new partner, repeating the process several times.

This is a brilliant way to incorporate content into the very first activity of your program. Participants are immediately presented with positive content that explores the very theme for which they have gathered today. You can find inspirational quotations at such websites as www.brainyquote.com and www.values.com. Just input the keyword of your choice and a multitude of powerful quotations and inspirational messages are generated. As an example, imagine that one of the themes of your next event is teamwork. I would generate enough cards for everyone attending (plus a few extras just in case), including the following quote that is currently hanging on my office wall:

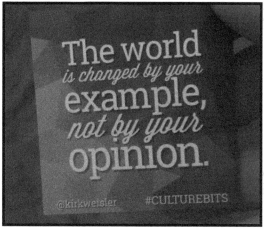

"Here's my advice for every day – a little teamwork and a lot of teamplay." —Jim Cain

The reflection and exploration of each message can be a significant part of this activity. To help participants with this process, you can write some of the following questions on the back of each card, or on a flip chart or white board that is easily visible to the group.

What do you think the author of this message was trying to convey with their words?
When was this message written? What was going on in the world at that time?
How would you rewrite this message in more modern language?
What words are most important in this message?

My friend and colleague Kirk Weisler (www.kirkweisler.com) is an inspirational guy. Kirk has a spot on his website where you can read his collection of T4D (Thought for the Day) quotations, inspirations and messages of all kinds (including the one shown here on his business card). Kirk wins my award for positive attitude, and his website reflects that admirable quality.

1-6 HAVE YOU EVER?

An active way to get to know each other and share common experiences.

In this active icebreaker, up to thirty participants form a large circle with each person standing on some type of place-marker, such as an index card. If you happen to have more than thirty people, I recommend creating multiple circles. One person stands slightly inside the perimeter of each circle, on a differently colored index card and becomes the first speaker. This speaker then says the phrase, "Have you ever…?" and completes the sentence by sharing something that is true for them. For example, "Have you ever… played sports in high school?"

At this point, anyone in the group who has played a sport in high school must change location. While each person is seeking a new location to stand, the speaker also attempts to find a new location. At the completion of each round, the person standing on the differently colored index card becomes the speaker for the next round.

There are two variations of this activity that I enjoy. First, before sharing their "Have You Ever" content, have speakers introduce themselves to the group and invite the entire group to greet them. Second, anytime a speaker has done something that no one else in the group has done, they receive a standing ovation of applause from the group.

I also like to give the speaker a very visible location to stand, just inside the perimeter of the circle. A speaker in the center has their back to half of the circle at any time. Near the perimeter, the speaker has a better chance of being heard by a majority of the group. Keeping the maximum circle size to about thirty participants also enables the majority of the group to easily hear the person speaking.

Have You Never? You can flip the focus of this activity from things that you have done to things that you have never done, by changing the phrase "Have you ever…?" to the phrase "Have you never…?" For example, "Have you never… ridden in a limo?" "Have you never… been to Spain?" "Have you never… scored 100% on a math test?"

You can find this activity and many more in the book *100 Activities That Build Unity, Community & Connection* (ISBN 978-1-60679-374-9) by Jim Cain, available from www.amazon.com and the American Camp Association bookstore at www.healthylearning.com.

1-7 DOODLES

Complete each illustration below by drawing, writing, sketching, scribbling or doodling something in each square.

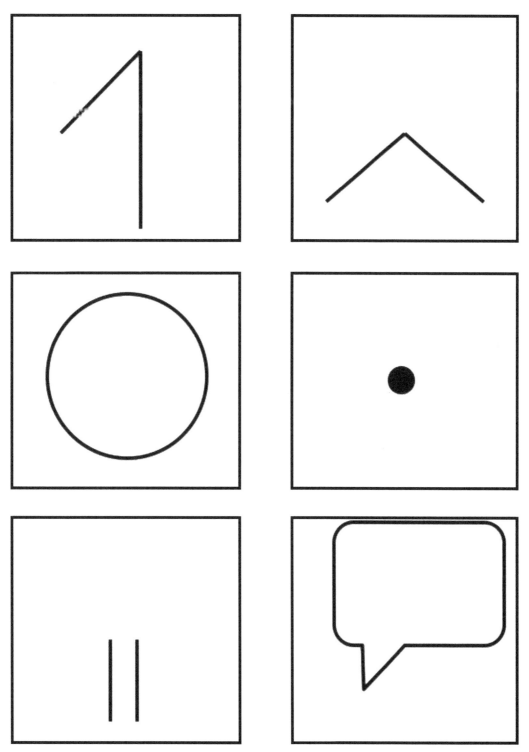

1-7 DOODLES

Doodle (n.)—*an absentminded scribble that can have significant meaning.*

On the previous page you'll find a ready-to-copy sheet with six doodle frames. Make copies of this page for each of your participants and invite them to complete each illustration by drawing, writing, sketching, scribbling or doodling something in each of the six squares. Provide a variety of artistic drawing instruments such as colored pencils, pens, markers and crayons. When everyone in your group has completed the task, present the following information, square by square, and discuss the questions at the end of each commentary.

SQUARE 1: IMAGINATION

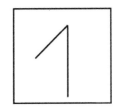

> *Imagination is more important than knowledge.*
> —*Albert Einstein*

> *Use your imagination not to scare yourself to death but to inspire yourself to life.*
> —Adele Brookman

This block illustrates how you use your imagination. If you draw numbers here, you have a mathematical imagination. If you draw objects, such as a golf flag, sailboat or kite, you are inventive. If you draw natural objects, such as a tree, you enjoy nature in your world. Question: What have you dreamed of that has yet to become reality?

SQUARE 2: FOUNDATION

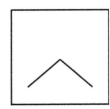

> *If you have built castles in the air, your work need not be lost;*
> *that is where they should be. Now put the foundations under them.*
> —Henry David Thoreau

This block illustrates your foundation or support system in life. If you draw a house or barn, you have a classic foundation based on structure. If you draw irregular geometric patterns or objects, your foundation is often chaotic and changing. If you draw people or faces, you pull support from other people in your life. Question: Who can you depend upon for support?

SQUARE 3: SELF-IMAGE

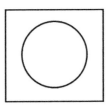

> *One of the multiple intelligences defined by Howard Garner.*

This block is how you see yourself. If you draw a face, it is your own self-image! If you draw objects, those objects speak of what you believe defines your life. A clock denotes attention to the passing of time. A pizza, awareness of food. A coin reflects a focus on things financial. A ball, spiral, balloon or target, playfulness. Question: Name one thing that you can do really well.

SQUARE 4: CREATIVITY

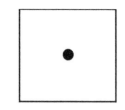

Creativity is the power to connect the seemingly unconnected.
—William Plomer

To invent, you need a good imagination and a pile of junk.
—Thomas A. Edison

This block gives insight to your creative process. If you draw simple shapes with minimal lines, your creative process is simple and straight-forward. If you draw multiline patterns or complicated illustrations you are a complex thinker and probably know how to program your DVR or create your own app or web page. Question: What have you invented or thought about inventing?

SQUARE 5: HOPES, DREAMS, AND ASPIRATIONS

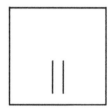

The biggest adventure you can ever take is to live the life of your dreams.
—Oprah Winfrey

This block reveals your hopes, dreams and aspirations. If you draw something vertical, such as a ladder, rocket ship, tall building or tree, you have high hopes. If you draw something like a fence or doorway, you see barriers to moving forward. If you draw natural objects, such as a tree or flower, you dream of wide-open spaces. Question: What is a goal you have set for yourself to accomplish in the next five years? Ten years? Twenty years?

SQUARE 6: WHAT'S ON YOUR MIND?

What would you write here as your personal quotation?
—You

This final block is your personal statement. It reveals a word or message that you find important. Hello and Hi are both common, but other words often appear. If you draw only outside the thought balloon, you are a maverick and like to play without rules. If you draw in bold letters, you are confident in public. If you combined words and pictures, you are comfortable expressing yourself. Question: If you could have any bumper sticker on your car, what would it say?

There is absolutely no scientific data connecting your doodles here to any of the six characteristics I've mentioned. This is simply a playful way to discuss some interesting details of both art and human nature. Have fun and don't take the answers or yourself too seriously.

You can find this activity and many more in the book *100 Activities That Build Unity, Community & Connection* (ISBN 978-1-60679-374-9) by Jim Cain, available from www.amazon.com and the American Camp Association bookstore at www.healthylearning.com.

1-8 A PERSONAL PYRAMID

A simple technique for sharing your values and beliefs.

Here is a very simple but powerful way of inviting your audience to share their values and beliefs with a partner. Begin with a collection of cards on which words of character have been written. Then ask each member of your audience to create a six-card pyramid, based upon the following criteria.

The three cards at the bottom form your foundation. These cards express three traits that you currently possess. The two cards on the next level identify two traits with which you sometimes struggle or find difficult. The final card at the top of the pyramid is something to which you aspire.

After each participant has created their own personal pyramid, invite them to present it to a partner or a small group and explore each level of the pyramid together.

Here are a few words that you might consider using for this activity:

Citizenship	Cooperation	Patience	Flexibility	Humor
Resourcefulness	Leadership	Integrity	Humility	Trust
Perseverance	Gratitude	Tolerance	Teamwork	Grit
Responsibility	Confidence	Courage	Creativity	Faith
Determination	Commitment	Tenacity	Wisdom	Love
Positive Attitude	Playfulness	Honesty	Stability	Hope
Appreciating Diversity	Competency	Inspiration	Optimism	Honor
Sustainability	Helpfulness	Resiliency	Stability	Skill
Common Sense	Truthfulness	Endurance	Fairness	Joy
Community Service	Enthusiasm	Motivation	Reliability	Caring
Accountability	Adaptability	Self-Control	Fortitude	Empathy
Communication	Compassion	Imagination	Respect	Kindness
Cheerfulness	Dependability	Authenticity	Diversity	Balance

You can use the Teamwork & Teamplay Training Cards (available from www.healthylearning.com, www.training-wheels.com or www.trainerswarehouse.com) for this activity or create your own deck of words from the list provided, with index cards. You can also invite your participants to create a collection of cards for this activity using words of their own choice.

1-9 ARE YOU MORE LIKE?

A quick way to meet people and explore choices.

This activity is a variation of The Big Question, found earlier in this chapter. For this icebreaker, participants are asked to make a choice. Explanations are not required, but invited. For example, which are you more like—a sparkler or a firecracker?

Invite each of your participants to take (or create) a question card and find a partner. One person in each group of two reads the question on their card and their partner answers it. Then the other partner reads the question on their card and the first person answers it. When the conversation is complete, partners switch cards with each other (so now they each have a new question) and raise their new card high above their head (the sign for *I'm looking for a new partner*). Next, form a new partnership with anyone holding a card high in the air and the activity continues.

Here are a few examples of questions for this activity. Are you more like:

Bookstores or Libraries • Words or Numbers • PC or Mac • Car or Truck • Odd or Even • Football or Soccer • Spicy or Mild • Caffeinated or Decaffeinated • Lobster or Shrimp • Text Message or Voice Message Software or Hardware • A Firecracker or a Sparkler • Dine In or Carry Out • Professional Sports or Amateur Sports • Walking or Running Escalator or Elevator • Speaking or Listening • Paper or Plastic • Canoe or Kayak • Student or Teacher • Bagel or Donut • Camper or Tent Crayons or Finger-paints • Backpack or Briefcase • Bacon or Sausage Pancakes or Waffles • Salt or Pepper • Carpet or Wooden Floor • Roller Skates or Ice Skates • Peppermint or Spearmint • Window or Aisle Weekday or Weekend • Star Wars or Star Trek • Day or Night • Candle or Flashlight • Lemon or Lime • Stop Light or Stop Sign • Hotel or B&B

I like to play a fast-moving version of this activity that I call a *frenzy*. The goal in this version is for everyone in the group to meet each other in just three minutes. The speed of this version minimizes the awkwardness that sometimes occurs when two strangers meet for the first time. Playing fast is an excellent way to meet many people quickly and without hesitation. This can be especially helpful when your audience is not familiar with each other.

You can find dozens of these questions on the *Teamwork & Teamplay Training Cards*, available from www. healthylearning.com, www.training-wheels.com or www.trainerswarehouse.com, and even more in the book *Are You More Like?—1001 Colorful Quandaries for Quality Conversations* (ISBN 978-1-8854-7341-9) by Chris Cavert and Susana Acousta.

1-10 DRAW ME YOUR STORY

Exploring the concept that a picture is worth a thousand words.

This get-acquainted activity invites partners to learn about each other by drawing pictures rather than speaking. I like to use this activity when my group contains multicultural people that do not speak a common language. First, present each group of two people with several large index cards and a few colorful markers or crayons. Next, ask them to take turns drawing a picture of each of the following items:

The house where you first lived	Your family	Your favorite hobby
Something you wish for	Your job	A sport you enjoy
A map of where you now live	Your vehicle	Your favorite food
Your ideal vacation location	Your pet	Your best friend

You can complete this entire activity in complete silence, or after completing the drawing part of this activity, you can invite partners to ask each other questions about their drawings and share insights.

I first experienced a version of this activity at an Outward Bound International Symposium in Ontario, Canada. Andy Martin, author of *Outdoor and Experiential Learning* (ISBN 978-0-5660-8628-X), shared this activity from his collection of holistic and drama-based learning, many of which are part of the Inner Touch program of Outward Bound in the Czech Republic.

I had the opportunity to travel to Guilin, China and work with the talented staff of a youth camp. After two weeks together, the group had grown quite close. As one of their many closing activities, the camp leadership, staff and campers each contributed to creating a mural detailing in graphic illustration all the major events of their experience together.

If you enjoy this activity, you might also enjoy reading *Show Me A Story—40 Craft Projects and Activities to Spark Children's Storytelling* by Emily Neuburger (ISBN 978-1-6034-2988-7).

You can find this activity and many more in *100 Activities That Build Unity, Community & Connection* (ISBN 978-1-60679-374-9) by Jim Cain, available from www.amazon.com and the American Camp Association bookstore (www.healthylearning.com).

1-11 BEST / WORST / FIRST

Icebreaker questions for groups of three.

My favorite way to introduce this activity is to present one-third of the audience with an index card on which the following information has been written. Then invite them to find two additional partners and form groups of three, discussing the questions on their card. This simple technique will place one-third of your audience in a leadership role, as they organize and perform the activity.

Best / Worst / First

Collect two other people and discuss the following information:

What was your BEST meal ever?
What was your WORST summer job?
Tell me about your FIRST day of work.
What is the BEST book you have ever read?
What was the WORST movie that you still watched from beginning to end?
What would be your ideal FIRST date?

If time allows, you can form new groups of three and discuss the following questions found on the backside of each card.

Where was the BEST hotel you have ever visited?
What was the WORST weather you have ever experienced?
What was the FIRST thing you ever purchased using a credit card?
What day of your life was the BEST ever?
What was the WORST food you have ever eaten?
What was the FIRST time you traveled outside the country?

1-12 STATISTICAL TREASURE HUNT

A mathematical group discovery activity.

The challenge of this activity is to add up the total score for each item below for every member of your group. Then compare your group's score with the score of other groups. Take time during the completion of this activity to discuss some of these quantities with the members of your group.

Total number of lottery tickets you have ever bought

The average number of books you read each year

The number of friends you have on social media

The number of brothers and sisters you have

The number of countries you have visited

The number of languages you can speak

Your height in inches (or cm)

The number of pets you own

Total Score = _____

1-12 STATISTICAL TREASURE HUNT

A mathematical group discovery activity.

Here is an icebreaker that incorporates mathematics. Present each group of six participants with a copy of the statistical treasure hunt criteria (found on the previous page). Instruct them to add up the total score for each item on the list for every member of their group.

Encourage each group to take time during the completion of this activity to discuss some of these quantities with the other members of their group. For example, when discussing how many siblings there are, which group member has the most? Or, do any of the various siblings in the group have the same first name? Explore opportunities to learn about each other, find commonalities and celebrate every category that builds unity, community and connection.

If you elect to create your own statistical treasure hunt sheet, be sure to include categories that are specific to the age, industry or interests of your participants.

The final tallies for each group can often vary by orders

of magnitude, depending on the criteria being investigated. Choose topics that create conversation, such as the number of countries you have visited (and which one was your favorite).

You can find this activity and many more in the *Teamwork & Teamplay International Edition* (ISBN 978-0-9882046-3-8) by Jim Cain, available from www.amazon.com, www.training-wheels.com and the American Camp Association bookstore at www.healthylearning.com.

1-13 X MARKS THE SPOT

A test of your group's observation skills.

I like to plan a few activities for my events that can begin even before the official start of the program. This is a great way to engage participants the minute they arrive.

Begin by writing a large X on an index card and then placing this card somewhere visible from the meeting space. Before the start of your program, invite everyone to casually search the area until they locate the X card. Instruct them not to give away the position of the card, or move it. When they have discovered the location of the X card, they can take a seat.

Depending on the observations skills of your group, you can modify the size of the object used in this activity. I sometimes use wooden letters available at most craft stores. Coins of various sizes work well, too. There are even artists that place "found art" in their workshops and wait to see who will discover them during the event. You can search Pinterest.com for many more examples of found art.

When I was a kid and found myself at the dentist's office, they occasionally had *Highlights Magazine*. One of the features of the magazine was a line drawing of a scene in which various familiar objects (a hammer, a face, a chair) would be carefully drawn into the scenery. A list of all the "hidden" objects was provided and I tried to find as many objects as I could. For your next event, take a photograph of a dozen or so objects (make copies of this photo for each "search party" group) and then place these objects around your meeting location. Before the program begins, invite everyone who arrived early to form small groups and search for these objects (but do not move them from their hiding place). You have now created a three-dimensional treasure hunt. In addition to the photograph of objects, you can also provide a clue for each object, such as "the thing you seek is near a week," for an object you hide near a calendar. Happy hunting!

For many years Reverend Gabe Campbell was the featured speaker at the Ohio State 4-H Leadership Camp. Gabe had an amazing collection of group activities and was one of the first speakers I witnessed who combined group dynamics, games, storytelling and training in one amazing experience. One morning at this camp, we all gathered together for a session with Gabe. Chairs had been placed in pods of three throughout the training space, but before we found a seat, Gabe asked us to walk around until we found a nickel he had placed somewhere on the floor (without giving away the location to anyone else). For several minutes the group milled about, until one by one, people began to take their seats. Eventually everyone found the nickel and a seat, and the program officially started. Gabe pointed out that if we are observant, and know what we are looking for, we just might find it—and he used that metaphor as the start of his workshop. A teachable moment indeed.

In many of the game books of the early 1900s you'll find a similar activity known as Huckle Buckle Beanstalk. In this game, the object is for players to find a hidden object and then return to a central location, sit down, and say "Huckle buckle beanstalk," denoting that they have found the object, but without giving away its location.

1-14 CROSSWORD NAMES

Four ways to play with names.

Start this activity by presenting each group of six people (seated around a table or comfortably seated on the floor) with a collection of index cards and markers. Invite each person to take the same number of index cards as letters in their first name and to print one capital letter on each card. Jim, for example, would need three cards, one with a J, one with an I, and the third with an M printed on it. When everyone in the group has completed their cards, challenge the group to create a crossword puzzle–like collection of letters, spelling out each person's name in the group, with all cards connected to each other.

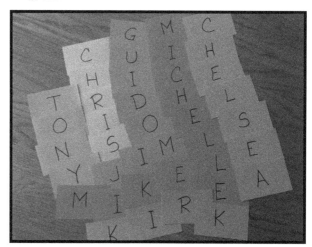

Then invite the group to shuffle the letter cards and see how many different words they can create using the letters available. Encourage each group to keep track of their word count. Highest number of words (three letters or longer) wins! These words will come in handy for the fourth version of this activity.

Next, challenge each group to create the longest single word (most letters) they can with the letters they have available.

Finally, as a fourth version of this activity, invite each group to again create a crossword puzzle, but this time making words with the letters available, rather than names. Encourage each group to continue playing this fourth round until they have no letters remaining.

I discovered an interesting teachable moment with this Crossword Names activity. If your team happens to create words such as *teamwork*, *accountability*, *engagement* or other positive words, notice that these words are only possible with contributions from multiple members of the group. The word *teamwork*, for example, consists of letters taken from the name cards of several members of the group. Metaphorically this suggests that teamwork requires the contribution of the entire group to happen. What positive words can you create from the members of your next team?

My friend and colleague Chris Cavert and I are always creating new activities. Crossword Names is one of Chris's most recent activities using index cards, which he offered to me for inclusion in this book. Thanks Chris! You can find several index card activities in Chris's book *Portable Teambuilding Activities* (ISBN 978-1-939019-14-1) and more great ideas at www.fundoing.com.

1-15 STORY CARDS

An artistic technique for storytelling.

Story Cards are a way to illustrate some of the most significant events of a person's life. For this icebreaking activity, provide your audience with a variety of index cards, tags or other interesting paper and colorful writing tools, stickers and (my favorite) scrapbooking embellishments. Next, invite them to draw five events from their life and then be prepared to share and discuss these illustrations within a small group of four to six people.

Story Cards enable people to express themselves visually and verbally. I've chosen major milestones in life for my version of Story Cards. You might consider other themes, including first day of school, your work team, your sport team, things you collect, what inspires you, your favorite foods, your favorite animals, places you have lived, or your favorite books, poems, songs, movies, etc.

Be sure to allow adequate time for everyone to present and discuss what they have created.

If you like, you can choose more topics for inclusion in this activity, so that the final artistic index card is crowded with content. But be aware, the greater the number of images, the longer it will take for each participant to present their card to their audience.

Over the years, I've discovered some interesting activities that make it easy for participants to tell their personal story. I included the activity Wrapped Around My Finger in the *Book of Raccoon Circles* (ISBN 978-0-7575-3265-8), which invites participants to introduce themselves to their small group and continue talking until they have completed wrapping a piece of string or climbing webbing (known as a Raccoon Circle) around their index finger.

Next comes a storytelling rope activity where the length of the rope is the entire lifeline of the storyteller. As the storyteller walks along the length of the rope, they tell some of the major events in their life. Other members of the group join the storyteller as they walk along the length of the rope. When the storyteller reaches the location of the present day in their life timeline, they mention something they are looking forward to in their future.

For the book *100 Activities That Build Unity, Community & Connection* I included a storytelling activity that I created for a training workshop. I needed a no-prop activity that I could share in limited space, so I invited participants to link elbows with two other partners and take ten steps together while telling their partners ten significant events that have occurred in their life. After using this activity a few times, I trimmed the list down to just five significant events and named the activity The Walk of Life.

But of all the techniques I've seen, used or experienced, one of the most profound techniques I've discovered was included in my book *Rope Games* (ISBN 978-0-9882046-1-4). Story Ropes are the creation of Marge Malwitz and you can read about them at www.margemalwitz.blogspot.com. Included there are videos, photographs and dozens of stories about the Story Rope experience, where participants use a variety of colorful and creative objects to weave a rope that tells the story of their life!

If you enjoy these storytelling activities, see the book *Show Me A Story—40 Craft Projects and Activities to Spark Children's Storytelling* by Emily Neuburger (ISBN 978-1-6034-2988-7) and try the activity The Box in the book *100 Activities That Build Unity, Community & Connection* by Jim Cain (ISBN 978-1-60679-374-9).

1-16 BELIEVE IT OR NOT

A game of interesting disclosure.

This simple icebreaking activity is an excellent way for participants to share interesting and unique experiences in their lives. To prepare for this activity, you'll need several index or playing cards, one of which has been altered to contain the phrase "Believe it or not." The rest of the cards are either blank index cards or unmodified playing cards.

Invite each member of your group to select a card at random from those available. The person selecting the Believe It or Not card is invited to share something interesting about themselves, such as "I have a twin brother." This statement can be true or false. The other members of the group can then ask three questions, after which they must decide whether to believe the speaker or not. After this vote, the speaker then reveals whether their statement was true or false.

Then, collect the cards, shuffle them, redistribute them and invite the next person holding the Believe It or Not card to reveal something unique or unusual, and the activity continues.

Believe It or Not is one of the few activities I know that can be played over and over again with the same audience, and the level of disclosure and discovery increases as participants become more and more familiar (and trusting) with the other members of their group. Initially participants share simple and typically nonrevealing disclosures, but as time passes, familiarity and trust increase within the membership of a group, and deeper and more significant disclosures occur.

Over the years, I've heard some amazing "Believe it or not" statements from the members of my audience. One participant mentioned that "my heart is on the other side"! Which turned out to be a true statement. Another suggested that he was Superman (and proceeded to show us his full-size chest tattoo of the classic S of Superman). But what is most interesting about Believe It or Not is the opportunity for participants to share some of the things that make them truly unique.

———————————

Long before Believe It or Not was an index card activity, it was one of my favorite Raccoon Circle (rope) activities. It was originally called Believe It or Knot, because the person nearest the knot on each rope was the one to speak in each small circle group.

You can find a collection of Raccoon Circle activities at www.teamworkandteamplay.com, and nearly 200 Raccoon Activities in *The Revised and Expanded Book of Raccoon Circles* (ISBN 978-0-7575-3265-8) by Jim Cain and Tom Smith. This book is also available in Chinese and Japanese. Contact author Jim Cain for more information about these international editions. You can also find some additional Raccoon Circle activities in *The Teamwork & Teamplay International Edition* (ISBN 978-0-9882-0463-8) by Jim Cain, translated into sixteen different languages in one single book!

Also, visit the Teamwork & Teamplay website to download a free PDF document with more than a dozen Raccoon Circle activities, icebreakers and games, at www.teamworkandteamplay.com.

1-17 BROKEN TOKENS

Token (n.)—A visible or tangible representation (a symbol) of a fact or feeling.

A Broken Token is an object that has been cut into two (or more) pieces. When all the pieces are reunited, the token becomes whole again.

I like to use the Broken Token activity as a creatively random way to form groups at the start of a program. With a little preparation, you can create groups from two to ten people with ease. First, you'll need to decide what group size you would ideally like to create. Next, you'll need to collect sufficient index cards (of many shapes, sizes, colors and textures) and cut these into the same number of pieces as your ideal group size. Then mix all your broken index cards together in a large bowl and invite your audience to select one piece and then find the rest of their new group.

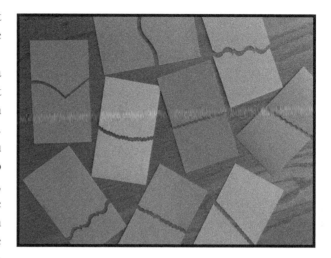

Index cards are not the only things you can use to make your broken tokens. You can also use comic strips, jigsaw puzzle pieces, wood blocks cut into unique shapes, playing cards that have been uniquely cut in half, paint color sample cards, cardboard pizza boxes, cereal boxes, nuts and bolts, photographs, pages from old books or magazines, advertisements, movie ticket stubs and postcards.

You can also add additional information to your broken tokens by adding words, pictures or instructions that become helpful only when all of the pieces are assembled.

As an example, consider a Broken Token in the form of a three-dimensional jigsaw puzzle made from a wood block. This particular block has a total of twelve pieces. You can make these blocks on a band-saw using different varieties of wood and different sizes of blocks. Some woods even have a distinctive smell.

One of the more interesting ways to cut index cards and other items into multiple pieces is with the unique scissors available at many craft stores. These scissors typically come in kits, with multiple styles of blades so that they cut unusually shaped and unique paths through your Broken Tokens.

1-18 THE QUESTION BOX

Selecting a question at random.

Here is a simple way to explore questions and answers with your next audience. Start by collecting interesting questions and writing these on separate index cards. Then place your collection randomly inside a suitable (and creative) box or drawstring bag. When your audience is ready, invite them to reach into the box, select one card and answer it aloud, or invite other members of the audience to answer the question.

For this activity, you can create a collection of question cards in advance or you can provide your audience with blank cards and ask them to each write an interesting question or two. For best results, you may want to suggest a topic or theme for each question card.

You can use The Question Box with your students, employees, workshop participants and even your family and friends. Place The Question Box on your dining room table and after dinner, invite each member of your family to select a question or two, and then discuss the answers with everyone present at the table.

INTERESTING QUESTIONS FOR THE QUESTION BOX

What currently impossible thing would you like to see become possible in your lifetime? Would you rather be an outstanding player on a mediocre team or a mediocre player on an outstanding team? What do you find most frightening about technology? Tell me about your favorite encounter with nature. What would you like to accomplish in the next ten years? Who is your most unusual relative or friend? What TV show do you wish they would bring back again? What are you waiting for? If each day became 25 hours long, what would you do with the extra hour? What is the very last thing you would be willing to give up? What is one talent that you would like to possess? Where do you most belong? When you have nothing to do, what do you like to do? What do you do best? If you were on a game show, what category of questions would you like to be asked? What is the most unusual job you have ever had? When was the last time you were surprised? What is the farthest you have ever traveled from home? What do you like most about your friends? What are you passionate about? Which five foods do you eat the most? In 100 years, do you think the world will be better or worse? What was your favorite breakfast cereal when you were young? What class in your entire education has proven to be the most useful in your life? Which of your clothing do you consider the most comfortable? What have you saved in a box for years but cannot seem to part with? What book that you have read is your absolute favorite? Who do you trust? If you didn't have to go to school (or work), would you?

You can use the questions above and on the next page to create your own Question Box, and for other question-based activities in this book, such as The Big Question, Where Do You Stand, It's Your Choice and Are You More Like?

ADDITIONAL QUESTIONS FOR YOUR QUESTION BOX

What is the loudest noise you have ever heard? Where does all the stuff you make in your dreams go when you wake up? If you could have 1 million of anything (except money), what would you choose? When was the last time you were really surprised? Name one thing that everyone should do in their lifetime. Sum up your entire life in just five words. What is the greatest number of people you have ever crammed into a single vehicle? If your time machine was working, would you go forward or backward in time? What are you most looking forward to? What do you want to be doing ten years from now? What makes you laugh? Who is the best role model you have ever met? If you could be fluent in another language, which language would you choose? What is the most fun you have ever had? If you could invent a new holiday, what would you call it, and when would it be? Name three things for which you are thankful. What is your favorite leisure time activity? If you could make a free long-distance call right now, whom would you call? Of all the words people use to describe you, which one do you like the most? When was the last time you received a hand-written note in the mail? When was the last time you wrote a hand-written card or letter? If you had the money, time and skills, would you rather build a house, a boat, a car or an airplane? What is the most daring thing you have ever done? When was the last time you changed your mind about something? Name five foods that you have never eaten. Name five foods that you would never eat, even if you were very hungry. Have you ever eaten food from a box or can that was way past the expiration date? What is the greatest value or belief that guides your life? What things make your life overly complicated? If you could do anything for your birthday this year, what would you like to do? What famous singer would you like to sing a duet with? If you could have a "do over" opportunity, what moment in your life would you choose? Which electric device in your home would you like to replace with a more current model? If you could wake up tomorrow morning having gained one ability or talent, what would it be? What are you famous for? If you were in the circus, what would be your dream act to perform? In your opinion, what is the greatest piece of music ever recorded? Which of the following would be more fun: to live in a tree, to live in a cave, to live on the moon or to live on a houseboat? Money, happiness or fame—choose one. If you could be the spokesperson for any product in the world, what product would you choose to endorse? If you were offered a sixty-second spot during prime-time television to say or promote anything you wanted, how would you use the time? What is the store you go to the most? What movie have you seen more than once, and why? Name three things you really like about yourself. What can you do in your dreams that you cannot do in real life? What is the longest line you have ever stood in for a long time? Have you ever seen the Northern Lights? If you could recover one item that you have lost or misplaced, what item would you choose? What is the best advice you were ever given? What would make your life easier? What is something that you appreciate now, that you didn't appreciate at all before? If you could organize the ultimate concert with three bands, which groups would you select to perform? Have you ever saved someone's life? Tell me about someone who was kind to you. What mistake have you made that has made you a better person? When was the last time you did something for the first time? Would the movie of your life be a comedy, a drama, an action/adventure flick or a romantic tear-jerker? What was the last song you whistled? On a scale of 1 to 10, how difficult is it for you to ask for help? What is something you have dreamed about doing for a long time, and why haven't you done it yet? In what period of your life do you feel you experienced the most personal growth or change? If 100 people were chosen at random, how many do you think would be leading a more satisfying life than yours? Would you rather be overdressed or underdressed for any occasion? If you could ask a crystal ball the answer to just one question about your future, what question would you ask? Name three people that you would like to emulate. If you were an entry in the dictionary, under which word would people find you? What is one item that you own, that you really should throw away, but probably never will? If you could own another home, where would you want it to be located? What advice would you give to your twenty-one-year-old self? Do you dream in color or black/white? Have you ever received a great idea through a dream? If you were a dog, what would your name be? How would you describe yourself in one word? What gift would you like to leave for future generations?

You can find 156 questions in the *Teamwork & Teamplay Training Cards* (ISBN 978-0-9882046-2-1) available from www.healthylearning.com, www.trainerswarehouse.com and www.training-wheels.com.

1-19 THE TO-DO LIST

A unique way to encourage participation.

The planners for many workshops, conferences, retreats and summer camps try to create an experience that is not only educational, but also one that creates connection between those attending. The To-Do List is a way to encourage a higher level of engagement and participation for every participant for both the content and social connection components of the event.

The next time you have a workshop, conference, retreat or summer camp, create your own To-Do List filled with a unique list of interesting things for participants to do during the event, especially activities and events that build an atmosphere of unity, community and connection. You can place all of these activities on a single index card and distribute to your audience or maintain a bowlful of these cards (with one To-Do item on each card) at registration and encourage your attendees to visit the bowl often and select a card (and then return the card when they have completed the task).

Have lunch with three other people that you do not know well • Invite someone to join you for a workshop today • Try some different food for lunch today • Enjoy a yoga workshop today • Shake hands and introduce yourself to someone new • Talk to people in elevators • Share a coffee with someone you don't know (yet) • Talk to someone near you about the content of a workshop • Find the highest lookout point nearby and take a panoramic photograph • Take three different elevators or stairwells to get to your room • Take a taxi, Uber or Lyft, city bus, or other public transportation to a location nearby, and invite someone to join you • Make plans to share a ride back to the airport with a new friend • Tell someone about a positive restaurant experience you've had so far this week • Dance with a partner • Take the elevator to a different floor and walk (up or down) to your next workshop location • Visit a local café/bookstore and enjoy a drink and/or book • Ask someone what kind of tree/plant/flower is growing in the lobby • Find someone with luggage just like yours • Find a nature item you can identify and tell someone else about it • Do something nice for someone at the conference without them knowing it was you • Find something with a hole in it • Share your newspaper with someone else • Pick up a piece of litter and throw it away • Find a comfortable place to relax and invite others to join you • Tip someone well • Sing a song • Get really excited about something • Personally thank a keynote or workshop presenter • Listen to someone tell a wonderful story • Avoid looking at your smartphone for at least two hours • Laugh out loud •

You can choose the number of challenges on the To-Do List for your next event according to the time and opportunities available for your participants. Look specifically for activities that require more than a single person. Be adventurous. List fun things to do. Encourage participants to join in.

1-20 THE SOAP BOX

Getting to know your teammates.

In the corporate world, new teams are formed frequently to work on specific projects. The amount of time required for a team to move through the stages of group development* can be altered (shortened) by spending some valuable time at the very beginning of the project building open communication, trust and teamwork. The Soap Box is a simple way for every member of a new team to share some valuable information with the group. Questions can vary, but here are a few of my favorite ones:

My name is _____, and I prefer to be called by the name _____.

What I bring to the table is (my skills for this project) _____.

The thing I am looking forward to most on this project is _____.

I wish _____.

You can count on me to _____.

(and the optional question) I'd just like to say _____.

With this simple collection of questions and statements, each member of the group can quickly state several pieces of valuable information that will help the team to start off on the right foot. Write the above questions on a large index card and allow speakers to hold this card while sharing their information.

————————————

I invented The Soap Box primarily for corporate clients to help newly formed teams get to know each other's strengths, talents and personalities. You are welcome to vary the questions as appropriate for your audience but try to keep the total number of questions to five or less, so that each person is only required to talk for a few minutes.

For another interesting and valuable activity to build open communication and unity at the beginning of a team's time together, see "21 Questions for Building Positive Relationships" in Chapter 7 of this book.

*The stages of group development are based upon the research of Bruce Tuckman. These stages include the forming, storming, norming, performing and transforming (or adjourning) stages. For more information about this work, see the following articles:

"Developmental Sequence of Small Groups," Bruce Tuckman, 1965, *Psychological Bulletin*, Number 63, pages 384-399. The classic original paper.

"Stages of Small Group Development Revisited," Bruce Tuckman & Mary Ann Jenson, 1977, *Group and Organizational Studies*, Number 2, pages 419-427. In this paper, the transforming stage was added.

1-21 LINKS OF CHAIN

A group formation activity

After using this activity a few times to organize a large group into a single circle, I discovered that this activity is actually a great way to creatively split a large group of people into smaller groups. Imagine that you have an audience of fifty people and you would like to randomly organize them into five groups of ten people each. Simply shuffle your handmade deck of fifty cards and pass them out to your audience. On each card, two phrases are found: your current identity and who you are looking for. The task is for everyone to find all the people in their group.

I like to create cards with specific themes, such as literary figures, movie actors, singers, scientific terms, computer lingo, animals, tools, vegetables, kitchen appliances and other familiar subject matter. Consider this collection of ten cards with athletic themes:

> You are a baseball bat, find a pair of downhill skis.
> You are a pair of downhill skis, find a boomerang.
> You are a boomerang, find a bowling ball.
> You are a bowling ball, find a golf club.
> You are a golf club, find a tennis racket.
> You are a tennis racket, find a skateboard.
> You are a skateboard, find a basketball.
> You are a basketball, find a swimming pool.
> You are a swimming pool, find a bicycle.
> You are a bicycle, find a baseball bat.

If you happen to need five identical groups of ten people, I recommend using five unique themes for each collection of ten cards. This will avoid players fitting into more than a single group and simplify the group formation process.

> You are a strawberry, find a lemon.
> Usted es fresa, encontrar un limón
> Sei un fragola, trova un limone.

If you have ever shopped in the giant blue and yellow store (Ikea) then you have probably encountered a product or object called by an entirely different (Swedish) name. If you happen to have a multicultural audience, you can try this activity in a variety of languages and encourage participants to share their knowledge of other languages as each team gathers the team members they need. You can also consider making each card multicultural by including several language translations on each card, as shown in the illustration. For this particular card, I used the free Google Translate app available for smartphones. On the following page, you can find information for ten cards, translated from English into Spanish and Italian.

TRANSLATIONS FOR THE LINKS OF CHAIN ACTIVITY

English	**Spanish**	**Italian**
You are a ___, find a ___.	Usted es ___, encontrar un ___.	Sei un ___, trova un ___.
Strawberry – Lemon	Fresa – Limón	Fragola – Limone
Lemon – Grape	Limón – Uva	Limone – Uva
Grape – Melon	Uva – Melón	Uva – Melone
Melon – Pineapple	Melón – Piña	Melone – Ananas
Pineapple – Apple	Piña – Manzana	Ananas – Mela
Apple – Orange	Manzana – Naranja	Mela – Arancio
Orange – Lime	Naranja – Lima	Arancio – Lime
Lime – Mango	Lima – Mango	Lime – Mango
Mango – Banana	Mango – Plátano	Mango – Banana
Banana – Strawberry	Plátano – Fresa	Banana – Fragola

In the no-prop activity book *Find Something To Do!* (ISBN 978-0-9882-0469-7), I included the technique known as Core Groups to allow smaller groups to conveniently find each other, even while mingling in a space with hundreds of people.

After using the Links of Chain activity to form groups, invite each group to create an easily visible hand motion and auditory sound that is unique. Encourage everyone in each group to practice both the sound and motion of their group. Then, later in the program, when you again need to convene the same small groups, simply yell, "Core groups!" and your audience will immediately fill the room with a cacophony of sounds and motions as group members reunite with the other members of their group.

TEAM CHALLENGES

CHAPTER TWO

This chapter is filled with thirty-seven teambuilding activities that utilize index cards and occasionally a few additional props. These activities focus on such skills as teamwork, communication, trust, creative problem solving, leadership and character. Enjoy!

NO.	ACTIVITY NAME	TEACHABLE MOMENT	IDEAL GROUP SIZE
2-1	Quotes in Order	Sensemaking	Groups of 6–15 people
2-2	Match Cards	Character, Values	Multiple groups of 10
2-3	The Lighthouse	Communication, Trust	Multiple groups of 2
2-4	Word Circles	Teamwork, Problem Solving	Any
2-5	Where Do You Stand?	A Mathematical Challenge	Any
2-6	Blind Find	Communication, Trust	Multiple groups of 3
2-7	Three Chairs	Win-Win Scenario	Divide into 3 groups
2-8	Sabotage	Communication, Trust	6-8 people per group
2-9	The 15th Object	Problem Solving	Any
2-10	Snowflakes and Butterflies	Tearable Art	Any
2-11	Acronyms and Abbreviations	A Linguistic Challenge	Multiple groups of 3
2-12	Back Writing	Communication	Multiple rows of 5 people
2-12½	Back Writing 2.0	Communication Styles	Multiple rows of 5 people
2-13	Reach for Your Dreams	Goal Setting	Multiple groups of 5
2-14	Hieroglyphics	A Linguistic Challenge	Multiple groups of 3
2-15	Thirteen Clues	A Logic Puzzle	Multiple groups of 5
2-15½	Einstein's Riddle	A Legendary Puzzle	Any
2-16	Alphabet Soup	Teamwork	Multiple groups of 10
2-17	Interference	Communication	Groups of 20–40
2-18	Next!	A Sequential Activity	15–20 People
2-19	Changing Places	Puzzling Teamwork	Multiple groups of 6

NO.	ACTIVITY NAME	TEACHABLE MOMENT	IDEAL GROUP SIZE
2-20	Tangrams	Problem Solving	Groups of 5
2-21	Stepping Stones	Problem Solving	Partners, small groups
2-22	The Proper Sequence	Linguistic Literacy	Any
2-23	The Transportation Card	Teamwork	Small groups
2-24	Build It	Communication	Multiple small groups
2-25	A Card Tossing Challenge	Problem Solving	Any
2-26	Paper Pushers	Physical Challenge	Groups of 3 or 4
2-27	Pass / Fail	Problem Solving	Groups of 10–20
2-28	Part of the Rainbow	Communication	Groups of 12
2-29	A Perfect Match	Communication	Groups of 12
2-30	It's Your Choice	Making Tough Decisions	Any
2-31	Everything on the Tray	Teamwork / Memory	Multiple small teams
2-32	The Beast	Communication / Creativity	Multiple small groups
2-33	Connections	Identifying Commonalities	Any
2-34	Expressionist Teambuilding	Teamwork / Problem Solving	Groups of 12
2-35	Four in a Row	Win / Win Solutions	Small teams

2-1 QUOTES IN ORDER

A linguistic challenge for groups.

The goal of this linguistic challenge is for a team to place various word cards in the proper sequence to replicate a familiar or inspirational quotation. You'll find a Piet Hein quotation mixed in the first photograph and correctly sequences in the last one below.

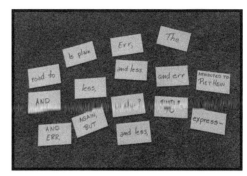

Each school year many teachers place inspirational posters in their classrooms, but after a few weeks, most students barely look at them. Corporations post motivational posters, but they soon become unnoticed by the workforce. Quotes in Order engages participants by challenging them to make sense of the quotation as they struggle to properly sequence what at first appears as a random jumble of words. According to Edgar Dale (and others) the greater the engagement during the learning process, the greater the retention of the information itself.

I personally like to present each team member with one or more cards from the selected quote and encourage them to move as needed to correctly sequence the quotation. This technique ensures a higher level of engagement and team commitment, at least for each person holding a card.

You can also use Quotes in Order as an individual challenge, rather than a team effort. Simply place each word of your selected quote on an index card, shuffle this deck of cards, and present to the individual of your choice, inviting them to place the word cards in the correct order. For a higher level of difficulty, consider translating the quote into a foreign language, or modifying the font on each card, or printing each card in tiny (4-point) print and providing a magnifying glass or optical loop. If you happen to enjoy creating Escape Room challenges, Quotes in Order can be an interesting way to provide an initial starting conundrum or riddle to your audience.

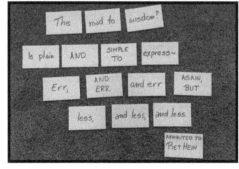

You can find quotations at Internet websites such as www.quotationspage.com. These sites allow you to search using key words such as *teamwork*, *leadership*, *communication*, *trust*, etc. Then create your own Quotes in Order activity props by transferring these quotes to index cards, with one or two words per card. As an example, consider the following quote:

The illiterate of the 21st century will not be those who cannot read and write, but those who cannot learn, unlearn and relearn.
—Alvin Toffler

The activity shown on this page incorporates the process of sensemaking into the problem-solving process. As participants struggle to make sense of the words provided, they engage more deeply. And if they happen to spend thirty seconds or more to figure out the correct order of the quotation, that is sufficient time to move the content from their short-term memory over to their long-term memory.

2-2 MATCH CARDS

Using the memory game to teach absolutely anything!

Match Cards are a variation of the matched-pair memory game. Twelve different word pairs are written on twenty-four index cards and these cards are randomly placed face down on a table. You will need one collection of these cards for each group of approximately ten people. At the beginning of the activity, one team member approaches their table and turns over any two cards, revealing the words. If the words match, the cards are placed in their original position face up. If the words do not match, the cards are turned face down in their original position. Then the second person repeats this process. The first team to turn over all twenty-four cards is the winner. But the real value of this game is that the same cards used as props during the game become the debriefing tool at the completion of the game.

In the first stage of the debriefing process, ask each person to select one card that contains a word or phrase they believe is important. Then invite everyone to explain why the word or phrase they chose is important to them. In the second stage, ask each group to decide which five words of the twelve words present are the most important words to them. Turn some cards face down but leave five cards face up, containing the five words or phrases selected by the entire group. In stage three, ask the group to decide which word of these five cards they could absolutely not live without.

While the actual words and phrases presented on the cards are important, it is the discussion that happens within the group that is often the most valuable component of this activity. Here are examples of some words you might include in your cards:

Teamwork • Honesty • Respect • Appreciating Diversity • Character • Integrity • Helpfulness
Positive Attitude • Leadership • Responsibility • Communication • Trust • Grit • Cooperation
Balance • Creativity • Courage • Empathy • Kindness • Flexibility • Common Sense • Wisdom

The Teamwork & Teamplay Training Cards have twenty-six different word pairs that you can use for this activity (and sixteen more activities, too!). You can purchase these cards from Training Wheels, Inc. (www.training-wheels.com) and Trainer's Warehouse (www.trainerswarehouse.com).

A few years ago I presented a series of teambuilding workshops for a major corporation. In one department of about thirty people, the culture had eroded to the point where the daily stress was overwhelming. After using a variety of team and community building activities, I happened to present Match Cards, using a collection of twenty-four index cards on which I had written words of character, such as respect, responsibility, integrity, communication, leadership and teamwork. While the activity itself had the desired effect, it was the debriefing after the activity that truly transformed the group. This was one of the most powerful teambuilding experiences I have ever witnessed and all it required was a collection of twenty-four index cards and some words of character.

2-3 THE LIGHTHOUSE

A two-person communication activity with consequences.

To prepare for this communication activity, you'll need to scatter a dozen or more index cards on the floor or ground, within a defined area. Then invite groups of two to work together to navigate from one side of the space to the other, without making contact with any of the index cards. One partner (the lighthouse) has their eyes open and is allowed to give verbal commands from outside the perimeter of the play space. The other partner (the ship) must navigate with their eyes closed (or be blindfolded), following the instructions provided by their sighted partner. Once a player has crossed the play space, partners switch roles and the activity is repeated.

For additional levels of challenge, consider some of the following alternatives: Identify what each index card represents by writing the name of various flotsam and jetsam (wreckage floating in the sea and discarded cargo found in the water) on each card, such as a half-sunken rowboat, a life preserver ring, a floating soda bottle or a plastic rubber ducky. Also include one or two valuable objects and encourage each pair to collect one of these cards, without touching any others. In addition to identifying various objects, you may also create a list of consequences for contacting any particular index card, such as returning to the beginning and starting again or taking two steps to the right before continuing. It may require multiple crossings to retrieve all the valuable objects in the area.

You can make interacting with the index cards more challenging by placing each index card on top of a cup or other small cylindrical object. Even the slightest wind can displace such cards. For the ultimate challenge, create a one- or two-level index card tower and instruct each person to retrieve one index card from this tower, without knocking over the remaining cards.

If you happen to have more than two people, consider inviting them to all work with their partners at the same time. The addition of other "boaters" in the water at the same time requires an even higher level of communication and focus between partners.

Over the years, this activity has been known by many names, including Minefield, Air Traffic Control and more recently GPS Navigation, but the basic idea of one person helping another person navigate a space filled with obstacles remains the same. Personally, I like the lighthouse metaphor—a beacon of light existing to help weary travelers safely reach their destination.

2-4 WORD CIRCLES

A linguistic puzzle for teams.

Word Circles are an interesting linguistic puzzle. Individual words are written on separate index cards and groups are challenged to rearrange these cards to create combinations (word pairs) that not only make sense, but also create a circle. For example, the seven words found in the left column below can be rearranged to complete a word circle with the following word pairs: *game over, over time, time out, out field, field goal, goal post, post game.*

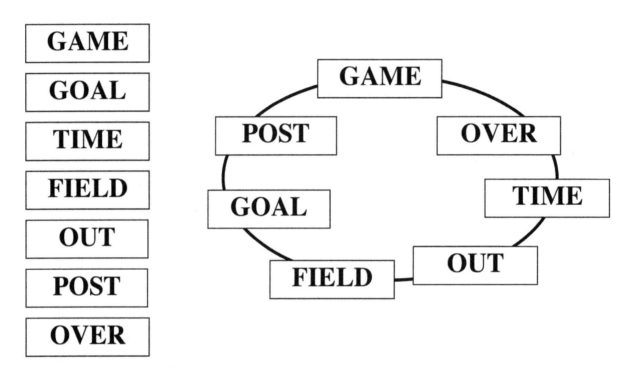

The goal of this linguistic challenge is to form a complete circle using all the word cards. Some combinations (such as *game field* in the example above) may sound correct, but if they do not contribute to creating a complete circle with all the cards available, they are not the correct combination.

In addition to the individual word cards used in this activity, add three additional "help cards" for the group to use at any time they wish. As the number of word cards increases, these help cards allow the group to gain valuable information from the facilitator. Here are a few help card examples.

Tell us one combination	Answer one yes or no question	Is this combination correct?

On the next page you'll find a collection of puzzle words that you can use to create Word Circles for up to twenty-five people. Don't forget to include a few help cards with Word Circle puzzles that contain fourteen or more words.

WORD CIRCLE PUZZLES

Place one of each of the following words onto an index card. Consider using different colors of index cards (or markers) to keep track of each different set. Place a small number on the backside of each card to help you remember how many cards are in that particular set.

3 Cards   Switch – Yard – Light   (switch yard, yard light, light switch)

5 Cards   Office – Party – Time – Out – Post

6 Cards   Time – Travel – Log – Book – Shelf – Life

7 Cards   Game – Over – Time – Out – Field – Goal – Post

8 Cards   Street – Light – Post – Game – Day – Time – Out – Side

11 Cards   Book – Smart – Car – Pool – Table – Setting – Down – Play – Time – Travel – Guide

12 Cards   Ball – Game – Over – Time – Out – Side – Walk – Man – Power – Station – Break – Fast

14 Cards   Front – Door – Man – Power – Lunch – Break – Down – Play – Time – Off – Key – Chain – Lightning – Storm

17 Cards   Ring – Tone – Up – Swing – Set – Down – Play – Ball – Game – Day – Light – House – Work – Out – Cast – Off – Key

21 Cards   Spring – Break – Fast – Pace – Car – Wash – Day – Dream – Team – Work – Week – End – Note – Book – Store – Front – Yard – Light – Sleeper – Sofa – Bed

25 Cards   House – Warming – Dish – Pan – Cake – Walk – About – Time – Frame – Work – Book – Shop – Front – Line – Up – Lift – Off – Key – Board – Foot – Race Horse – Play – Pen – Light

Chris Cavert and Chip Schlegel are two of the creative minds behind Word Circle puzzles. You can find a dozen of these puzzles in Chris's book *Portable Teambuilding Activities* (ISBN 978-1-939019-14-1). Jim Gladstone also describes a different version of word circles, which he calls "looping" in his Chain Reaction activity found in the book *Gladstone's Games To Go* (ISBN 978-1-9316-8696-3).

2-5 WHERE DO YOU STAND?

A mathematical challenge for groups of eight.

Here are several human-sized puzzles that explore mathematical skills, creative problem solving and movement. The puzzles shown are designed for teams of eight. You can modify any of these puzzles for smaller or larger groups by adding or removing squares. You can create each of the patterns shown on this page using individual large index cards or large paper plates (as place markers) or by drawing with sidewalk chalk on a concrete floor, permanent marker on a tarp or using masking tape to create the grid pattern. Make the size of each grid square 16 inches (40 cm) on a side.

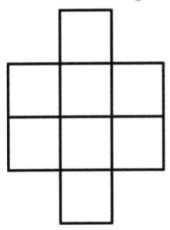

Begin by assigning team members numbers from one to eight. Participants can either remember their number or wear a button, badge or sticker showing this number. After a brief planning period, teams are introduced to the grid pattern and asked to locate each team member in one of the squares. The only restriction is that no two sequential numbers can be placed on squares that adjoin horizontally, vertically or diagonally. For the empty grid pattern shown on the left side of this paragraph, one possible solution is shown on the right side.

Some patterns are simple enough for participants to see a solution immediately. Others may require some trial-and-error problem solving, perseverance, tenacity or just plain luck.

After accomplishing the first grid pattern, allow time for a debriefing session, followed by another brief planning session when the group encounters the next grid pattern. Here are several variations of Where Do You Stand? grids for eight people. One of these does not have a solution. Why?

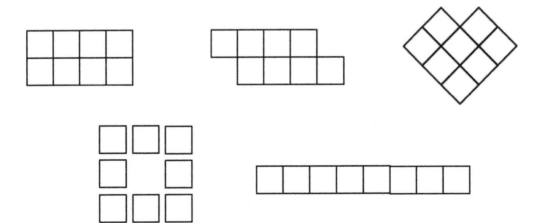

A variation of this activity first appeared in the book *Teambuilding Puzzles* by Mike Anderson, Jim Cain, Chris Cavert and Tom Heck (ISBN 978-0-7575-7040-7) available from Kendall/Hunt Publishers. *Teambuilding Puzzles* has become a valuable reference for Escape Room puzzle design.

2-6 BLIND FIND

A Communication Activity for Groups of Three

For this simple communication activity, there are three specific roles. One person in each group of three has the role of seeker. This person has the job of physically finding an index card in the available playing space, while blindfolded or with their eyes closed. A second person is the communicator. This person can speak but is also blindfolded so they cannot see. The third person in each group is able to see but cannot speak. This person's job is to communicate nonverbally to the communicator who tells the seeker where to find the index card.

Arrange the play space by removing any hard obstacles in the area, but feel free to leave soft toys, pillows, balloons and other harmless distractions. Then place blindfolds on both the seeker (who typically crawls on hands and knees during this activity) and the communicator (who is typically seated) before placing the index card within the activity space. Then begin the activity.

If you happen to have more than one team of three people participating in this activity at the same time, provide a few extra players to keep seekers from crawling into each other. After a seeker has located the index card, invite teams of three to change roles with each other and play again.

If you would like to increase the intensity of this activity, replace the index cards for each group with a kitchen timer or cell phone with the timer app activated. Before beginning this version, ask each group to estimate how long it will take to accomplish the task. Then set their timer for the time they have selected. The challenge then becomes to find the object before time runs out.

Be creative (but safe) in your placement of each team's index card. Hanging an index card from the ceiling via a string will require seekers to stand and reach upward. Locating the index card inside something, such as paper bag or below an empty cardboard box are additional possibilities.

To improve the outcome of this activity, provide each group with two minutes of planning time at the beginning of each round, allowing them to discuss their strategies and communication techniques.

For a slightly more boisterous version of this activity, see the activity Pirate's Treasure in Chapter 3. In this version of Blind Find, two teams compete to finish first with often hilarious results.

As an alternative to finding a single index card in this activity, teams can work together to find multiple index cards with words on them and then rearrange these cards to spell out a significant message or inspirational quote.

2-7 THREE CHAIRS

Creating a win-win solution.

This activity presents an interesting debrief since most groups tend to compete for resources in this activity, rather than searching for a win-win solution. Begin the activity by dividing your group into three equal parts. Each group is then provided with an index card on which is written one of the following commands:

Place all the chairs in the room in a circle.

Turn all the chairs in the room on their side.

Move all the chairs to one corner of the room.

After each group has been given their command, encourage them to quickly perform the task they are assigned. Chaos typically happens as the three teams try to gather as many resources (chairs) as they can to complete their task. This chaos leads to a perfect opportunity to debrief the activity with a discussion about achieving win-win solutions when practical, which in this case might involve placing all the chairs on their side, in a circle, in one corner of the room.

 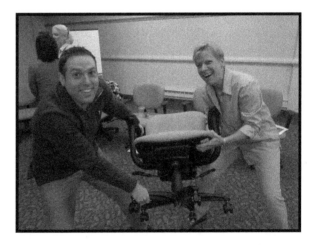

This activity works best if you have these three essential elements: twenty to thirty chairs, a room with four corners and twenty to thirty competitive participants.

I discovered this activity in Europe where it is very familiar with trainers and facilitators there. You can find this activity and fifty other activities in *The Teamwork & Teamplay International Edition* by Jim Cain (ISBN 978-0-9882046-3-8) available from www.healthylearning.com and www.training-wheels.com. This book contains fifty-one team activities and translations in sixteen languages including Chinese, Japanese, Russian, Turkish, Greek, Hebrew, Danish, Thai, Mongolian, Spanish, French, German, Dutch, Italian, Portuguese and English.

2-8 SABOTAGE

A group challenge that requires communication, teamwork and trust.

To prepare for this team construction activity, you'll need to create a visual model of a collection of various sizes, colors and patterns of index cards (or playing cards) in advance. I recommend making the model permanent by using glue to hold each card in position. This also ensures that no one can modify the position of each card during the activity. Then place this model in an out-of-the-way place in the room so that members of your audience must intentionally walk over to view it. Then provide each group with an identical collection of various size, color and patterns of index cards (about twice as many as your original visual model contains). Each group is then given the task of creating a replica (copy) of the original visual model using the supplies they have, with the following guidelines:

1. Each member of the group is individually presented with an index card on which is written the following information: "You are NOT the saboteur." Group members are not to share the content of the card they have been given with other members of their group. This step will leave open the possibility that someone in the group may be sabotaging the efforts of the rest of the group. Groups typically consist of six to twelve participants.

2. One member of the group at a time can travel to see the visual model, and then return to the group with advice on how to construct the replica (copy) of the original. Each member of the group typically makes only one trip to view the model.

3. When all groups have completed their replica, bring the original visual model closer so that each group can compare their copy to the original.

4. Discuss the results of the challenge and the performance of each group as part of a postactivity debriefing session.

This activity can be performed with a variety of physical objects, including index cards, playing cards, dominoes, construction toys (e.g., Lego®, Duplo®, Tinkertoys® and K'Nex®) or wooden blocks.
For this particular activity, I typically do not include a true saboteur in each group. This reality often leads to some very interesting discussions during the debriefing stage of the activity as participants try to understand the behaviors and performance of each person in their group.

There are three techniques that can be used to increase the difficulty of this challenge. First, place the visual model on a Lazy Susan turntable and rotate the model after each viewing. Next, cover a different part of the model for each participant so they can only see a portion of the whole on each visit. Finally, include a time limit for the activity.

———————————

I have encountered many activities that incorporate some version of the saboteur effect, but one of the first documented versions can be attributed to Tim Bond, author of the 1986 book *Games for Social and Life Skills* (ISBN 978-0-7487-0339-5). If you cannot find a copy of this book (published in the UK), I recommend searching on the website www.allbookstores.com, where you can generally find used copies at reasonable prices, even for out-of-print books.

2-9 THE 15TH OBJECT

A creative problem-solving opportunity for groups.

Learning "the rules of the game" is an important skill in life. By observing a situation, we gather knowledge, the ability to analyze the situation and an understanding of what is happening. Here is a challenge where the opportunity is not only to learn the game, but to discover the key to winning every time.

Begin by placing 15 index cards in a straight line on a table. Ask for a volunteer from your audience to play with you and explain the rules of the game. In each round, a player can remove one, two or three cards. Then their opponent removes one, two or three cards. This continues until the final card is removed. The goal is NOT to take the last card.

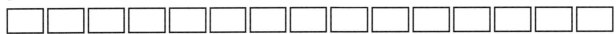

For the fifteen-card configuration shown, the player that controls the tenth card typically wins the game. To guarantee control of the tenth card, a player needs to control the second and sixth cards as well. If you increase the number of cards to sixteen, a player would need to control the third, seventh, and eleventh cards to guarantee a win. For fourteen cards, controlling the first, fifth and ninth cards are required to win. These cards are the keys to winning.

Like any magic or sleight-of-hand trick, repetition is a good technique for testing your analysis of the situation. With each repeated performance, you can gather a few more clues, test a few more hypotheses, increase your knowledge of the puzzle and refine your guess of which objects are keys to control the outcome of the game. Learn well and you can win every time!

Consider how my friend and colleague Kirk Weisler used this activity to create a teachable moment for his audience. Kirk was invited to assist with a wilderness therapy program in a remote area of the Rocky Mountains. After a long travel by four-wheel-drive vehicle, snowmobile and eventually snowshoes, Kirk and a replacement set of counselors met up with a dozen or so at-risk youth from the program. While the outgoing counselors were packing up to leave, Kirk sensed the need to bond the new counselors with the program participants. He gathered fifteen stones and placed them on a table in the main camp lodge. "I've got a game," he said, "and it takes knowledge and skill. Who wants to play?" One of the young participants accepted Kirk's offer and sat down opposite him at the table. Kirk explained the rules of the challenge and in the first round, Kirk won (no surprise there). At this point, a few of the other participants began to gather around and watch the game. Round two, Kirk wins again. But this time, there is some conversation among the participants. Round three, Kirk wins again. But something is definitely happening. At this point, Kirk asks the group, "So why do I win, every time?" After a brief discussion and various comments from the group, both respectful and some less than, someone offered, "You know something we don't." Bingo, thought Kirk, now is the time for a teachable moment. "Who else around here knows things that you don't right now?" Kirk asked. Eventually the counselors were identified. "The good news here," said Kirk, "is that I want you to be able to win at this game. I <u>want</u> you to beat me. I want you to be able to win, <u>every time</u>. All you need is some knowledge. Knowledge is power, and I want you to have some. Now these counselors that are here with you, they have some knowledge, too, and the really great news is, they want to share it with you. They want you to win in the biggest game of all, life itself." At this point, Kirk explained that there were key objects in this game, and that those who controlled those keys controlled the outcome of the game. He also talked about keys to life, and how they controlled the outcome of that "game." Knowledge is power. Get some!

2-10 SNOWFLAKES AND BUTTERFLIES

A communication activity with artistic possibilities.

This simple activity demonstrates how important listening is to the communication process. Begin by providing each person with a large index card (or colorful piece of construction paper). Ask them each to close their eyes, and then provide the following verbal instructions.

"Please follow each of my instructions. For this first round, you may not ask questions. Fold the paper in half and tear off the lower right corner. Fold the paper in half again and tear off the top left corner. Fold the paper in half again and tear off a tiny piece of the lower left corner and the lower right corner. Now unfold your paper, open your eyes and compare your snowflake to all the others."

Typically, each snowflake is different. Even though the instructions were fairly simple and everyone started with the same materials, the end result can vary greatly. Next, let's try making a butterfly.

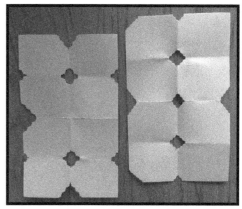

"Please follow my instructions exactly. Fold your paper in half and tear off each of the four corners. Fold your paper in half again and tear off a small piece in the middle of this folded line. Fold the paper in half again and tear off more of one of the corners already missing a piece. Now unfold your paper, open your eyes and compare your butterfly to all the others."

Even with prior experience, the appearance of the butterflies in this activity can vary quite a bit. Discuss these differences with your audience. Then, as a final test, try a variation of this activity known as Tearable Art. Invite participants to keep their eyes open but hold the paper behind their back as they fold and tear a new design of their own choosing.

At the completion of this activity, invite participants to write down their insights directly on their snowflakes and butterflies and display their creations on a wall in the training space, so that everyone can see them.

There is a frequently misused communication theory known as the 7% rule. Combining the statistical results of two communication studies, Professor Mehrabian suggested that communication is only 7% verbal, and that the other 93% of communication is composed of 55% body language and 38% tone of voice. This theory is greatly debated, especially when foreign languages are present.

You can create your own scientific study with this activity by presenting each participant with three forms of instructions. First, present each participant with written instructions (words only, no illustrations). Second, this same information is presented verbally by the instructor. Finally, verbal instruction with visual examples is shown at each stage of the process. Then determine for yourself which communication technique produced the best results with the members of your group.

2-11 ACRONYMS AND ABBREVIATIONS

A linguistic challenge for multiple small teams.

SCUBA (the best acronym ever!) *Self-Contained Underwater Breathing Apparatus*

Acronyms and abbreviations are part of our daily lives and yet these phrases have become so common and familiar that we sometimes forget exactly what the individual letters stand for.

For this activity, place a single acronym or abbreviation on the front side of an index card (and the answer on the back side). You'll find a list of over forty of these on the next page. Then place about a dozen of these cards face up on a table and invite your group to view the cards and collectively identify the meaning of each acronym or abbreviation.

As an alternative to using index cards for this activity, create a single page of twenty or more of the following acronyms and abbreviations and make copies for each group of three people. After about five minutes, encourage each small group to "double their brainpower" by combining with another nearby group to form a new group of six people.

To reduce the competition that sometimes occurs when teams are working on a challenge with other teams nearby, try the following technique. After doubling the brainpower of each group of three, creating a group of six, invite one person from each group of six to come together as "ambassadors" for their group. When the ambassadors gather together, they can discuss the phrases they have solved and look for help in the ones they still need to decode. After a minute or two, send the ambassadors back to their groups and allow another minute or two to finish the activity before sharing the answers below. A significant teachable moment in this activity is realizing that none of us is as smart as all of us. Teams that work together can accomplish much more than any single individual can working alone.

Some of the abbreviations and acronyms in this list are chronologically challenging—that is, they are familiar to some age groups (such as texting abbreviations like LOL and IMHO) but less familiar to others. This can be a great opportunity for people of different ages (and other diversity factors) to work together, appreciating the knowledge that their group members have and are willing to share.

2-11 ACRONYMS AND ABBREVIATIONS

None of us is as smart as all of us!

Place one of the following abbreviations or acronyms on each index card (with the corresponding answer on the back of each card).

1. NASA — National Aeronautics and Space Administration
2. SETI — Search for Extraterrestrial Intelligence
3. NASCAR — North American Stock Car Auto Racing
4. LASER — Light Amplification by Simulated Emission of Radiation
5. VOIP — Voice Over Internet Protocol
6. ROI — Return on Investment
7. TNT — Trinitrotoluene
8. PDF — Portable Document Format
9. WiFi — Wireless Fidelity
10. SASE — Self-Address Stamped Envelope
11. DVD — Digital Versatile (Video) Disc
12. RSVP — Respondez S'il Vous Plait
13. NATO — North Atlantic Treaty Organization
14. UNICEF — United Nations International Children's Emergency Fund
15. FLOTUS — First Lady of the United States
16. TASER — Thomas A. Swift Electronic Rifle
17. AC / DC — Alternating Current / Direct Current
18. RADAR — Radio Detection and Ranging
19. ISBN — International Standard Book Number
20. OSHA — Occupational Safety and Health Administration
21. FBI — Federal Bureau of Investigation
22. AWOL — Absent Without Official Leave
23. BBC — British Broadcasting Corporation
24. CBS — Columbia Broadcasting System
25. MTFBWY — May the Force Be With You (Star Wars)
26. CPR — Cardiopulmonary Resuscitation
27. WD-40 — Water Displacement – 40th Attempt
28. 3M — Minnesota Mining & Manufacturing
29. M&M's — (Forrest) Mars & (Bruce) Murrie
30. BMW — Bavarian Motor Works
31. ZIP code — Zone Improvement Plan Code
32. GEICO — Government Employees Insurance Company
33. NABISCO — National Biscuit Company
34. LLAP — Live Long and Prosper (Star Trek)
35. HTML — Hypertext Markup Language
36. JPEG — Joint Photographic Experts Group
37. AM/FM — Amplitude Modulation / Frequency Modulation
38. AM/PM — Ante-Meridiem (before midday) / Post-Meridiem (after midday)
39. L.L.Bean — Leon Leonwood Bean (the founder)
40. CVS — Consumer Value Stores
41. A&W — (Roy) Allen & (Frank) Wright (root beer)
42. JCPenny — James Cash Penny
43. NASDAQ — National Association of Securities Dealers Automated Quotations

2-12 BACK WRITING

Communication with a unique writing technique.

One of the great things about this index card activity is that you begin with blank index cards and let your audience do the artwork themselves!

Communication is an essential life and business skill, especially when face-to-face conversation is not possible and people use technology (such as telephones, fax machines, messenger services, mail delivery, pagers, email, text messaging and social media) to transport their message. Even with these technological resources, our communication sometimes misses the mark. This activity will help your group explore communication and identify ways to improve that communication in the future.

Begin this activity by forming multiple lines of five participants, seated in chairs. Present the person sitting in the front chair with a collection of five index cards and a colorful marker. Next, show each of the people sitting in the back chair the first of these illustrations.

The challenge here is for the last person in each row (line) to view a drawing or sketch created by the facilitator and then transfer this information to the members of their group by drawing this image one time on the back of the person directly in front of them (using their index finger). This person then passes the image received to the next person in line, until it finally reaches the first person in line, who transfers this information onto an index card. Once all groups have finished, the facilitator reveals the original drawing and each group compares their version to the original.

The basic equipment required for this activity includes chairs for all participants (although in informal or outdoor settings, participants can be seated on the floor or ground), five large index cards per group, a bold marker (pen) for each group and a flipchart with markers (for the facilitator).

As with many team activities, the value of this activity comes not just from participating, but in the discussion that follows, especially when it relates to the challenges of effectively communicating across great distances, time zones, languages and cultures.

After each round, invite everyone to rotate to a new position within their group of five. This is easily accomplished if everyone moves forward one position, and the first person in each line moves to the back position. This rotation allows each member of the group to experience all the different levels of communication (an important point that will become a useful debriefing discussion later). Four illustrations are shown, for the first four rounds of this activity. For the fifth round, use an illustration that is meaningful to your participants.

Begin with simple drawings of no more than ten lines or elements. Even at this level of simplicity, many groups cannot correctly transfer the image through four of their team members without significantly altering the final "message." Here is an example of participant-generated artwork.

A Script for Back Writing

Consider the following script to assist you in introducing and facilitating Back Writing for the first time. Begin the script once you have seated your participants into columns of five people each.

Try to imagine just fifty years ago, when folks in New York needed to communicate with folks in Los Angeles. What communication options did they have? There was of course the telephone, telegrams, US Mail, and a few private delivery companies. Now let's set the clock forward 50 years to the present day. In addition to those earlier services, we now have cell phone, fax machines, teleconferencing, voice messaging, texting, social media, overnight delivery, and a host of new technologies that help us connect. But even with these innovative technologies, has communication really improved? Not really.

Luckily, there is a new technology that we'll employ today. Raise your right hand and extend your index finger. This is your new word processor. In a moment, I'll share an illustration with the members of your team in the back row. They will communicate the content of each illustration to you, by drawing that picture on your back, just once. Why only once? Because when you hit <send> on a text message or email, it's gone! After you receive the illustration, you pass it along to the next person, and the next, until it finally reaches the front person, who then transfers this image to an index card. Then we'll check to see how much your copy looks like the original.

It is ok to tell your recipient, "Ok, here it comes." But it is not permissible to say, "Hey, it's a tree." In other words, only your index finger can be used to communicate the image, not your words.

Then begin with the first image. When all columns have completed their drawing, let everyone see what the first person has drawn, and then share the following information:

It appears as though not all the details of our message have been successfully transmitted. Notice however, that this method of communication is one directional. But we know that good communication is two directional. Turn to the persons behind you and tell them two important components. First, what was good about what they did. Second, what they could do to be even better. You might say, for example, "Could you press a little harder?" or "Could you draw a little slower?" Give them some feedback.

Continue rotating the members of each team with each illustration. When you have completed this activity (after five or so rounds), you can instruct participants to form circles within their group of five and invite persons to share a personal story of when communication may have fallen apart for them, or any personal insight related to effective or noneffective communication.

In addition, in small groups or with the entire audience, review this activity by asking some of the following questions:

What did you do to improve your communication technique in this activity? Did practice improve your performance? How is this activity similar to the communication in your organization, department, classroom or corporation? What valuable insights can you take away from this experience? If you were asked to advise a new employee how to effectively communicate within your organization, what insights would you offer them?

During a 4-H conference in Colorado, I met speaker and author Tom Jackson for the first time. The activity presented here, Back Writing, is a variation of Tom's activity Back Art which he shared in both his workshop and his book, *Activities That Teach* (ISBN 978-0-9160-9549-5). You can find even more valuable teaching and training activities in Tom's other books: *More Activities That Teach* (ISBN 978-0-9160-9575-4) and *Still More Activities That Teach* (ISBN 978-0-9664-6335-8). For even more training ideas from Tom, visit www.activelearning.org.

2-12½ BACK WRITING 2.0

Communication with multiple techniques.

This variation of Back Writing incorporates some additional communication techniques beyond those in the previous activity. It also provides a before and after image for comparison, as a method of measuring communication effectiveness.

Research has shown that communication is composed of three (some say more) distinct parts. Some research claims that only 7% of spoken communication is verbal and that 93% is nonverbal. Others claim that about 7% to 15% of what is said is attributed to the actual words used. While 38% to 40% of the message is the inflection or tone of the voice, and 45% to 55% is attributed to the body language and expressions shared during the exchange.

Back Writing 2.0 incorporates multiple communication techniques as a message (image) is passed from participant number five to participant number one.

Back Writing 2.0 begins with five people sitting in a column (line), all facing forward, with plenty of space between each other. The fifth (last) person in line is shown an index card with a simple image on it. This person then describes (whispers) what they have seen to person number four. Person number four then draws this image on the back of person number three, using their index finger as an imaginary pencil. Person number three passes the information on to person number two by "texting" the information (words only) to them on an index card. Player number two then draws the image as a series of dots or "points" on the back of player number one. Player number one then transfers the image as received to an index card (so that everyone can see their results).

The results of these four communication techniques are then evaluated by each team, and groups are invited to brainstorm ideas for making each form of communication better in future rounds.

While each of the distinct parts mentioned are helpful components of communication, some may question whether the percentages are truly correct. Take for example, Abraham Lincoln's *Gettysburg Address,* one of the most well-known speeches of all time. Most people encounter this historical speech in written form since no recording of the original speech is available. Even with no record of Lincoln's tone or body language that day, his words still have significant impact!

2-13 REACHING FOR YOUR DREAMS

A personal goal-setting activity with group involvement.

You can begin this activity by organizing your audience into groups of six to eight people. Then present each person with an index card and invite them to write down a goal they have for themselves. Depending upon your audience, this could be a personal goal, a professional goal, or any other goal they are willing to make public. Then ask each group to step inside a rope circle. I like to use a circle made from 1-inch- wide tubular webbing approximately 15 feet (4.6 meters) long, known as a Raccoon Circle.

From a standing position at the perimeter of each rope circle, invite participants to take one giant step and place their index card goals on the floor at this distance, then return to the interior of the circle. When everyone in the group has returned, ask each person to share their goal with the group. Next, invite each person to attempt to retrieve their goal cards, without physically touching the space outside of the rope circle. While a few athletic participants may be able to stretch the distance required to retrieve their card, for some members of the team this will be an impossible task, unless they ask for help! Working together, most groups are able to help each person reach their goal card successfully.

When everyone has retrieved their card, invite them to discuss how working together enabled them to reach their goal. How might this same method be used in real life to reach the goal written on each card? Is getting help to reach your goals possible? Practical? Helpful?

In this case, the metaphor of having your teammates help you achieve your goals is profound. Many of the goals we set for ourselves could use a little outside help. In the end, we have to achieve (grasp the card) ourselves but having some assistance along the way from our friends is indeed helpful.

In *The Revised and Expanded Book of Raccoon Circles* (ISBN (978-0-7575-3265-8) by Jim Cain and Tom Smith, you'll find over 150 interesting and playful ways to use a Raccoon Circle as part of your teaching, training and facilitating programs. You can also download (and freely share) a digital copy of over a dozen Raccoon Circle activities in PDF format at the Teamwork & Teamplay downloads page: www.teamworkandteamplay. com/downloads.html. You can also find Reaching for Your Dreams and many more activities with rope in the book *Rope Games* (ISBN 978-0-9882046-1-4) by Jim Cain.

2-14 HIEROGLYPHICS

A linguistic challenge for multiple small teams.

Feel free to make copies of the Hieroglyphic word puzzles shown on the next page. You will need one copy of this page for each group of three people. Sharing resources is part of working together as a team. Allow each group of three to work on this challenge for about five minutes, and then encourage each small group to "double their brainpower" by combining with another nearby group (to form a group of six).

One of the teachable moments in this activity is realizing that none of us is as smart as all of us. If we work together, anything is possible.

One of the variations I like for this activity helps to reduce the competition that sometimes occurs when teams are working on a challenge with other teams nearby. After doubling the brainpower of each group of three, creating a group of six, I invite one person from each group of six to come together as "ambassadors" for their group. When the ambassadors gather together, they can discuss the word puzzles they have solved and look for help in the ones they still need to decode. After a minute or two, I send the ambassadors back to their groups and allow another minute or two to finish the activity, before sharing the answers below.

Rather than printing all the word puzzles on a single page, consider placing one of each of these puzzles on a separate index card. Then scatter these cards around the room and invite groups to move about, solving each puzzle they encounter along the way.

Here are the solutions to the word puzzles of the opposite page.

1. Scrambled Eggs
2. Traveling Overseas (over C's)
3. Forum (4 UM)
4. Split Second Timing
5. H2O = Water (from H to O)
6. Just Between You and Me
7. Line Up (in Alphabetical Order)
8. More Often Than Not
9. Long Time – No See (no C)
10. Forget It (Four 'Get It')
11. One if by land, two if by sea (C)
12. Blanket = Blank It
13. Look Both Ways Before Crossing
14. A Little Bit More
15. No One (No 1)
16. Eraser (E racer)
17. Last But Not Least
18. That's Beside the Point
19. Tuna Fish (two nafish)
20. United States
21. Love at First Sight
22. No U Turn
23. Partly Cloudy
24. The Start of Something Big
25. Tennessee (10 S C)
26. Just Under the Wire
27. Banana Split
28. Quit Following Me
29. Unfinished Business
30. A Bad Spell of Weather
31. Painting by Numbers
32. Feedback (FEED backwards)

2-14 HIEROGLYPHICS

A Linguistic Challenge for Groups

Decode each of these cryptic messages and write the true word or phrase beneath it. For example, Hieroglyph 14 decodes as "a little bit more."

1. GESG

2. Traveling
   —————
   CCCCCC

3. 2 UM + 2 UM

4. TIMING   TIM ING

5. HIJKLMNO

6. YOU/JUST/ME

7. EILN PU

8. Often, Often, Often,
   Not, Not

9. T   I   M   E
   —————————————
      abdefgh

10. Get It Get It Get It Get It

11. IF LAND   IF IF C

12. _____ it

13. LOOK KOOL CROSSING

14. bit **MORE**

15. 0, , 2, 3, 4, 5

16.

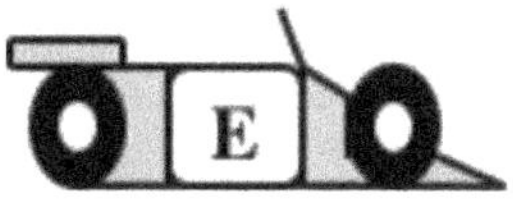

17. L/EAST

18. • THAT'S

19. nafish nafish

20. IDAHOHIO

21. SIGHT LOVE
    SIGHT
    SIGHT

22. TRN

23. clo

24. **SOM**

25. SSSSSSSSSSC

26. Wire
    ————
    Just

27. BAN ANA

28. ME QUIT

29. Busines

30. Wheather

31. Mona Lisa 123

32. DEEF

You will find this activity and many more in the books *100 Activities That Build Unity, Community & Connection* (ISBN 978-1-60679-374-9) and *Teambuilding Puzzles* (ISBN 978-0-7575-7040-7).

2-15 THIRTEEN CLUES

A mystery presented in thirteen pieces.

Present each group of four people with the clues shown on the next page and invite them to solve the mystery using just the information provided. You can write one clue on each of thirteen index cards or simply copy the next page. If you plan to use index cards and make multiple sets for your audience, I recommend making each set from a different color of index card.

The mystery presented here is in the form of a logic puzzle. The solution can be found using a Sudoku-like grid with some combination of the three known factors: places 1 through 6, the names of the bakers and the six flavors of pie. One example is shown in the photo below, featuring the six flavors of pie on the horizontal axis and the five pie makers on the vertical axis. The potential places are then listed from the information provided (apple = 1st prize, peach = 2nd prize, cherry = 6th prize, blueberry = 5th prize, leaving only 3rd and 4th prize; chocolate placed one place higher than pecan, so chocolate = 3rd prize and pecan = 4th prize).

Next, we need to eliminate some of the possibilities shown on the grid. Andy made the chocolate or pecan pie, eliminating all other fruit pie flavors for Andy (so we place Xs there). Sarah did not receive 1st or 6th prize, so cross those off for her. Betty placed lower than Andy (so we can cross off 1st, 2nd and 3rd place for her) and higher than Dave (so we can cross off 6th place as well). Betty placed lower

	APPLE	CHERRY	CHOCOLATE	PEACH	PECAN	BLUE BERRY
SARAH	X	X	X	2	X	X
DAVE	X	6	X	X	X	5
BETTY	X	X	X	X	4	X
ANDY	X	X	3	X	X	X
ELLEN	1	X	X	X	X	X

than Andy (who either took 3rd or 4th prize), meaning Betty took 4th or 5th prize, and higher than Dave (who either took 5th or 6th prize). We know that the person taking 5th prize also takes 6th prize, so Dave is the double pie baker, winning 5th and 6th prizes. Ellen is the only pie maker left in the first column and wins 1st prize for her apple pie. Betty wins 4th prize for her pecan pie and Andy is one place above her, in 3rd place, for his chocolate pie, leaving the final pie maker Sarah in 2nd place with her peach pie. Whew!

The *Teamwork & Teamplay Training Cards* have four different mysteries to be solved, including the one presented here. For the initial printing of these cards, the County Fair mystery was complete, except for one clue (that was mistakenly omitted by the printer), rendering the puzzle unsolvable. That clue is presented in this version of the Pie Contest. Happy solving!

You can find this and three other mysteries to solve on the *Teamwork & Teamplay Training Cards* (ISBN 978-0-9882046-2-1) available from www.training-wheels.com.

THE COUNTY FAIR PIE CONTEST

A mystery in thirteen pieces.

Using the clues below, see if your team can solve the mystery.

Judges awarded prizes for first, second, third, fourth, fifth, and sixth place.

The judges awarded first prize to the apple pie.

There were six entries in the pie contest at the county fair.

Ellen's pie was one of the best she ever made.

Betty's pie placed lower than Andy's pie and higher than Dave's pie.

Andy has never entered a fruit pie in the county fair.

Sarah did not receive either first or sixth prize.

Sarah substituted brown sugar for regular sugar in her pie.

Who baked which pie? What prize did each pie win?

One person won two prizes, for fifth and sixth place, and one of these was blueberry.

The chocolate pie placed one place higher than the pecan pie.

The cherry pie was so sour the judges did not place it in the top five.

The peach pie won second prize.

2-15½ EINSTEIN'S RIDDLE

Can using index cards make you as smart as Einstein?

There is a unique test, proposed by Alan Turing in his 1950 paper, "Computing Machinery and Intelligence," based upon what he refers to as the "imitation game." In Turing's theoretical test, one person is asked to decide if they believe they are communicating with another person or a computer. This possibility brings up an interesting question: What question could you ask to determine if you are talking to a person or a computer? My answer would be simple, text in Einstein's Riddle. Most references to this riddle state that only 2% of the population can successfully solve this puzzle, so a correct solution would infer that there is a 98% possibility that you are talking to a computer.

But I found a method (using index cards) that can greatly increase the probability of success in solving Einstein's Riddle. This classic riddle is a mystery presented in eighteen parts (sixteen separate clues, plus two more essential clues in the final questions). First, let's present the classic version of Einstein's Riddle, and then I'll illustrate how to solve it with index cards. Because of the classic nature of this riddle, I have chosen to present it in as close to the original form as possible, which includes the reference to both alcohol and cigarettes. This version dates back to the early 1960s and includes sources such as *Life International* magazine (December 17, 1962) and many others as the puzzle became more well known. If references to alcohol and cigarettes are less than appropriate for your audience, you can replace these topics with other, more suitable references, such as beverages and food. Jeremy Stangroom does this in the version he presents in his book *Einstein's Riddle—Riddle, Paradoxes, and Conundrums to Stretch Your Mind* (ISBN 978-1-5969-1665-4).

THE CLASSIC FORM OF EINSTEIN'S RIDDLE

1. There are five houses, each painted a different color, in a row.
2. The inhabitant of each house has a unique national heritage (country of origin), owns a different pet, drinks a different beverage and smokes a different cigarette.
3. The Englishman lives in the red house.
4. The Spaniard owns a dog.
5. Coffee is drunk in the green house.
6. The Ukrainian drinks tea.
7. The green house is immediately to the right of the ivory house.
8. The Old Gold smoker owns snails.
9. Kools are smoked in the yellow house.
10. Milk is drunk in the middle house.
11. The Norwegian lives in the first house.
12. The person who smokes Chesterfields lives in the house next to the person with the fox.
13. Kools are smoked in the house next to the house where the horse is kept.
14 The Lucky Strike smoker drinks Orange Juice.
15. The Japanese smokes Parliaments.
16. The Norwegian lives next to the Blue House.

Questions: Who drinks water? Who owns the zebra?

The key to solving Einstein's Riddle is to create a series of solution grids and enter as much information as you know. I also like to keep track of which clues (number 1 through 12) I've used. For example, from the classic form of Einstein's Riddle, the following information is known: The nationality of the first house is Norwegian (clue 11), the beverage of the middle house (number 3) is milk (clue 10), and since the Norwegian lives next to the blue house, the color of house number 2 is blue (clue 16). We use clue 1 (the five houses) and clue 2 (each category is unique) to create the first solution grid.

Solution Grids for Einstein's Riddle

House	1	2	3	4	5
Color		Blue			
Nationality	Norwegian				
Beverage			Milk		
Cigarette					
Pet					

From the clues we know that:

House colors include: red, green, ivory, yellow, blue

Nationalities include: English, Spanish, Ukrainian, Norwegian, Japanese

Beverages include: coffee, tea, milk, orange juice. And from the question: water.

Cigarettes include: Old Gold, Kools, Chesterfield, Lucky Strikes, Parliaments

Pets include: dog, snails, fox, horse. And from the question: zebra.

Clue Number	1	2	3	4	5	6	7	8	9	10	11	12	13	14	15	16
Clues used so far:	X	X								X	X					X

The next step in our solution process is to determine which answers are possibilities for specific locations in our grid. Possibilities for each of these grid locations are reduced to an abbreviation (the first letter of each possibility). From clue 3, the English person can live in houses 3, 4 or 5;, and each of those houses could be red. From clue 5, coffee can be drunk in houses 1, 4 or 5. From clue 6, the Ukrainian can reside in houses 2, 4 or 5. From clue 7, the green house can only be 4 or 5, and the ivory house can only be 3 or 4.

The next deduction is a bit more complicated. Since the green house is immediately to the right of the ivory house, and the ivory house can only be house 3 or 4, then the Englishman cannot live in house 4 (because if the ivory house is number 3 then the green house is number 4, leaving the English person in house number 5; and if the ivory house is number 4 then the green house is number 5, leaving the English person in house number 3).

Next, the Norwegian does not live in the blue house, nor the red or ivory or green house, so must live in the yellow house, and by clue 9 smoke Kools. Identifying the first house color as yellow also eliminates coffee as a choice of beverage in this house. And, since orange juice is connected with a Lucky Strike smoker (and the Norwegian in house 1 smokes Kools), then the only beverage left as a possibility for house 1 is water.

From clue 13, a horse is kept in the house next to the Kool smoker, so house 2 has a horse. From clue 14, Lucky Strike cigarettes and orange juice can go in houses 2, 4 or 5. From clue 4, the Spanish person can live (with a dog) in house 3, 4 or 5. From clue 8, the Old Gold smoker (with snails) could live in house 3, 4 or 5. From clue 15, the person from Japan smoked Parliaments, and can only live in houses 2, 3, 4 or 5. This leaves only one clue left to explore.

From clue 12, the Chesterfield smoker can live in house 2, 3, 4 or 5; and the fox owner can live in house 1, 3, 4 or 5. The only pet available to house owner number 1 is a fox, so that identity is now known (eliminating houses 3, 4 and 5 as potential homes for a pet fox, and eliminating Chesterfield cigarettes from homes 3, 4, and 5). This choice also makes sense because it is typically accepted that one person would drink water and a different person would own the zebra.

The final piece of solution grid information (so far) comes from the question "Who owns the zebra?" With the pet identities known for houses 1 and 2, the zebra must reside in house 3, 4 or 5.

House	1	2	3	4	5
Color	Yellow	Blue	R, I	G, I	R, G
Nationality	Norwegian	U, J	E, S, J	U, S, J	E, U, S, J
Beverage	**Water**	T, OJ	Milk	C, T, OJ	C, T, OJ
Cigarette	Kools	Chesterfield	OG, P	LS, OG, P	LS, OG, P
Pet	Fox	Horse	D, S, Z	D, S, Z	D, S, Z

At this point some additional deductions are possible, such as the fact that the Japanese person smokes Parliaments, eliminating the nationality of Japanese from the owner of the second house, identifying this owner as Ukrainian and drinking tea.

Here is the moment when index cards can be very helpful. Simply recreate the solution grid pattern shown here, using colored index cards for all the known entries, and white index cards for each of the "possible" entries. Then simply insert various combinations for each missing entry.

Let's begin with an attribute that only has two possibilities. If we insert red as the color of the house number 5, we infer that house is occupied by a person of English nationality. That requires that house 3 is ivory and house 4 is green, which requires that the beverage of house 4 is coffee and house 5 is orange juice. This requires that Lucky Strikes are smoked in house 5. This eliminates a pet dog in house 5, and since the snail owner smokes Old Gold, house 5 has a pet zebra.

House	1	2	3	4	5
Color	Yellow	Blue	Ivory	Green	Red
Nationality	Norwegian	Ukrainian	S, J	S, J	English
Beverage	**Water**	Tea	Milk	Coffee	Orange Juice
Cigarette	Kools	Chesterfield	OG, P	OG, P	Lucky Strikes
Pet	Fox	Horse	D, S	D, S	Zebra

At this point, our first attempt fails. Since the Spanish person owns a dog, the only pet choice left for the Japanese person is a snail. But we already know from clue 8 that the snail owner smokes Old Gold, while the Japanese person smokes Parliaments. This is a contradiction. If we return to our original assumption and switch the English person from house 5 to house 3, you'll find everything drops into place nicely (and correctly) as shown in this solution grid to Einstein's Riddle.

House	1	2	3	4	5
Color	Yellow	Blue	Red	Ivory	Green
Nationality	Norwegian	Ukrainian	English	Spanish	Japanese
Beverage	**Water**	Tea	Milk	Orange Juice	Coffee
Cigarette	Kools	Chesterfield	Old Gold	Lucky Strike	Parliament
Pet	Fox	Horse	Snails	Dog	**Zebra**

If you like the idea of solving logic puzzles like this one using index cards, there is an interesting app with the title iCardSort (by E-String Technologies, Inc.) that allows you to create virtual index cards and move them around on screen. I used this app to create all the virtual index cards necessary to correctly solve Einstein's Riddle.

2-16 ALPHABET SOUP

A sequential activity that requires teamwork

There are two version of Alphabet Soup presented here. The first version is a classic teambuilding activity that can be done indoors or out. The second is a tabletop version that requires less running but faster reflexes.

For the classic version of Alphabet Soup, you'll need to prepare a few props. First, you'll need twenty-six index cards that each have one capital letter of the alphabet printed on them in large, easy-to-read block letters. Randomly place these cards face-up on the ground or floor, with sufficient space around each card to easily walk between them. Next you'll need two pieces of rope—one to act as the start/finish line for each round and a second rope to encircle the twenty-six alphabetic index cards. Place these two ropes about 10 feet (3 meters) apart. You'll also need a stopwatch for this activity, and a score card (flip chart, clipboard, or other easily visible writing surface). Time begins each round when the first participant crosses the line and finishes when the last person returns.

The challenge of this activity is for teams to touch each of the twenty-six cards in alphabetical order, one at a time, for time, with the following restrictions:

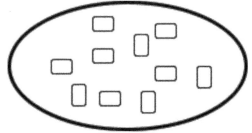

1. Only one participant at a time can be within the perimeter of the circle.

2. The cards must be touched in order.

Before beginning each round, invite each team to establish a time goal. When finished, compare the estimate to the actual performance. In addition to the actual time required to complete each round, errors (such as touching a card out of order or having more than one person within the perimeter of the circle at the same time) carry a five-second penalty for each occurrence.

This version of Alphabet Soup requires some general problem solving and group decision making, plus a physical component as team members rush from the starting line to the circle enclosing the twenty-six alphabet cards, and finally some goal setting. In each successive round, teams typically improve both their estimation of the time required to complete the task and the actual time necessary.

The table top version of Alphabet Soup is a smaller version of the original, perfect for an indoor setting. Using 3x5 index cards, create one card for each of the twenty-six letters of the alphabet and place these cards face-up on a table in random order. No need for any additional rope around the cards, as the edge of the table will work just fine as the perimeter. Then place a short rope 6 feet (2 meters) away from the table to serve as the start/finish line for each round.

For both versions of Alphabet Soup, encourage many participants in each team to take an active role, physically making contact with several of the alphabet cards during each round.

I included Alphabet Soup in my very first teambuilding book *Teamwork & Teamplay*, coauthored with my friend and colleague Barry Jolliff over 20 years ago. It remains one of my favorite ways to get groups moving and working together, indoors and out.

2-17 INTERFERENCE

A full-volume communication exercise.

Interference is a wonderfully loud communication exercise that begins with three distinct teams. Team 1 (The Senders) occupy the leftmost space on the playing field. They verbally (and generally quite loudly) transmit a message that has been presented to them written on an index card. Team 2 (The Receivers) occupy the rightmost space on the playing field and are tasked with listening (and receiving) the message transmitted by Team 1 (The Senders) located about 20 feet (6 meters) away. The final group, Team 3 (The Interferers), occupy the middle space of the playing field and are tasked with interrupting the communication process by blocking the signal (generally visually and verbally) between the Senders and the Receivers. A rope barrier is placed on the ground between each team.

Team 1	Team 3	Team 2
The Senders	The Interferers	The Receivers

The messages transmitted by Team 1 (The Senders) are typically short coherent quotes or other simple phrases of about a dozen words or less. Team 1 has exactly one minute to transmit the information. Team 3 (The Interferers) try their best to block the information being transmitted by Team 1 toward Team 2. This can take the form of visually blocking the line of sight between Team 1 and Team 2 members, or verbally increasing the noise level to cancel out Team 1 voices. Team 2 has what some consider the most difficult task, trying to separate the signal (the message) from the noise (the interference) and make sense of it to capture the information being sent by Team 1.

For this particular activity, play three successive rounds, with three different messages. After each round, invite team members to change locations (Team 1 becomes Team 2, Team 2 becomes Team 3, and Team 3 becomes Team 1). After three rounds, debrief the activity by asking teams how they overcame the interference and which role they enjoyed the most and why.

You can search for interesting messages on the Internet at creative websites like www.quotationspage.com, which allow you to search for key words (such as *communication*, *listening*, *interference*, etc.). One of my favorite messages for this particular activity is: "In order to listen, you must first become quiet." There is something rather hilarious about a collection of Senders screaming at the top of their lungs the word 'quiet!'

This activity is extremely noisy, so an outdoor (or noise protective) environment is recommended. To increase the challenge level of this activity, increase the space between the Senders and the Receivers, or double the number of interferers occupying the middle space, or play with diminished lighting to reduce visibility, or increase the number of words in each message, or blindfold the Receivers, or change the language of the message being transmitted.

You can find this activity and many more communication activities in the no-prop teambuilding activity book *Find Something To Do!* (ISBN 978-0-9882-0460-7) by Jim Cain, available from www.healthylearning.com and www.training-wheels.com.

2-18 NEXT!

A sequential challenge that requires a variety of team skills.

This unique activity requires each member of a group to complete their assignment in sequence in order for the team to succeed. You can prepare for this activity by creating the sequential cards for Next! found on the following pages. There are two versions of the activity to choose from, each with twenty-six tasks in total. If you have a group larger than twenty-six people, you can split the group to a more manageable size using multiple decks of Next! cards. I would advise you to create each deck using a different color of index card. After creating the cards required, randomly distribute all of them (some people may have more than one card). Then explain the basic rule of the activity. When someone in the group performs the first task listed on your card, you should perform the response listed. The goal is to make it through every card, in proper sequence, without making a mistake.

To begin the activity, the facilitator (very obviously) claps twice. This will begin the chain reaction of events that sequentially reaches the final task (everyone joining hands in a circle and somebody saying, "We're done!").

There are several typical errors that can occur during this activity. Sometimes groups make it to the end of the activity sequence but may have skipped several tasks along the way. Sometimes the action stops, because someone misses hearing their clue. Sometimes participants present the correct sequential response, but their voice level may be insufficient to be heard by others in the group. Sometimes players lose focus or become distracted. These are all real-life situations that can happen in any assignment that requires a team to complete the task. If any of these errors occur, ask everyone in the group to review the content of their card and try again,

I like that this activity explores many of the skills necessary for groups to succeed, including leadership, listening, communication, accountability, problem solving, group cohesiveness, attention to detail and teamwork. This activity is a very convenient and concrete way to demonstrate how every member of a group can contribute toward a goal that benefits everyone in the group. This activity seems to work best when all group members can see each other (such as seated in a circle).

2-18 NEXT!

When somebody claps twice, stand up and say, "Good morning, everybody."

When somebody says, "Good morning, everybody," instruct everyone to move over one seat.

When everyone has moved over one seat, say, "It's a mistake" and instruct everyone to move back to their original seat.

When everyone moves back to their original seat, pull out your cell phone, hold it to your ear, and say, "I think you have the wrong number."

When somebody says, "I think you have the wrong number," invite everyone to ballroom dance with a partner.

When everyone is ballroom dancing, shout out, "I just won tickets to the Superbowl!"

When somebody shouts out "I just won tickets to the Superbowl!" ask everyone to find a new seat and place both hands on their head.

When everyone is seated with their hands on their head, say, "I'm thirsty."

When somebody says "I'm thirsty," stand up and pretend to paddle a canoe around the room.

When somebody begins paddling an imaginary canoe around the room, ask everyone to sing "Happy Birthday to You!"

When everyone is finished singing "Happy Birthday," ask everyone to smile at their neighbor.

While everyone is smiling at their neighbor, instruct everyone to stand up and march around the room.

While everyone is marching around the room, invite them to stop where they are.

When everyone marching stops where they are, make a loud sneezing sound.

When somebody makes a loud sneezing sound, say, "Looks like allergy season is here again."

When somebody says, "Looks like allergy season is here again," say, "Two can play at that game."

When somebody says, "Two can play at that game," instruct everyone to stand back-to-back with a partner.

When everyone is standing back-to-back with a partner, stomp your feet and invite everyone to join you.

When everyone is stomping their feet, shout out, "Shhhhhh!" very loudly.

When somebody says, "Shhhhhh" very loudly, shake hands with the person next to you and say, "Nice to meet you!"

When somebody says, "Nice to meet you!" silently raise your hand high above your head, and wave.

When somebody raises their hand high above their head and waves, go to the middle of the group and make the letter Y with your body. Stay there.

When somebody makes the letter Y, grab two other people, stand next to the Y, and make the letters M, C, and A.

When somebody makes the letters of YMCA, say loudly, "I think we are almost done."

When somebody says, "I think we are almost done," instruct everyone to join hands in a circle.

When everyone joins hands in a circle say, "That's it. We're done!"

In addition to the activity itself, there is also an opportunity for postactivity reviewing and reflection, which can bring additional value and insight to this and indeed any activity. For this activity, reviewing questions might include:

Discuss how difficult or easy it was to reach the goal. What skills were needed to complete the task? What did individuals do that contributed to the success of the group? What happens when someone does not do their part? What are some ways that a group can support its members as they strive to reach their goals? What types of communication were used in this activity? Were any modifications made by the group that assisted them in the completion of the activity?

During the reviewing or reflection component of this activity, some groups brainstorm techniques to help them successfully complete the task at hand. For example, if participants are allowed to mingle before the facilitator claps twice, they could seat themselves in order so that it becomes a bit more obvious which task follows another. Players may also be allowed to switch cards with another participant, so that each player can perform a task they are confident about completing.

One of the differences between the original version of this activity and the updated version is that the original version had a majority of tasks performed by a single individual, and the modified version suggests tasks that require more people to accomplish each assignment, which increases the distractions in the room, additionally challenging participants to focus on the task at hand. Confusion, chaos, disorder, shifting priorities and focus are all real-life events that can impact the successful completion of a task, especially one in which the contributions of multiple people are required.

As a variation of this activity, you can use a stopwatch as a performance metric, to record the time required to complete each round. But be sure to discuss with your audience if they believe speed is important, and if so, which is more important, speed or accuracy?

I discovered this activity by Anne Stevenson and Patty Hupfer Riedel from Carl (Energizer) Olson, which he included in his book *Impact! Activities to Enhance Teaching & Learning.* Anne, an Extension Professor at the University of Minnesota and her sister Patty, a chemistry teacher at Pius XI High School in Milwaukee, Wisconsin developed the activity in 1995 and were gracious enough to allow me to include both the original version of their activity, which they call When Someone Claps Twice, and the modified version which I have entitled Next! Thanks Anne, Patty and Carl.

On the next page, you'll find the original version of this activity, created by Anne Stevenson and Patty Hupfer Riedel.

WHEN SOMEONE CLAPS TWICE

(The original version of Next! by Anne Stevenson and Patty Hupfer Riedel)

When somebody claps twice, stand up and say "good morning".

When somebody says "good morning", get up and turn off the lights.

When somebody turns off the lights, yell "It's dark in here!"

When somebody yells "It's dark in here!" get up and turn on the lights.

When somebody turns on the lights, stand up and spin around twice.

When somebody spins around twice, make a loud cow (mooing) noise.

When somebody makes a cow (mooing) noise, stand up and say, "I'm glad to be here!"

When somebody says "I'm glad to be here," stand up and flap your arms like a bird.

When somebody flaps their arms like a bird, stand on your chair.

When somebody stands on a chair, say "Get down from there!"

When somebody says 'Get down from there!", make a loud sneezing sound.

When somebody makes a loud sneezing sound, feel the forehead of the person next to you and shout "Somebody get a Doctor!".

When somebody shouts "Somebody get a Doctor!", sing "Mary Had a Little Lamb" in a loud voice.

When somebody sings "Mary Had a Little Lamb," walk around the leader/teacher 2 times.

When somebody walks around the leader/teacher two times, laugh really loud.

When somebody laughs really loud, stomp your feet for 5 seconds.

When somebody stomps their feet, do a cheerleading move and say "Rah! Rah! Rah!"

When somebody does a cheerleading move and says "Rah! Rah! Rah!", tell us what time it is in a loud voice.

When somebody tells us what time it is, shake hands with the person next to you and loudly say, "Nice to meet you!"

When somebody says, "Nice to meet you!", say "I have a question".

When somebody says, "I have a question", yell: "The answer is seven."

When somebody says, "The answer is seven," go to the front of the room and make the letter Y with your body. Yell out "Y" and stay there.

When somebody makes the letter Y, grab 2 other people, go to the front of the room, stand next to the Y and make the letters M, C, and A, then sing "YMCA."

When somebody sings "YMCA", hop on one foot for 5 seconds and yell "I am a rabbit."

When somebody says "I am a rabbit," say "Here comes Peter Cottontail!".

When somebody says "Here comes Peter Cottontail!", give everybody a piece of candy!

2-19 CHANGING PLACES

Working together to make all the right moves.

For these human-sized puzzles, use large index cards as place markers and your audience as the playing pieces. Each of these puzzles incorporates creative problem solving for every member of the team. Let's start with the classic teambuilding puzzle known as Traffic Jam.

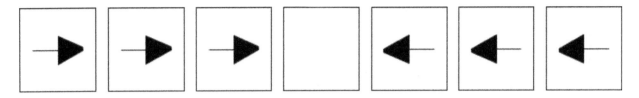

This team challenge is a shuttle puzzle that can be performed with human participants, and also as a tabletop puzzle with wooden pegs or coins. Start with the index card pattern shown. Three participants stand on the left side of the pattern, three participants on the right, with each group facing the center. The challenge is for each group to switch sides with members of the opposite group.

A few rules apply to how participants can reposition themselves during this activity. A participant can move into any open space. A participant can jump (move around) a member of the opposite team, into an open space. A participant cannot pass a member of their own team. Participants cannot back up. If a participant reaches a position from which no one can move forward, the system becomes "locked" and the entire group must return to the beginning to try again. There is no penalty for trial-and-error attempts, but try to be as efficient as possible and learn from any mistakes that occur.

It takes a minimum of fifteen moves to complete the above challenge. Groups achieving success to this challenge can be further challenged by demonstrating that they can repeat their performance a second time, without talking. As a final, high-level challenge, invite your group to complete this activity without breathing! That is, asking everyone in the group to simultaneously take a breath and hold it, start and complete the relocation, before anyone needs to breathe again. Good luck!

One of my favorite variations of Traffic Jam is to place the seven index cards in a curved pattern (like a smile). This allows participants to see each other and the entire playing field during the challenge, compared to the straight-line version above which allows only limited vision, especially for the participants in the back positions.

The next (and slightly more difficult) variation of Changing Places comes in the form of the letter M. The goal of this puzzle is for the team on the left side to change places with the team on the right side. No jumping is allowed in this puzzle, but participants can slide into any open space. A participant can move any number of spaces in one turn, provided they slide only along the lines connecting each location. You can create the M version of this activity with large index cards as place markers and sidewalk chalk (or masking tape) to show the lines connecting each card.

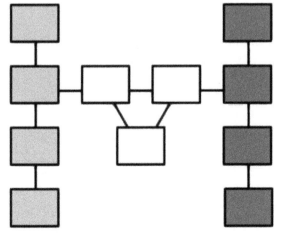

The final variations of Changing Places are the formations shown below. In these configurations, two teams attempt to change locations. Each move consists of sliding into any open position or jumping over (around) any other person. Players can jump members of their own team and members of the opposite team as well.

For the first arrangement (with sixteen people) a minimum forty-six moves are required to complete the transfer. You can reduce the number of people and the number of moves required by using the middle pattern (which requires only ten people) or the smaller double square pattern (with just six people).

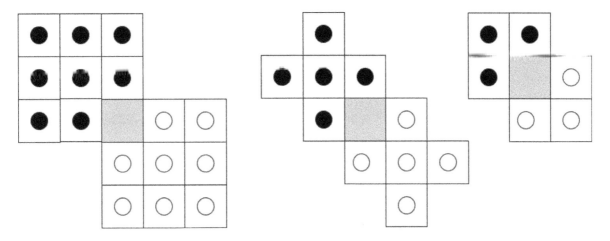

REINVENTING THE PAST AND MAKING IT BETTER

I have more than a thousand books filled with icebreakers and games of all kinds. Some of the games and activities mentioned in those books are so old they become new again. I'm never surprised when I pull out a classic (some might say ancient) activity and participants claim they are playing it for the first time! This brings up two good points. First, if you play a game (as written) and it doesn't produce the results you were hoping for, then you have the right to change something about the game to make it work for you. Change the size of the group, change the prop, change from indoors to outside, change something that will improve the game. Second, some games have been around for a long time. Just because they are old doesn't mean they aren't great. Try some oldies but goodies now and then. Some games are so old, they are brand new to the latest generation! If you present such a game, and you are excited about it, your audience will be excited about it, too.

As an example, the teambuilding challenge Traffic Jam has been around since the 1980s and as a wooden tabletop puzzle long before that. Adding the elements of not talking and not breathing to this challenge renews the activity. Don't be afraid to try some old games and see if you can make them new again. Visit www.archive.org and search for puzzles, games and amusement books from the 1800s. You can download (for free!) dozens of electronic book formats filled with interesting games from the past, all of which are just waiting for you to bring them into the present.

Each of the puzzles presented here can be used to encourage trial and error solutions, learning and adapting from our mistakes. You can further encourage the concept of an experimental laboratory by offering the group ten minutes to make as many attempts (and mistakes) as possible before a final trial for all the marbles. The concept of "failing forward," that is, learning from our mistakes, improving our processes, and becoming better as a result of trying, is well supported by using these puzzles. You can learn more about this concept by reading *Failing Forward: How to Make the Most of Your Mistakes* by John C. Maxwell (ISBN 978-0-7852-7430-8).

2-20 TANGRAMS

Modern variations of an ancient puzzle.

A tangram is a dissection puzzle made from seven flat pieces, which are assembled to create various shapes. Invented during the Song Dynasty of China (960–1279 AD), the tangram is one of the most popular dissection puzzles in the world.

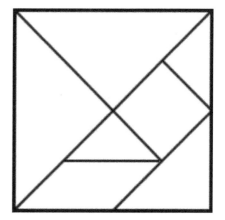

You can make the classic seven-piece tangram puzzle shown here with a pair of scissors and a large index card. First cut the index card into a square, and then into the seven pieces illustrated.

Now see if you can produce the following shapes using all seven of the tangram pieces.

In addition to the classic tangram pattern familiar to all, you can modify the manner in which you dissect a square to produce other collections of seven pieces. Try creating these tangram variations and see if you can still produce some of the shapes presented above with these modified tangram sets.

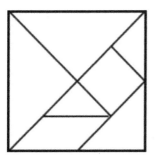
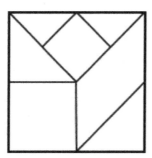
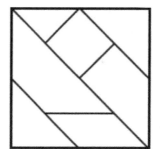
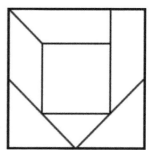

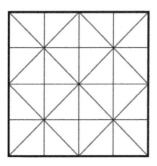

The four patterns shown above are not the only ways to dissect a square into seven pieces. Use the grid shown on the left as a pattern for making your own interesting and unique collection of seven-piece puzzles. You'll discover that some dissections are more difficult to reassemble into the shapes shown above.

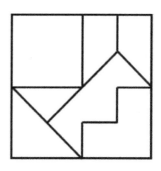

MORE WAYS TO USE TANGRAMS TO CREATE TEACHABLE MOMENTS

Underwater Tangrams. While this activity actually takes place on dry land, it does require some underwater skills. Begin with the entire team standing around the perimeter of a rope circle (about 30 feet [10 meters]) in diameter. In the center of the circle, seven large tangram pieces have been placed in random order. The task for the group is to correctly assemble these tangram pieces into a shape provided by the facilitator. The challenge is that team members can only enter the circle one person at a time, and they must hold their breath for the duration of the time they are inside the circle. The circle is essentially an imaginary swimming pool and the tangram pieces are considered "underwater." Since participants cannot hear underwater, communication can only occur on dry land (outside the perimeter of the circle). By requiring participants to only enter the circle once (for as long as they can hold their breath), facilitators encourage all group members to become involved in the solution process.

Tangrams for Exploring Diversity and Uniqueness. Construct the four different seven-piece puzzles shown on the first page of tangram activities, using a different color of index card for each puzzle.

After providing each group of three to five participants with one of the above collections of geometric pieces, ask them to create various shapes, and see how many of these same shapes can also be made by each of the other groups, using their own unique pieces. You can ask some of the following questions to your group: *What shapes or patterns do we all have in common? What shapes or patterns can each group uniquely make? Is it important that all groups are the same?*

Notice that each of the four patterns, though different, have several pieces in common with each of the other patterns.

Tangram Communication. As a communication activity, you can provide one person or small group with a tangram pattern already assembled. The task is to verbally communicate to other participants or groups how to recreate this same pattern using their own tangram pieces. Initially, try this version with one-directional information only (that is, with only the presenter talking). Next, try another pattern, but this time allowing feedback and two-way communication between presenter and tangram builders.

Tangram Variations. You can make tangrams from a variety of materials (index cards, wood, plastic, paper, foamboard, cardboard, magnets, cloth, leather, stained glass, stone). With the right forethought, you can assemble your tangrams on the ground, on tables, on walls (using spray adhesive or tape), on the ceiling, on a refrigerator (using magnets), on overhead transparencies (for projecting to a large audience) or anywhere else you can find the right combination of tangrams and space.

Hints and Clues. One of the most helpful techniques to assist a team solving a tangram puzzle is to offer to place one or two pieces in the correct position, at the team's request. You can also provide an outline or framework to further identify the space the tangram puzzle should fill.

For More Information. You can find dozens of interesting tangram sites on the Internet, such as www.tangram-channel.com. For more tangram patterns, see the book *Tangram Puzzles—500 Tricky Shapes to Confound & Astound* by Chris Crawford (ISBN 978-0-8069-7589-X).

You can find even more ways to use tangrams as team challenges in the book *Teambuilding Puzzles* (ISBN 978-0-7575-7040-7) written by Mike Anderson, Jim Cain, Chris Cavert and Tom Heck for Kendall/Hunt Publishers (www.kendallhunt.com). This book contains 100 puzzles for teams and has become an essential resource for the design of escape rooms and other teambuilding challenges.

2-21 STEPPING STONES

Walking on index cards.

Moving individuals or teams from Point A to Point B is a time-honored component of many teambuilding activities. But making that journey memorable and creating a teachable moment in the process is the critical difference between an average teambuilding activity and a great one. Here are several variations for using large index cards as stepping stones in this series of transportation challenges.

First, as a challenge for individuals, give each participant two or three large (5x8) index cards and invite them to move from Point A to Point B, a distance of perhaps 20 feet (9 meters), using only these cards and without touching the floor with their feet and without sliding the cards along the surface of the floor. With three cards, the task is fairly easy. With two cards, a bit more problem solving is required, as well as balance and agility.

Second, for teams of two, give each team of partners a total of three large index cards and invite them to travel from Point A to Point B. This version of Stepping Stones is likely to incorporate more teamwork and creative problem solving. If you wish to include empathy in your outcomes for this activity, blindfold one of the partners in each group. Be sure to keep the total distance covered by each team fairly short for this version of the activity.

Third, for teams of four to eight people, provide each group with one index card per person and invite them to stay in constant contact with each other and with the index cards on the floor. Any card positioned on the floor and left uncontacted by a participant is likely to "blow away" in the wind. Any participant unconnected to the team will likely do the same. Stay safe—stay connected!

Fourth, for teams of four to eight people, present each group with one index card per person and ask them to transport a set (loaded) mouse trap on an index card from Point A to Point B. Anyone holding an index card with the mouse trap on it cannot move their feet, but they can pass this card to another person. For this activity, you can either provide each person with an index card and pass the mouse trap from card to card or just place the mouse trap on a single index card and pass this card from person to person, until the destination is reached.

Finally, one of the more unique ways to use an index card in a transportation activity is to place it between your knees and attempt to walk to a specific destination without allowing the index card to drop and without touching it with your hands during the crossing.

If you'd like to increase the difficulty for any of the variations mentioned, consider challenging contestants to transport a paper cup filled with water, or an empty 5-gallon bucket, or a large cardboard box filled with something unusual (such as the debriefing props for the end of the activity), or a bowling ball, as they move from Point A to Point B.

You can also invite your participants to write down the skills they can contribute to the team on their personal index cards. Use these cards during the activity as transport devices and as a debriefing tool at the completion of the activity. *Which skills were used during the activity? How could more of the team's collective skills be used on a daily basis?*

2-22 THE PROPER SEQUENCE

Working together to produce a coherent story.

Many of the tasks in our daily lives require the ability to absorb information and process it in a meaningful way, so that information can be used in a productive manner. We read the newspaper and collect information about our community and our world. We read the weather report and that information might potentially change our plans for the day. We read the sports section for the results of last night's game and have an emotional response to the final score. We read an editorial piece or a letter to the editor, and decide if we agree or disagree with the author. Sometimes we read an article that makes no sense to us, so we search for more information… all to make sense of what is going on in the world around us. We struggle to take in information and create something coherent from a collection of often less-than-coherent pieces.

The Proper Sequence takes advantage of our ability to make sense of something that is presented incoherently (that is, without logical or meaningful connection). Forensic scientists and detectives excel in this field because they can take disconnected clues and information and combine these things to produce a coherent conclusion.

Jigsaw puzzles are a visual version of the Proper Sequence. Such puzzles are presented incoherently (disassembled) and the user is challenged to assemble them into a coherent image. Quotes in Order, an activity found earlier in this chapter, is a literary example, where participants are presented with seemingly disconnected words and phrases and challenged to assemble these words into a coherent (and meaningful) quotation. The books *Zoom* and *Re-Zoom* by Istvan Banyai, mentioned in Chapter 7 of this book, are playful examples of presenting images to a group and asking them to place these images in logical order.

The content I like to use for this activity is a familiar story (which creates a literary or word-centered challenge) or a series of clues (which require not only sensemaking but logical deductions from these clues as well). The activity Thirteen Clues, presented earlier in this chapter, is a literary challenge with a mathematics-based solution.

Three of my favorite stories for this activity are *The Blind Men and the Elephant* by John Godfrey Saxe (a Vermont poet and humorist), *A Little World—A Book About Tolerance* by Joanna Carolan and *All I Really Need to Know I Learned in Kindergarten* by Robert Fulghum. You'll find the complete text for *The Blind Men* in this chapter as part of activity 2.29, A Perfect Match. You can dissect each of these stories into individual words, phrases or sentences and place them onto large index cards. You can also do the same with song lyrics, poetry, popular quotations, DIY project instructions, cooking recipes, stories and classic speeches (such as the *Gettysburg Address*).

According to the Cone of Learning, proposed by Edgar Dale in 1946, the greater the intensity of the learning experience, the greater the retention of that information by the student. And that information was widely accepted, until new research in differentiated learning (according to each student's learning style) became popular. Suffice to say that when students struggle to make sense of an ambiguous situation, they tend to retain that experience and information as a result.

The process of organizing information and putting it into a coherent, logical and meaningful order is known as sensemaking. You can find out more about this foundation of organizational science in the book *Sensemaking in Organizations* (ISBN 978-0-8039-7177-6) by Karl E. Weick.

2-23 THE TRANSPORTATION CARD

Index Cards as Transport Devices

While an index card is much smaller than a standard tray, it can still be used to transport some interesting things, such as a glass of water, an action figure or toy, marbles or even a set mouse trap.

First decide which variation of a transportation card you wish to build. The first version consists of an index or playing card with several strings attached to the card. This version will allow more participants to be actively engaged in the transportation process. The second version is to simply use a single index or playing card (the larger the better) as your entire transportation device (no strings attached).

Next, decide what objects you would like to transport (or allow your audience to choose the object themselves). For most objects, an unmodified index or playing card works best, but for such things as marbles, you may want to punch a few holes near the center of each card to act as resting places for any objects which tend to roll around.

Finally, after creating your Transportation Card and collecting some interesting things to transport, you will want to identify an interesting transportation route for your audience to navigate. Walking through a doorway or passing Transportation Cards up a staircase can both be challenging. Be sure that the entire route is not too long. Transporting a set mouse trap, for example, should be limited to a reasonable distance of about 10 to 20 feet (3 to 6 meters).

Here are a few creative variations for the Transportation Card. Challenge your next audience by requiring that anyone touching the card (or string attached to a card) cannot move their feet. This will require more handoffs between participants as the contents of the transportation card move from one location to another. You can also challenge teams to pass the object they are transporting from one Transportation Card to another without anyone actually touching the item itself. Another variation is to invite your audience to transport a sand-filled (plastic) egg timer. The team must complete the transportation route before the sand timer runs out, effectively adding a time constraint to the challenge. You can also replace the index or playing card with a bandana and use this flexible cloth to transport some interesting objects. Finally, modify the Transportation Card with multiple strings so that only a single string remains. Challenge individual participants to transport an object by dragging the Transportation Card along the ground, using the single string attached to the card. The more rugged the terrain, the more care will be needed to successfully traverse the course.

The initial idea for the Transportation Card game from the creative mind of Jon Grizzle. Jon shared his original version of the activity, using a laminated playing card. I suggested that a hotel key card might be even more durable, especially when you want to drill holes and attach strings to the card. You can find more creative ideas from Jon in his new book *Team Building A La Card: Affordable Adaptations of Team Activities* (ISBN 978-1-5448-5349-9) available from www.amazon.com.

One of the more unusual things I have discovered about creating teambuilding props and activities is that many of the teambuilding props available are actually inefficient machines. Marble tubes, for example, used to transport a collection of marbles from one location to another, are incredibly inefficient, but teamwork overcomes that inefficiency and makes relocating a few marbles interesting, engaging, and fun. So, if you want to create something new, say an index card transportation device, just be sure your device is inefficient by design and let teams figure out for themselves how to overcome that inefficiency (with teamwork) and get the job done!

2-24 BUILD IT

A colorful construction and communication activity.

You can begin preparation for this activity by organizing your audience into teams of six people each. Then ask each team to find a partner team, and designate one team the design team and the other the manufacturing team. Each team is then given an identical collection of index cards of various sizes, shapes, colors and textures plus a few other stationery items such as scissors, tape, staples, paper clips, crayons, markers and pens.

The design team is tasked with assembling twelve index cards in a unique and creative manner. When complete, this design becomes the model which the manufacturing team will attempt to replicate. The only constraint is that the manufacturing team cannot directly view the design model. Instead, one member at a time (from the design team and the manufacturing team) can meet (away from each model) and discuss how to construct the replica, for one minute per session. These team members then return to their respective teams for one minute before another pair of teammates discuss the project. Six team members are on each team, with six meetings total. After a final two-minute construction period for the manufacturing team, the replica model is transported next to the original design model, and a discussion begins on the results of the communication process.

To increase the challenge of this activity, try a few of these modifications. Increase the number of participants and cards on each team. This will allow for additional visits between the design and manufacturing teams. In addition to the index cards, include a collection of stickers that can be attached to cards in specific places, or colorful pens. In addition to providing scissors for cutting and trimming index cards, you can also provide creative paper punches (available at most craft stores) and allow teams to make folds in their index cards as well.

For many teambuilding facilitators, the preferred building materials for Build It are Lego® kits, wooden blocks, tangrams, Tinkertoys® or some other collection of construction toys. Personally, I like the cost advantage of using index cards, plus the creative opportunity for modifying index cards with scissors, stickers, hole punches and folding. The final designs when using index cards are often beautiful and can be used as table centerpieces when your audience breaks for lunch.

Technology has come to play a significant role in this activity. Once, while using construction toys as building materials, the manufacturing team produced an exact replica of the original design, down to the last detail. When I complimented them on their performance, they pulled out their cell phones and showed a collection of photos they had texted between the design and manufacturing teams. Using the resources available is part of the creative process. Well done, students!

2-25 A CARD TOSSING CHALLENGE

Creative problem solving.

One of the trademarks of an outstanding team challenge is one that allows for multiple correct solutions. Another is the ability to clearly state the challenge in only a few words. Any activity that is easy to explain but not necessarily easy to solve is a good example of a potentially excellent team challenge. The Card Tossing Challenge presented here contains all of these critical components. The challenge is to modify a standard index card so that when released, it travels the farthest distance possible.

Some typical modifications include adding additional weight (such as attaching a coin or metal washer to the card), cutting the card into a circle, dropping the card from a greater height, adding wings, mailing (or shipping) the card to a distant location, and folding the card into a paper airplane.

As a variation of this activity, instead of attempting to toss a card the farthest distance, challenge your audience to see if they can modify an index card to land as close to a specified target as possible. Oddly enough, wadding the card into a paper ball is one of the simplest ways to modify the trajectory. Dropping index cards from a balcony to a target on the floor below (or into a bucket) is a fun challenge as well.

A few years ago, I found a partially deflated helium balloon wedged into a tree in my backyard with a colorful streamer and an index card attached to it. On the card, I discovered a hand-written note from an elementary student in St. Catharines, Ontario, Canada (about 80 miles west of my home), but in an entirely different country. Included on the card was the student's name, school, grade and a few questions, such as where the balloon was found, and my favorite book title. There was a prize for the student whose balloon flew the furthest distance.

It just happens that the next day I was traveling to Scotland. So (prankster that I was back then) I took that index card and balloon with me to Scotland, and a week later, I mailed a photograph of the balloon (taken in front of Edinburgh Castle) and the card with my answers back to the school in St. Catherines. I don't actually know the results of the contest, but I like to think that the student who crafted the balloon I found might be amazed at how far the balloon traveled (albeit with a little help from me and a jet airplane or two).

2-26 PAPER PUSHERS

The fine art of moving paper around

This is one of the more physical challenges in this book. It is hard to believe that something as lightweight as an index card can be used to produce such a high level of physical exertion.

For this activity, begin by forming teams of three or four people. Next create a "starting line" using a piece of painter's masking tape (the blue kind that is easy to remove) or a long piece of rope. Then explain that the challenge for this activity is for each team to push an index card as far beyond the starting line as possible, with nothing more than their hands touching the space beyond the line, and then retreat completely behind the line. If contact is made with the floor or ground beyond the starting line with any body part other than hands, that team is invited to try again.

Most teams try to build some sort of bridge-like structure using their bodies as the main structural components, and then allowing other team members to crawl over them, pushing the index card as they go. The greater the number of players on each team, the greater the level of physical exertion required. And don't forget, teams not only need to push the index card as far as they can, but they also need to retreat behind the starting line again, without making contact with the floor or ground with anything other than their hands, for their index card placement to count!

One of the most difficult things about Paper Pushers is the amount of time required for any particular player to have their body weight on their hands. Techniques that minimize the total amount of time for the entire team generally push their card farther. Rather than building a bridge-like structure (with team members climbing over each other), try using a windshield wiper approach (where teams build their complete structure behind the starting line, and then rotate (like a windshield wiper) this structure, pushing the index card as far as they can in the process.

One of the more unique variations of Paper Pushers is rather than having teams push an index card as far as they can, place several index cards (or prizes) in front of the starting line and challenge teams of three or four players to reach for these items and return them behind the starting line. Teams successfully retrieving their card or prize get to keep it!

Over the years, I've used a wide variety of things to push beyond the starting line—from an unsharpened pencil to a toy car to a five-gallon bucket of water filled to the brim. One of the advantages of using an index card in this activity is that each team can write their team name and their estimate of the total distance they think they can push the index card beyond the starting line and then compare this estimate to the actual distance they were able to move the card.

2-27 PASS / FAIL

Finding the secret criteria.

Criteria (n., pl.)—A principle or standard by which something may be judged or decided.

This activity encourages participants to discover the secret criteria that determine an acceptable (pass) or unacceptable (fail) transfer of an index card to the facilitator.

To prepare for this activity, collect four different varieties of index cards that vary by size, shape, color and line pattern. You will need a total of about three times the number of cards as the number of participants in this activity. Shuffle this collection of cards and invite everyone in your audience to select two of these cards, leaving the remaining cards randomly distributed in a pile on the floor in the middle of a circle of chairs. Next invite everyone to take a seat, including the facilitator.

Explain that the challenge of this activity is to discover the secret criteria that determine whether the transfer of an index card between a participant and the facilitator is considered acceptable (pass) or unacceptable (fail). Inform your audience that there are exactly two elements to an acceptable transfer, and that both of these need to be identified by the team.

Then invite anyone seated in the circle of chairs to pass a card to the facilitator. Participants may stand and walk the card to the facilitator or pass a card around the circle to the facilitator. Encourage all participants to observe the delivery technique of each and every index card, striving to figure out the criteria that determine an acceptable transfer.

The facilitator (of course) knows the pass/fail criteria for this activity. For those transfers not meeting the secret criteria, the facilitator dramatically rips these index cards in two and drops them to the floor. Acceptable (pass) transfers are simply regarded with the phrase "Thank you" as the facilitator adds these cards to the pile of additional index cards in the center of the circle.

To determine the secret criteria, participants must utilize a finite but dwindling supply of index cards. After participants have exhausted their personal supply of cards, they can continue the game using the additional index cards on the floor in the center of the circle.

Participants can suggest at any time what they believe the criteria are for this challenging activity. There is no penalty for a wrong guess, but recommend to your audience that they test any particular theory they may have before suggesting it.

My personal favorite criteria for an acceptable transfer are, the index card must be passed with the left hand (by the participant) and only cards of a specific color (yellow) are acceptable. All other cards and transfer techniques are unacceptable.

Some of the teachable moments in this activity include working with limited resources to define and solve a problem, teamwork, communication, creative problem solving, testing hypotheses, observation and team dynamics.

The original version of this activity, which can be found in the book *Essential Staff Training Activities* (ISBN 978-0-7575-6167-2) by Jim Cain, Clare Marie Hannon and Dave Knobbe, was called Pop It, and utilized balloons instead of index cards. Acceptable transfers were recycled into a pile in the center of the circle while unacceptable transfers were dramatically popped with a push-pin thumbtack.

2-28 PART OF THE RAINBOW

Do you see what I see?

Over 7.6 billion people now populate our planet. That means there could be over 7 billion different points of view. Part of the Rainbow tests that theory using a collection of colorful index cards to see if people with different points of view, different visual abilities and other diversities, can come to a consensus on which two index cards are most alike (or even identical) in color.

For this activity, you will need a collection of colored index cards or an artistic collection of index card stock from a craft or paper store. You can also use a spectrum of paint chip cards from your local paint store, or a collection of construction paper from your local stationery supply store.

To prepare for this activity, take one index card (the target card) and place it on a wall (about eye level) in one room. Then place a collection of fifteen index cards with a diversity of color on the wall of an adjoining room. These locations should be chosen so that no one can see both the target card and the collection of cards at the same time. The cards in the diverse collection should also have an identifying number or letter at the bottom of each card, for easy identification.

Invite your audience to gather in the room with the target card. One participant at a time can visit the room with the diverse collection of cards, for up to one minute. When they return, another participant can visit the other room.

Encourage each participant to choose up to three candidate cards from the diverse collection that could be a match for the target card. When everyone has visited the room with the diverse collection of cards, ask them to come to a consensus on which single card is the best match for the target card. Then ask one or two people to revisit the diverse collection room and confirm the group's opinion. The final task is to move the target card to the diverse collection room and confirm the result.

The primary difference between the cards in this activity is color, but you could also include cards with different sizes, shapes, features (such as rounded corners), folds or other distinguishing characteristics. If you want to increase the challenge for this activity, place the cards in rooms with little or no lighting, and provide a flashlight for participants to carry between rooms and view the cards in each room. You can also change which room your participants begin the activity. See if your next audience performs best starting in one room versus the other.

The first time I share this activity with a group, I like to select a target card with a familiar primary color (red, blue, green or yellow) and make the diverse collection a rainbow of possibilities. Most folks are unlikely to mistake blue for red, but you never know. For the second round, I increase the challenge by making the target a subtle shade of blue or green and all of the diverse collection slightly different shades of this same color.

Some group members may try to use more than just their eyesight and memory to record the target color by comparing the target to a piece of clothing they are wearing or taking a smartphone photograph. Both of these are creative problem-solving possibilities.

Part of the Rainbow explores the possibility that two or more people can look at the same things and yet see something different. This can lead to some very interesting discussions as your group explores such things as a common vision and what consensus or agreement will look like for this group.

The original version of this activity, which can be found in the book *100 Activities That Build Unity, Community & Connection* (ISBN 978-1-60679-374-9) by Jim Cain, utilized paint chip cards (which can be found in most paint supply stores). Paint chip cards cover a wider variety of colors and hues, including dozens of colors that are within a few shades of the target color, making the paint chip version of this activity quite a bit more difficult.

2-29 A PERFECT MATCH

Can you find the identical twin?

A Perfect Match is a communication and problem-solving activity where blindfolded participants are challenged to determine which of the two objects they hold are identical twins.

You can prepare for this activity by cutting, trimming, hole punching and folding ordinary index cards into a collection of eleven different shapes. The twelfth shape is an exact copy of just one of the eleven other shape possibilities. For example, if houses are your theme, you can cut, trim, punch and fold ten different house profiles, and then place two index cards together to create two additional houses that are identical.

Once you have created the playing pieces, blindfold twelve of your participants and invite them to be seated in a circle. Additional team members can be observers standing behind this collection of players. Once all participants are seated and blindfolded, the facilitator passes out one of the index card shapes to each person. Players can then discuss the index card shape they are holding, but they cannot pass their shape to another player or touch anyone else's index card shape. The goal is for the group to determine which two of the shapes they possess are identical twins (exact replicas of each other).

This activity will generally take ten to twenty minutes for a group to complete. Up to twelve people can participate. Additional participants can act as observers and then share their observations during the debriefing component of this activity. To complete this communication activity, participants must use precise language and identify key differences in each of the shapes (or objects) they hold. Debriefing points can include observations about leadership within the group, finding a process that works for the team, communication and listening.

You can make your own collection of Perfect Match objects using index cards, cardboard, action figures, toys, plastic animals, wooden shapes and other craft supply objects. A Perfect Match kits and instructions are available from www.teamworkandteamplay.com.

A Perfect Match was originally published in the book *The Teamwork & Teamplay International Edition* (ISBN 978-0-9882046-3-8) by Jim Cain and utilized wooden blocks or three-dimensional action figures and toy animals for the playing pieces. With index cards, you can create a collection of playing pieces that is specific to the group you are facilitating. For outdoor educators, you can use objects from nature, such as trees. For corporate audiences, you can create replicas of their products, or common office supplies. For teachers, you can incorporate familiar teaching supplies or subject matter–related objects.

If you like to include stories as part of your teaching or training programs, I'd recommend *The Blind Men and the Elephant* by John Godfrey Saxe (a Vermont [USA] poet and humorist, 1816–1887) as the perfect story to share with the activity A Perfect Match. You can find versions of this poem online and at your local library, and on the next page of this book. And, if you prefer music, Natalie Merchant sang this complete poem in her album, *Leave Your Sleep*.

THE BLIND MEN AND THE ELEPHANT

By John Godfrey Saxe (Vermont poet and humorist, 1816–1887)

It was six men of Indostan, to learning much inclined,
who went to see the elephant, though all of them were blind.
That each by observation, might satisfy his mind.

The first approached the elephant, and happening to fall
against his broad and sturdy side, at once began to bawl -
"Bless me! But the elephant is very like a wall!"

The second, feeling of the tusk cried, "Ho! What have we here?
So very round and smooth and sharp, to me it's very clear.
This wonder of an elephant is very like a spear!"

The third approached the animal and happening to take
the squirming trunk with both his hands, thus boldly up and spake –
"I see," he said, "the elephant is very like a snake!"

The fourth reached out his eager hand, and felt about the knee.
"What most this wondrous beast is like is mighty plain," quoth he.
"It's clear enough the elephant is very like a tree!"

The fifth, who chanced to touch the ear, said, "even the blindest man
can tell what this resembles most; deny it if you can,
"this marvel of an elephant is very like a fan!"

The sixth no sooner had begun about the beast to grope;
than seizing on the swinging tail that fell within his scope,
"I see," he said, "the elephant is very like a rope!"

And so, these men of Indostan disputed loud and long,
each in his own opinion exceedingly stiff and strong,
though each was partly in the right, and all were in the wrong!

And the moral of the story is:

So oft in philosophic wars the disputants, I ween,
rail on in utter ignorance, of what each other mean,
and prate about an elephant, not one of them has seen!

2-30 IT'S YOUR CHOICE

Making tough decisions.

This activity explores making decisions, both individually and as a group. The facilitator shares some of the questions below and invites the entire audience to move to a location on the floor that reflects that decision. You can place a rope line down the middle of the group, and instruct your participants on which side to stand for each of two choices. Or you can create a layout for three choices (A, B and C) using hula-hoops or rope circles in three locations. Once a choice card is read, participants can move to the location that is connected to their choice, and then discuss their decision with others in that vicinity.

Would you rather: leave a written note, a voice message or a text message? Who would you rather meet in person: Abraham Lincoln, Leonardo Da Vinci or Mahatma Gandhi? Which disease would you rather cure first: Breast Cancer, Heart Disease or AIDS? Would you rather be a great athlete on a mediocre team, or a mediocre athlete on an outstanding team? Which of the following would qualify as the most valuable thing you have ever learned: the alphabet, learning to speak, the golden rule? Which holiday is your favorite: the Fourth of July, Thanksgiving, New Years Day? Would you rather go sky diving or deep-sea diving? Would you rather drive a car, a truck or a motorcycle? Would you rather cook your next meal over a campfire, in a microwave, or in a conventional oven? What determines your success in life: your heredity, your ability, your humanity? If you truly wanted to make a contribution to the world, would you rather be a politician, a teacher or an author? If your time machine was working, would you rather go forward or backward in time? Would you rather circle the globe by water (boat), by air (jet) or by ground (car, bicycle, foot)? Would you rather give up your cell phone, your television, or your computer? Would you rather watch a good movie, star in a good movie or write the script for a good movie? How many people would you like in your immediate family: less than five, between five and ten, more than ten? Which of the following things has the highest priority for "a good life": health, wealth, education, family or friends? You have an hour to spare before your next appointment. Would you rather pass that time in a hardware store, a grocery store, a clothing store, a bookstore, an electronics store, a stationery store or a gift shop? Would you rather invent something that saves lives, makes a ton of money, or pushes the limits of technology? If you could qualify for a major sporting event, which of the following events would you prefer: the Olympic 100-meter dash (over in ten seconds), the Boston Marathon (over in about two hours), or the Tour de France (twenty-one stages over twenty-three days)? If you could recover one item that has been lost, would you do this for yourself, for a friend or for a member of your family? Would you rather give advice or receive it? Would you rather be rich or famous? One hundred years from now, do you think the world will be better, worse, or about the same?

There are other playful variations of this activity in the first chapter of this book, with icebreaking questions. See the activities The Big Question and Are Your More Like? But the unique element of It's Your Choice is that each question requires a decision, some of which can be extremely challenging. The choices provide insight into the hearts and minds of the participants. Sometimes even the simplest choices can provide profound insights into human behavior and group decision making. Explore the possibilities and enjoy!

2-31 EVERYTHING ON THE TRAY

All of us are smarter than any of us.

This memory game is an index card variation of the classic Kim's Game first shared in the writings of Rudyard Kipling. The difference is that in this version of the game, teams are allowed to work together to identify all the items displayed in the box. Conduct this activity in two rounds, to emphasize the power of working together as a team.

For this activity, you'll not only need a supply of index cards and pencils, but also a tray with about a dozen diverse and interesting things. You can add such things as a fork, a wooden spool, a paperclip, a pencil sharpener, a toy, a kitchen utensil, tools, coins, a napkin and other things you can find around the house, office or school. Once your collection is ready, walk slowly around the room displaying the contents to your audience (for about ten to fifteen seconds) and then cover the contents.

Next, ask each member of your audience to take an index card and write down (with as much detail as possible) the contents they remember from the collection. You can also ask a bonus question of how many total objects were on the tray. In Round 1 of the activity, after everyone has written down all the objects they remember, redisplay the contents and let everyone score themselves for the number of objects they remember.

When it comes to accurately guessing the total number of objects on the tray (in Round 1), most people will forget to include the napkin or placemat on which the objects rest on the tray or even the tray itself.

In Round 2, produce a second collection of stuff, and again display this collection to your audience for about ten to fifteen seconds. Then ask everyone to take an index card and (again) write down as many objects as they can remember. When everyone has finished writing, invite everyone to find a partner, and compare answers, adding any objects that were missing from your first guess. Then double the size of each small team, from two people to four, and repeat the process. Finally invite everyone to share their individual list and generate a group list. For most teams, the accuracy of the group list is generally better than that of any individual list.

You can play another version of this game without index cards. Simply display the tray full of miscellaneous objects once and then remove several objects, mix up the remaining objects and display the tray again. Then ask the group to identify which objects were removed.

———————————————

If you are interested in the group-think process, read the book *The Wisdom of Crowds—Why the Many are Smarter than the Few* (ISBN 978-0-349-11605-9) by James Surowiecki.

2-32 THE BEAST

Recreating a masterpiece.

Here is a playful activity that is equal parts creativity, communication and construction. Begin by dividing each small group into three teams of two to five participants. The first team (the construction crew) takes one collection of index cards, markers, scissors, masking tape, staples, rubber bands and other office supplies and constructs "the beast," a ferocious three-dimensional creature that can be part dinosaur, part robot, part anything! This beast is best assembled away from the other two teams. While the first team is completing their creation, the second team (the duplication team) becomes acquainted with an identical collection of office supplies at their disposal. When the first team has completed their construction, the third team (the communication experts) visit The Beast, one at a time, mentally recording what they find there, and communicate this information to the second (duplication) team.

The goal is for the communication team to accurately assist the duplication team in creating an exact replica of the original Beast. No set time limit or number of visits to see the beast are dictated. The duplication team can request specific information from the communication team.

In keeping with the theme of this book, index cards and other office supplies have been used to construct The Beast, but in reality, many other things can be used (provided you can assemble two collections of identical supplies). Foam noodles, tarps, rope, balls, buckets, kitchen utensils, hand tools, cardboard boxes, paper bags, straws, duct tape, athletic equipment and other common and familiar things are ideal for this activity.

2-33 CONNECTIONS

Identifying connections—the beginning of teamwork.

Sometimes in diverse audiences, it can be easier to pick out the differences between members of the group than the similarities. The purpose of this activity is to focus on what commonalities exist, rather than the differences. If you happen to be working with a group that has significant differences between the members of the group, this can be a powerful way to prepare your audience to collaborate.

Begin this activity by presenting your group with a stack of index cards and inviting them to write the names of things on index cards, using one item per card and filling as many cards as they can. Collect and shuffle these cards and then deal three cards face up to your audience and challenge them to find a connection between these three things.

For example, the three words *basketball*, *bridge* and *buffalo* all begin with the letter B. A blender, a truck and a washing machine all have gears. Some trios are more challenging than others. What do the Goodyear blimp, the 1980's band Devo and professional basketball player Lebron James all have in common? They all come from Akron, Ohio.

I like to invite my audience to brainstorm a list of things for this activity, but you can also create a random list of things on the web at https://www.randomlists.com/things. At this site, you can enter the total number of things you want for your list and instantly get a list of things (with illustrations). Some use the things generated at this site to create a scavenger hunt list, but this web-based list generator works just fine for the game of Connections, too. The first list I generated from this site produced a collection of three things, including a blanket, a shovel and a cat. So, what do these things all have in common? That, my friend, is your task in the game of Connections! Good luck.

In addition to using random objects in the game of Connections, you can also "stack the deck" by adding specific words that have significance to your audiences. If communication is important, you can add words such as *clarity* and *transparency* and incorporate communication tools such as a telephone, telegram, email or other familiar things.

———————————————

The game of Connections can be especially useful for situations when you have significant differences between the members of a group. In addition to this game, I'd like to share an additional resource to help you when working with groups in conflict. The following information is not so much a conflict resolution curriculum but a collection of things you can do BEFORE you engage in conflict resolution with a group. The *Thought, Words & Deeds* curriculum is designed to build unity, community and connection with groups that are not quite there yet, by inviting them to think about it, talk about it and do something about it. You can download the complete curriculum for free on the Teamwork & Teamplay website (www.teamworkandteamplay.com) by clicking on the Downloads button on the main page. A majority of the activities presented in this curriculum can be found in the book *100 Activities That Build Unity, Community & Connection* (ISBN 978-1-6067-9374-9) by Jim Cain, available from www.healthylearning.com, www.amazon.com and www.training-wheels.com.

Happiness is when what you think, what you say and what you do are in harmony.
—Mahatma Gandhi

2-34 EXPRESSIONIST TEAMBUILDING

A masterpiece in under 60 seconds.

This artistic teambuilding activity explores creative problem solving. A collection of fifteen large index cards creates a visual masterpiece. The challenge is for a team to correctly place each of the fifteen cards in their proper location to complete the artwork in as little time as possible.

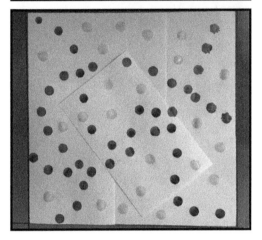

To prepare for this activity, you'll need to create your own artwork. I have chosen an abstract expressionist theme, influenced by the creative style of American artist Jackson Pollock. To begin, I arranged a collection of fifteen large index cards to completely fill a 20x20 inch (51x51 cm) square, which I had drawn onto an even larger piece of cardboard. Next, I fixed each of the fifteen index cards temporarily in place with double-sided tape. Then, I searched my basement for a collection of paints and sprayed, spattered and dripped a variety of colors onto these cards, producing the masterpiece shown.

After you have created your artwork and allowed your cards to dry, detach them from the painting backdrop, remove any remaining tape, shuffle them and prepare to challenge your audience.

Teams are to correctly locate each of the fifteen index cards in their proper location as quickly as possible. Before the first round, teams are asked to estimate the time required for them to complete the task. Then teams will have three attempts to demonstrate their ability to complete the task in the time they estimated, with adequate time for discussion and additional planning between each attempt.

Before adding paint to the fifteen index cards, I added some additional lines to several index cards as a hint to their location. Each of the four corner cards have "corner" illustrations on them, while each of the border cards have single lines near the border edge. I also added a few straight lines to some of the interior cards. You can add additional "clues" to your cards, including numbers, letters and shapes that extend from one card to another. You can also add holes in places that other cards will cover, or trim the corners of several cards for easy identification. You can further assist the completion of this activity by providing a frame for the index cards to fit within, such as a large sheet of poster board or cardboard.

I prefer to create the artistic puzzle shown in this activity without the pieces lining up along their edges. The randomness of this construction technique produces a more interesting and challenging puzzle than simply cutting a large piece of paper into smaller pieces.

American painter Jackson Pollock was famous for his unique style of drip and splash painting and a major figure in the abstract expressionist movement. You can create your own version of the cards required for this activity by letting Pollock's techniques inspire you. For more information, visit www.jackson-pollock.org.

A Story About Puzzles and Teamwork

While preparing the text for this activity, I was reminded of a story I shared in the book *Teambuilding Puzzles*, which I wrote with Chris Cavert, Mike Anderson and Tom Heck. The story was adapted from a tale told by my mentor and friend Denny Elliott of the Ohio State University Cooperative Extension Service, at 4-H Camp Ohio. The story describes the relationship between a father and son and incorporates a unique picture puzzle, very much like the Expressionist Teambuilding artwork described on the previous page.

The Puzzle Story

One Sunday afternoon, Mom decided to run a few errands, leaving her husband and their seven-year-old son together at home. Dad had a few projects to do that day, including finishing up some paperwork. As he sat working at the dining room table, his son played noisily nearby and managed to interrupt his poor Dad every few minutes. After thirty minutes of accomplishing almost nothing, Dad was ready to pull his hair out. "I've got to find something for Junior to do so that I can get some work done!"

As he gazed over at the Sunday newspaper, a plan formed in his head. He quickly glanced through the paper until he found a large picture on one of the pages—in this case, a full-color illustration of the earth. He removed this page from the paper and began tearing it into smaller pieces. After finishing this task, he presented his son with the puzzle and invited him to put the world back together. "That should keep him busy for a while," he said, and went off to finish his paperwork.

But within five minutes, his son was back. "I'm done, Papa," said the boy. Now this father always thought that he had a pretty smart son, but was skeptical that he could have finished the puzzle in such a short time.

When he stepped into the living room, however, he found that the puzzle was indeed completed, and in the correct order. "How did you finish this puzzle so quickly?" he asked his son. As the boy spoke, he began turning over each piece of the puzzle. On the reverse, there was a full-page photograph of his favorite professional sports team. "You see, Dad, if you can get your team to come together, then getting the rest of the world to come together is easy!"

In the teambuilding world, there is a familiar wooden frame version of this activity known as Cycle Time, where teams put together a collection of wooden frame pieces as quickly as possible. With each new attempt, teams are often able to reduce the time required to complete the task. In this case repetition (and familiarity) produced superior results. The Expressionist Teambuilding activity shown here is a more artistic version of the Cycle Time activity.

If you want to commission some truly interesting artwork for this activity, consider providing one of your favorite artistic children with paint and index cards and invite them to create a masterpiece. Ester Hoefsloot's children, Emma and Bente, created the artwork shown here.

2-35 FOUR IN A ROW

Finding a win/win solution.

Four in a Row is an excellent activity for visually demonstrating the value of cooperation rather than competition. You can prepare for this activity by creating a 4x6 grid on a large sheet of flip chart paper or on a small tarp. Each compartment of the grid should be about 6 inches square. Next assemble three different colors of 3x5 index cards. You'll need ten cards of one color, an additional ten cards of a different color, and four brightly colored wild cards of a third color.

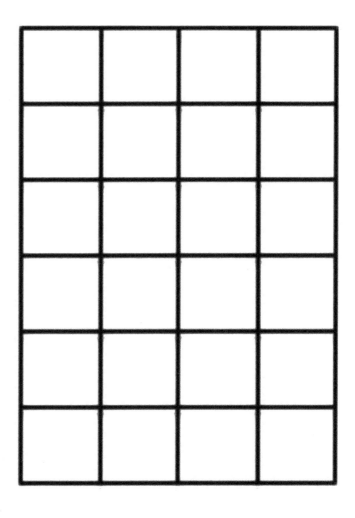

Next, split your audience into two teams and present each team with ten identical color cards plus two wild cards, for a total of twelve cards per team. Then introduce the activity.

Teams take turns placing one of their team's index cards in any of the twenty-four available compartments on the grid. Teams alternate until all cards have been played (and all the available spaces are filled). The team that creates the most four-in-a-row ball patterns (vertically, horizontally and diagonally) using their team's cards and any wild cards wins that round. Once placed on the grid, a wild card can be used by either team. Once a card is placed on the grid, it cannot be moved again during that round.

Initial rounds of this activity as generally competitive, as both teams try as much to block the other team as they try to create their own four-in-a-row patterns. Most teams typically place their wild cards in locations that only help their team. After just a few rounds, both teams quickly learn that by collaborating, they can typically create more four-in-a-row patterns for their own team.

The teachable moment for Four in a Row is that by collaborating it is possible for each team to create more four-in-a-row patterns than they ever could in a competitive environment. There are also elements of creative problem solving, pattern recognition, working within the structure and rules of the game and win-win possibilities.

The negotiation activity known as Win as Much as You Can incorporates some of the same rules, strategies and outcomes as Four in a Row. The value of collaboration versus competition is key to each of these activities, as is the opportunity for creating a win-win solution that is beneficial to both teams.

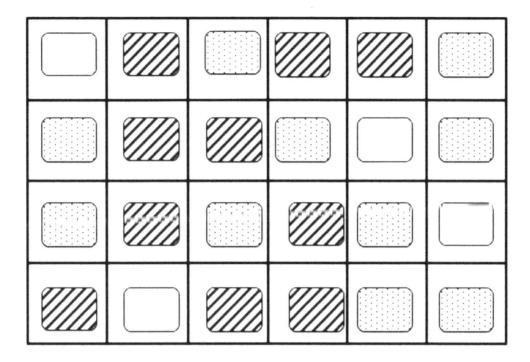

For the grid shown above, the score would be 2 for the polka-dot card team and 3 for the striped card team. Most of the wild cards (plain white cards) are placed to assist only one of the teams. For the grid shown below, the optimal placement of cards (especially the wild cards) creates a score of 7 for each team—much greater than either team could produce individually.

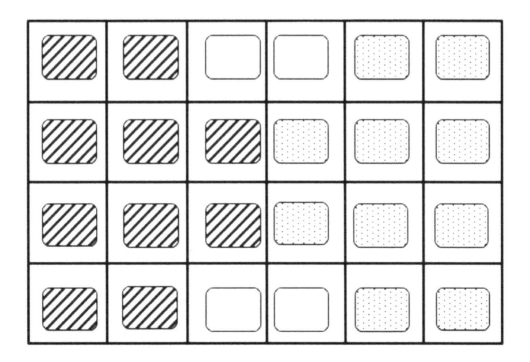

CHAPTER THREE

PUZZLES AND GAMES

This third chapter is a collection of forty-five unique puzzles and games that can be played with index cards and a few simple props. Not only are these activities fun, but many of them present significant teachable moments for you and your audience to explore together.

NO.	ACTIVITY NAME	TEACHABLE MOMENT	IDEAL GROUP SIZE
3-1	The Dice Game	My Favorite Dice Game	Multiple groups of 6–8
3-2	Kerfuffle	3 Minutes of Mayhem	20 or more people
3-3	Mrs. Right	Communication/Listening	Circles of 6–25 people
3-4	The Story Game	Quick Thinking and Action	Multiple groups of 8–15
3-5	Tora Tora	Anticipation, Fun	Multiple groups of 7
3-6	Birthday Cards	Mathematical Magic	Any
3-7	Math Magic	Mathematical Magic	Any
3-8	Non-Sequitur Slam Poetry	Literacy and Creativity	Any
3-9	Just One Word	Creative Problem Solving	Any
3-10	The Tangram Quilt	Creative Problem Solving	Multiple groups of 4–6
3-11	The Arrowhead Puzzle	Doing More with Less	Multiple groups of 4
3-12	Seven Folds	Extreme Origami	Any
3-13	Conundrum Cards	Adventures in Logic	Any
3-14	Three Houses and Three Utilities	Creative Problem Solving	Multiple groups of 4–6
3-15	Drawing in the Dark	Artistic Expression	Any
3-16	Alphabetically	Teamwork	Multiple small groups
3-17	Close All the Doors	An Architectural Challenge	Any
3-18	Tongue Twisters	A Linguistic Challenge	Any
3-19	Riddle Cards	Problem Solving	Any
3-20	Ultimate Tic-Tac-Toe	Gamesmanship and Strategy	Partners

NO.	ACTIVITY NAME	TEACHABLE MOMENT	IDEAL GROUP SIZE
3-21	Triplets	A Linguistic Challenge	Any
3-22	Card Tricks	Nine Card Magic	Any
3-23	Speed Spelling	Fast Words	Multiple small groups
3-24	The Walkabout Challenge	Balance and Poise	Any
3-25	Making Stuff Up	Literary Challenges	3–10 people
3-26	Directionally Challenged	Following Directions	Any
3-27	What Are We Yelling?	A Burst of Language	Multiple small groups
3-28	Sherlock Holmes	Investigation and Discovery	Any
3-29	The Internet Shopping Network	Seek and Ye Shall Find	Any
3-30	The Whole Story	Artistic Story Writing	5 or more people
3-31	Verbose Verbiage	A Linguistic Challenge	Any
3-32	Seven Dots	Creativity	5 or more people
3-33	Refrigerator Art	Artistic Expression	5 or more people
3-34	Why? Because!	Creative Problem Solving	5 or more people
3-35	Board Games	Games for Fun	2 or more people
3-36	The Jigsaw Hunt	Treasure Hunting	Any
3-37	Team Origami	A Super-Sized Challenge	Multiple groups of 4
3-38	Numeric Logic Puzzles	Logic and Numbers	Individuals or small teams
3-39	Squiggles	Team Art	Multiple groups of 2
3-40	Nursery Rhyme Headlines	Decode Each Message	Multiple groups of 4
3-40½	Nursery Rhyme Mysteries	Memory and Playfulness	Multiple small groups
3-41	Obscured	A Game I Invented!	Any
3-42	Snap Words	Knowing the Answers	Any
3-43	The Secret Word	Communication	Multiple groups of 6–8
3-44	Pirate's Treasure	Communication	Multiple groups of 4

3-1 THE DICE GAME

A frenetic table game for groups of eight people.

Gather your group and invite them to take a seat around a table, with a blank index card in front of each person, a single pen in the center of the table and one pair of dice.

The game begins as one player rolls the dice. If they happen to get doubles (two dice showing the same value), the group yells "DOUBLES" and that person grabs the pen. They begin writing the numbers 1, 2, 3, 4… as fast as possible on their index card. Meanwhile the game continues around the table, with each person rolling the dice. When another person rolls doubles, the table again yells "DOUBLES" and that person is given the pen and begins writing 1, 2, 3, 4… on their index card.

If the first player gets doubles again, and they managed to reach 17 on the last round, they begin with 18 and continue writing as fast as possible. The first person to write from 1 to 100 wins! But, when a player reaches 50, they must switch and write with their nondominant hand.

This game generally begins calmly enough, but after someone rolls doubles for the first time, the game takes on a much higher level of energy and excitement.

Tim Borton came to work with me as part of a summer internship for his master's degree. Tim taught me this game and I have enjoyed sharing it with people around the world. Tim mentioned that his father was one of the least competitive people he knew, but one year at Thanksgiving, while playing this game around the family dining room table, Tim's father leaped up onto the table to grab the pen when he rolled doubles. I like the loud and boisterous nature of the game and I'm sure your audiences will, too.

3-2 KERFUFFLE

Kerfuffle – A commotion or fuss, confusion, disorder
Hullabaloo – An uproar, clamor, brouhaha, pandemonium, mayhem
Hurly Burly – A busy, boisterous activity
52 Pickup – A terror inflicted by older siblings on younger siblings, involving the release and collection of playing cards

This high-energy activity has had many names over the years. I like the name Kerfuffle, but feel free to call the game anything you like. Begin with a collection of index or playing cards and write one of the tasks (found on the following pages) with permanent marker on each card. This is a great way to repurpose a used deck of playing cards, especially for those incomplete decks that you might have at home.

Next, collect about twice as many cards as you have participants. Gather your group together and toss the entire deck of cards into the air (so that they randomly float down to the floor). Then instruct each person to pick up a card and perform the task written there. Once they have completed the task, place that card on a "discard" chair in the center of the room and then choose another card from the floor. Participants are not to share the content of their card with others in the room.

The uproar in the room will be substantial as participants perform the various tasks written on the cards. This is a perfect activity for creating three minutes of boisterous activity between presentations or after a long period of audience inactivity.

I have chosen many of the tasks in my deck of Kerfuffle cards to require interaction with other participants in the group. This version creates substantial mayhem and also provides for an interesting teachable moment—namely, when you received your task card, did you complete your task first or help someone else complete the task on their card first?

You can play a quick version of this game (One and Done) by asking each person to complete just one task from the deck of cards available. You can also lengthen the game if players drop their card to the floor again, after they finish a task. Then others in the group can also find and perform that task. I recommend keeping the total time for this activity to less than five minutes so that the energy level remains high throughout the activity.

Over the years I've seen variations of this activity, sometimes called by different names and from many different sources (see *The Cokesbury Stunt Book*, printed in 1934). But several groups have recently reintroduced this activity under the name 52 Pickup. Project Adventure, High Five Learning Center and Training Wheels all have card versions of this activity that are a riot to play and enjoy.

Here are dozens of tasks that you can use to make your own Kerfuffle cards.

Get five people to each make a different wild animal sound.

Pretend to ice skate with a partner.

Pretend to roller skate with a partner.

Invent a new style of ballroom dance with a partner.

Conduct an orchestra with as many people as you can, playing imaginary instruments.

Wave both hands and yell "Yoo-hoo."

Secretly follow another person around the room for two minutes.

Organize eight people to sit or kneel in a circle.

Get five people to say "Shhhhh!" together.

Get four people to each do one letter of YMCA.

Make someone laugh out loud.

Skip around the room with a partner.

Line up five people tallest to shortest.

Get three people to laugh very loud with you.

Do ten push-ups or get ten people to each do one push-up.

Build a living Mt. Rushmore with four people, take a selfie.

Sing your favorite song. All of it!

Get four people to whistle a happy tune.

See if you can get everyone to clap at the same time.

Make race car sounds as you drive one lap around the group.

Get five people to each make a different farmyard animal sound.

Find someone who was born in the same state as you.

Waltz with a partner.

Get several people to stomp loudly around the room.

Get four people to sing the alphabet song ("a, b, c, d, e, f, g…..").

Trade cards with another person.

Shake hands with four people then yell "Yahoo!"

Find your closest twin and take a selfie with them.

Pretend to cry until someone asks you why you are crying.

Stare into someone's eyes for twenty seconds.

Run five circles around a single person.

If anyone approaches you, run away.

Shout out "Marco" until you hear someone say "Polo."

Point to the ceiling (or sky) and say "Well look at that" until someone else looks up.

Stand really, really close to someone for one minute.

Get as many people as you can to sing "Happy Birthday to You."

Collect as many shoes as you can and make a tower from them.

Moo like a cow until someone moos with you.

Find the tallest person in the room and greet them with "Howdy, Partner."

Pretend to jump rope solo, and then with two other people holding the rope.

Dribble an imaginary basketball around the room.

Laugh as loud as you can for ten seconds.

Swim around the room.

Link arms with three other people and walk around the room.

Row a boat around the room.

Pretend to be a quarterback and yell "Blue 54, blue 54, hike, hike" and throw a pass.

Paddle a canoe around the room.

Tell five people what your favorite food is.

Create a famous work of art and keep it until someone guesses what it is.

Ask someone to tie your shoe for you.

Listen for someone to moo, and then yell "Ye-Haw!"

Flap your arms like you are flying for one minute. Ask someone to join you.

Find three people whose watches (cell phones) all have a different time.

Find a person who is wearing the most jewelry and high-five them.

Hide behind another person until the game is over.

Find a person who has the longest hair and shake their hand.

Thumb wrestle with two other people. Best of three wins.

Wink at every person who makes eye contact with you.

Strike a yoga pose while saying "Inner peace, inner peace… ."

Close your eyes until someone asks if they can help you.

Shake hands with everyone in the room.

Count to twenty in any language you like.

Stand on one leg and get five people to join you.

Get four people to join your bobsled team, then circle the group.

Pretend to boldly juggle with a partner.

Ask people what time it is, and then say "No, that can't be right."

Dance wildly until someone smiles at you.

Act like your favorite animal until someone guesses what animal you are.

When someone approaches you, put your hand to your ear and say, "Do you hear that?"

Build a nest and squawk at anyone who approaches it.

Cheer someone on until they finish the task on their card.

Give five different compliments to five different people.

Do the chicken dance until two additional people join you.

Play rock, paper, scissors until you win three times in a row.

Make someone laugh without talking.

Talk-Talk Double-Double And-And Loud-Loud All-All The-The Time-Time.

Sing "I'm dreaming of a…." over and over until someone says "White Christmas."

Stand like the Statue of Liberty until someone guesses what you are doing.

Crow like a rooster five times.

Pretend to be reading a book until someone guesses what you are doing.

Broadcast music from your mobile phone.

Listen for someone to sing and go join them.

Find someone who was born the same year as you.

Throw (and catch) an imaginary boomerang, three times.

Take a photo of the group and text it to a friend.

Get on your knees, search the floor, then shout "I found it!"

Search the room for someone who needs help and help them.

Find someone taller and someone shorter than you. Take a selfie with them.

Throw this card (like a Frisbee) completely around the room.

Make a train with five or more people and circle the room while making train sounds.

Grab four people and do the bunny hop for one minute.

Find a helper, pick up a chair and carry it around the room.

3-3 MRS. RIGHT

A lesson in listening.

> *"There was a definite process by which one made people into friends,*
> *and it involved talking to them and listening to them for hours at a time."*
> —Rebecca West

When it comes to ranking the causes of communication problems and errors, listening skills are often near the top. The following activity is an interesting way to explore all four of the fatal assumptions of a leader suggested by Clarke and Crossland in the book *The Leader's Voice* (presented here with my suggestion* of one additional assumption). When a leader speaks, they assume:

1. That the audience is listening to the information being presented.*
2. That the audience understands the information being presented.
3. That the audience agrees with the information being presented.
4. That the audience cares about the information being presented.
5. That the audience will act accordingly using this information.

Let's explore this theory and see how such assumptions might play out during a communication activity that you can use at your next training program.

Begin by inviting your audience to stand in a circle. Give each participant a single index or playing card to hold. Inform your group that you are going to read a story and that they should listen carefully. Each time they hear the word "left" they should pass their card one person to the left. Each time they hear the word "right" they should pass their card one person to the right. Ready? Let's begin.

> *This is a story about Mrs. Right. Once upon a time Mrs. Right took her three children, Wendy Right, Bobby Right and Billy Right and left on vacation. They left on a Monday but returned home right before the holiday weekend. Now Wendy Right wishes they had never left, because she left behind a list of all the people she wanted to write to. Bobby Right was the first Right to find out he had left his cell phone behind, and Billy Right was left-handed but liked to write right-handed. Stop!*

At this point, how many participants have more than one card? How many have no cards? Do you think any of the five assumptions listed above may have contributed to the outcome of this activity? For example, was the audience listing? For the most part, yes. Did they understand the information being presented? Unless there is a significant percentage of the audience for which English is not their native language, it would seem that most did understand. Did they agree with the information being presented? Again, most likely. Did they care about the information? This is where it gets a bit tricky. Finally, were they willing to act accordingly on the information they were presented? Evidently not, or everyone would have a single card.

Mrs. Right is just a simple story with only two significant key words for which action is necessary. How then can it be that a talented workforce of people, with valuable skills, including communication, cannot perform this simple task? Perhaps the fatal assumptions listed above are not so rare after all. If a talented group of professionals can be less than fully successful in this basic task, it is going to take considerable work to ensure success with even more complicated and real-life situations and challenges.

This leads us to the following questions: What can we do about this? How can we be better at listening? How can we be better communicators? How can we ensure that we don't fall victim to the fatal assumptions listed above?

If we reconsider the five assumptions presented here, which ones require skills or tools that may be beyond our workforce's abilities or beyond their access? Let's consider these on a case-by-case basis.

Is the audience listening? Educators in Harlem, New York, identified reasons their students were having difficulties in class, and surprisingly found a variety of factors that they could influence to improve the situation. Some schools now serve breakfast prior to the start of classes. Students whose basic needs have been met are better able to focus in class. How different do you expect it is for professionals in the workplace? Are some workers distracted? Absolutely. Is there a way to negate these negative influences so that employees are able to focus and listen appropriately?

Does the audience understand the information being presented? How can we know for sure? Are there opportunities for questions or feedback from the audience? How can we make sure that communication is two-directional, not just one?

Does the audience agree with the information being presented? How can we assess their agreement or disagreement? Do we accept criticism? Are we spending more time defending our view than carefully listening to feedback from our troops?

Does the audience care about the information being presented? How can this be assessed? What incentives can we offer to increase their ability to genuinely care about this information?

Will the audience act on this information? Do they have the skills and tools necessary to perform this function? In the case of the index card activity presented here, most groups will still fail in this last step. How can we prepare our team to ensure that they can act appropriately with the information they are given?

Isn't it amazing how much valuable discussion can come from a single activity and a few index cards?

Mrs. Right is a variation of the Tom Jackson activity Pass Right / Pass Left. Tom is an amazing teacher and you can find hundreds of valuable activities in his books *Activities That Teach* (ISBN 978-0-9160-9549-5), *More Activities That Teach* (ISBN 978-0-9160-9575-4) and *Still More Activities That Teach* (ISBN 978-0-9664-6335-8). For even more training ideas from Tom, visit the website www.activelearning.org.

3-4 THE STORY GAME

Once upon a time....
....and they all lived happily ever after.

Here is a fun game that requires players to think and talk on their feet! Begin by writing a single word on a dozen or more index cards. Nouns are traditionally useful words for this activity, but you can also add additional words of importance, such as adjectives, verbs, mission statement words, character building phrases, and more. Be sure to use large index cards (5x8) and print the words in large block letters. Shuffle all your cards and pass out one card per person. Then invite each member of the group to take a seat in a circle of chairs facing outward. Once seated, invite everyone to hold

their card so that anyone passing in front of them can easily read the word shown.

The facilitator can demonstrate this activity by taking the role as storyteller the first time. The storyteller begins by walking around the circle, telling a made-up story as they go along. Of course, all stories begin with "Once upon a time...." Each time the facilitator (storyteller) mentions a word printed on one of the cards, the person holding that card stands up and follows the facilitator as they walk around the outside perimeter of the group. The storyteller should intentionally look at the various cards while walking around the circle and attempt to incorporate as many of these words as possible during the telling of their tale.

After what is likely to be a random story (which is part of the fun), the storyteller concludes with the phrase, "And they all lived happily ever after, the end!" At this point everyone tries to find a seat, including the storyteller. The one person without a seat becomes the storyteller for the next round.

After a few rounds, invite everyone to write a new word on their index card, and then continue the game. You can even encourage participants to write words specific to a historical event, children's book, quotation, mission statement, vision statement, core values or other collections of useful words.

This style of impromptu storytelling is a great way to practice public speaking. Some stories are hilarious and some storytellers manage to get almost everyone in the circle on their feet during the telling of their tale.

A second variation of this activity is played with the same collection of noun cards, in the following manner. Chairs are randomly distributed around the room. A storyteller begins telling a story while wandering around the room. Whenever the storyteller incorporates a word held by a member of the audience, that person stands up, runs around their chair and quickly sits down again. After incorporating a sufficient number of word cards from the audience, the storyteller concludes the story with, "And they all lived happily ever after, the end!" at which point everyone stands and moves to a new seat (which provides the storyteller with the opportunity to find a seat as well).

3-5 TORA TORA

A quick-response dice game.

Tora Tora is one of my favorite table games for exactly seven people, and all you'll need for this quick-response dice game are the following props: one index card and pen per person, six strings about 14 inches (35 cm) long with a wooden bead or button attached to one end, a hand-sized plastic salsa bowl and one large die (singular of dice)

Prepare for this activity by placing each of the wooden beads together in the center of a table, with the strings stretching outward (like spokes of a wheel) toward six of the players, who grasp just the end of their string. The seventh and remaining player then places the die into the salsa bowl and slams it down on top of the wooden beads (with the die inside it). The die thrower then quickly lifts the salsa bowl.

If the die displays a 1 or a 6, the six players holding a string must quickly pull their bead out of the center of the table. If any other number is showing (2, 3, 4 or 5), these players should do nothing.

If the die displays a 1 or 6, the thrower will attempt to slam the salsa bowl back down on the beads, capturing as many of them as possible. If any other number is showing, the thrower does nothing, except pick up the die and roll again.

The challenge of this activity is to quickly remove your bead if a 1 or 6 is displayed on the die. For any beads caught by the salsa bowl, when a 1 or 6 is showing, players are given a letter for their mistake. Players spell out the name of the game, T – O – R – A, T – O – R – A on their index score card. Eight mistakes during the game for any single player means the game is over. Players can also earn a letter for another kind of mistake. If they tug on the string when the number 2, 3, 4 or 5 is showing (by mistake), this too earns them a letter.

The thrower can also earn a letter for making a mistake. If the thrower rolls a 1 or 6 and do not capture any beads, they earn a letter. If the thrower rolls a 2, 3, 4 or 5 and still slams the salsa bowl down on the table, they earn a letter.

After five rolls, the thrower passes the salsa bowl to the next player, takes that person's string, and this new player becomes the thrower for the next five rolls.

Tora Tora is a high-intensity table game that is sure to fascinate your audience. It is largely a game of mistakes, where every mistake earns a player a letter. Variations of this game have been found in game books dating back as far as the late 1700s.

3-6 BIRTHDAY CARDS

A magical way to guess your birthday.

The unique collection of mathematical cards shown below and on the next page are designed to amuse and entertain. This collection of cards will astound your audience as you easily figure out the age, birth month, birth date and birth year of any member of the group. You can even ask a member of your audience to choose a number at random, and then easily reveal that exact number to them.

First, you'll need to create your own collection of number cards, like those shown on the following page. Then shuffle these cards and pass the complete deck to a member of your audience. Tell this person that you are going to correctly determine their age. Ask the person to identify each card that has the correct age (number) written upon it, and to keep these cards. Then pass back the remaining cards. Quickly scan the first number on each card, add these numbers together, and subtract the total from 127. The remainder is the age of your partner. You can also invite the person to just pass back the cards that contain the correct age, but this version is less "magical." For this

version, just add up the first number shown on each card. The total is the person's age. You can repeat this same technique to determine the birth month, birth date and birth year if you like, or any number the person chooses from 1 to 127.

The "magical" technique in this activity is that each card has a numerical sequence as the first digit on each card (in the upper left-hand corner). By adding up the first digits on the cards that contain the correct number, the dealer can correctly determine the number chosen by their partner. For example, my birthday is in December. Cards number 3 and 4 each contain the number 12. The first digits on cards 3 and 4 are the numbers 4 and 8. Eight plus four equals twelve! If all six cards were used, and only the cards NOT showing the number 12 were returned, the answer would be the addition of 1 + 2 + 16 + 32 + 64 subtracted from 127, or 127 - 115 = 12! Either way, the answer comes out the same, but when your partner gets to keep the cards that show the correct number, they are amazed that you can figure out the truth, even with cards that don't have that number on them. Magic!

Due to the digital nature of the cards displayed in this activity, the highest number possible is a function of the number of cards available. With four cards, you can reach a maximum of 15. Five cards will bring you to 31. Six cards will produce a maximum of 63 and seven cards will enable a maximum of 127!

You can create your own deck of magic Birthday Cards (sufficient to guess any number from 1 to 127) by drawing the numbers shown on the following page, on seven index cards.

BIRTHDAY CARDS

1	3	5	7	9	11
13	15	17	19	21	23
25	27	29	31	33	35
37	39	41	43	45	47
49	51	53	55	57	59
61	63	65	67	69	71
73	75	77	79	81	83
85	87	89	91	93	95
97	99				

2	3	6	7	10	11
14	15	18	19	22	23
26	27	30	31	34	35
38	39	42	43	46	47
50	51	54	55	58	59
62	63	66	67	70	71
74	75	78	79	82	83
86	87	90	91	94	95
98	99				

4	5	6	7	12	13
14	15	20	21	22	23
28	29	30	31	36	37
38	39	44	45	46	47
52	53	54	55	60	61
62	63	68	69	70	71
76	77	78	79	84	85
86	87	92	93	94	95
100					

8	9	10	11	12	13
14	15	24	25	26	27
28	29	30	31	40	41
42	43	44	45	46	47
56	57	58	59	60	61
62	63	72	73	74	75
76	77	78	79	88	89
90	91	92	93	94	95

16	17	18	19	20	21
22	23	24	25	26	27
28	29	30	31	48	49
50	51	52	53	54	55
56	57	58	59	60	61
62	63	80	81	82	83
84	85	86	87	88	89
90	91	92	93	94	95

32	33	34	35	36	37
38	39	40	41	42	43
44	45	46	47	48	49
50	51	52	53	54	55
56	57	58	59	60	61
62	63	96	97	98	99
100					

64	65	66	67	68	69
70	71	72	73	74	75
76	77	78	79	80	81
82	83	84	85	86	87
88	89	90	91	92	93
94	95	96	97	98	99
100					

3-7 MATH MAGIC

One simple operation is all it takes.

Here are two unique, magical equations. Even if numbers and math are not your favorite things, you should be able to perform one simple operation that will make the following equations yield the desired result. You can write each of these equations on index cards and share them with your next audience.

Perform one operation on the following equation so that the result equals 821.

$$1 + 6 + 906 + 101 - 9$$

Perform one operation on the following equation so that the equation becomes true.

$$IX = X + I$$

For many numerical puzzles, the term "operation" typically refers to a mathematical operation, such as multiplying, dividing, adding or subtracting; and it is possible to contrive some form of mathematical operation to yield the desired value for each of the above equations. But a simpler "operation" is simply to rotate each card 180 degrees and read the equation from this view, which reminds me of the following quote:

"If the only tool you have is a hammer, you tend to see every problem as a nail."
—Abraham Maslow

We are sometimes so prepared to use our favorite tool or skill that we can miss all the information that says we should be using a different tool or skill altogether. Before we begin working on the answer to a puzzle or problem, we should be sure to listen completely to the question first.

If you choose to print out the cards for Math Magic (instead of hand-writing these equations), be sure to use a font that can be viewed upside down and still appear correct.

3-8 NON-SEQUITUR SLAM POETRY

Something that doesn't make sense can still be beautiful.

This activity combines literacy, creativity and index cards. First, you'll need a book. Any book will do. Choose your favorite book or one at random. Next, you'll need a dozen index cards. On one card write the following numbers:

1. A number between 1 and 10
2. Ten random numbers between 1 and 100

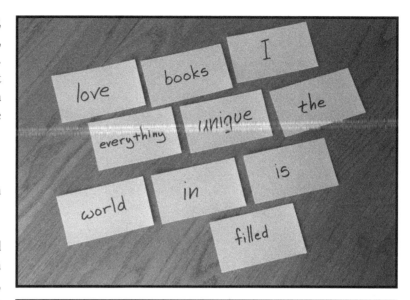

The numbers you have selected will help you "find" words within your book, and from these words, you can create your slam poetry. The first number (between 1 and 10) is the page number (in your book) where your poem begins. The ten random numbers (between 1 and 100) identify the words that you will use for your poem. Word number one is the first word that appears on the page, followed by number two, number three, etc. Continue adding words even if you need to turn the page to reach the numbers you have selected. Write each of these ten words on a separate index card.

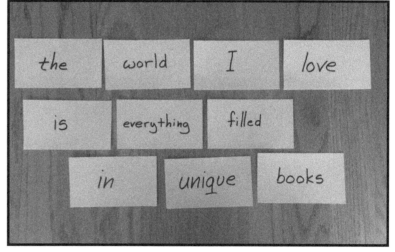

In the next step of the slam poetry process, select one of the words to be the title or theme of your poem. Then rearrange the remaining nine cards until they form a coherent (or incoherent!) message. When you are satisfied with the final order of words, print the title and poem on the final index card, and share it with your friends (or post it on your refrigerator door).

I performed the above process on the book you are now reading, using the numbers 1, 6, 17, 22, 27, 42, 46, 47, 50, 83 and 84. These numbers yielded the following words from the Introduction: *love, books, I, everything, unique, the, world, in, is, filled.* From these words, I fashioned the following poem:

The world I love is everything filled in unique books.

3-9 JUST ONE WORD

A classic puzzle of words.

This activity is both a linguistic challenge and a lesson in careful listening. Begin with eleven index cards and write the following capital letters, one per card: S, U, N, J, T, O, D, E, R, O, W. Then display these cards to your audience and (carefully) explain to them that with this collection of letters they should be able to create just one word.

While most audiences will struggle for a while trying to create a single eleven letter word, some creative groups will take the challenge literally (you should be able to create JUST ONE WORD)!

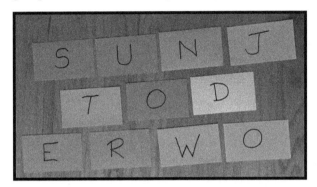 

Some puzzles are made more difficult because audiences may interpret what they believe the instructions are rather than completely listening to the directions provided. In this case, the solution is stated clearly at the beginning of the challenge, but most groups miss it entirely.

In addition to using index cards for this activity, you can also use wooden letters (available at most craft stores), toy wooden blocks, word puzzle tiles, magnetic refrigerator letters (available in toy stores), bulletin board stencils and other unique letters.

3-10 THE TANGRAM QUILT

Using tangrams to explore the theory of the four-color map.

This activity was created by Jim Cain as an interesting way to explore a variety of tangram-like shapes and the theory of the four-color map. You can prepare for this activity by creating the following four patterns of seven-piece tangram-like puzzles, from four different colors of large index cards.

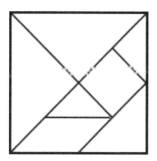 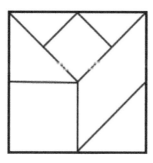 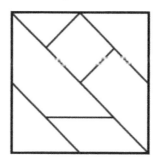 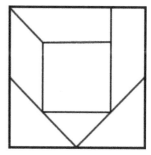

Next, place these complete puzzles to form a large square pattern. Now the challenge begins. See if you can relocate pieces from each puzzle, within the same large square pattern, so that no two pieces with the same color touch each other at more than a single point.

In the decade since I first presented this challenge, no one has offered a solution to this challenge. Many teams have come close, including those shown in the photos here. Your team could be the first to solve this challenging puzzle! And if you do, please email me a photo of your result at jimcain@teamworkandteamplay. com.

Your team could be the first to solve this puzzle. And if you do, please email me a photo of your result (jimcain@teamworkandteamplay.com).

The Tangram Quilt puzzle presented here was first published in the book *Teambuilding Puzzles*. It is a puzzle based upon the theorem of the Four-Color Map. While the four-color map theorem guarantees that it is possible to color any map geography with only four colors, this same theorem does not guarantee that any geometrical figures will go together to fill an enclosed space. This proof is up to you to resolve. Good luck!

For more mathematical background on the four-color map theorem, read *Four Colors Suffice—How the Map Problem Was Solved* by Robin Wilson (ISBN 978-0-691-11533-8).

3-11 THE ARROWHEAD PUZZLE

Doing more with less.

The Arrowhead Puzzle was created by Jim Cain for the book *Teambuilding Puzzles* (and is featured on the front cover of that book). It is one of those rare puzzles that is simple to construct and difficult to solve. The solution also creates a wonderful teachable moment related to doing more with less.

You can construct the seven pieces for this manipulation puzzle by enlarging and then tracing the pattern shown below onto four large index cards and then cutting these four arrowheads into a total of seven unique pieces (as shown below). Collect these seven pieces in a small bag until you are ready to share them with your audience.

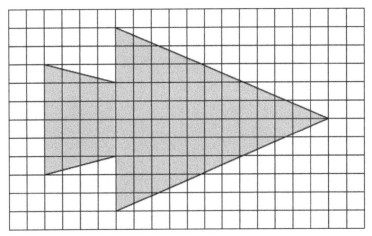 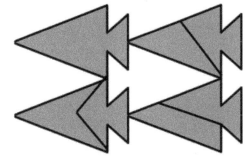

You will notice that one of the arrowheads is whole. This is an example of what a complete arrowhead looks like. There are sufficient pieces in the bag to create a total of five arrowheads. Each one of these arrowheads will be exactly the same size and shape as the whole arrowhead, and you will be able to see all five arrowheads at the same time. Ready, go!

The first thing your audience will notice is that there seems to only be sufficient pieces in the bag to create a total of four arrowheads, not five. At first, they may suggest that you, the facilitator, missed something or forgot to provide the proper number of pieces. Assure your audience that they do in fact have sufficient pieces to create a total of five arrowheads and to keep trying.

You can find this puzzle and 99 more in the book *Teambuilding Puzzles* (ISBN 978-0-7575-7040-7) by Mike Anderson, Jim Cain, Chris Cavert and Tom Heck, available from Kendall Hunt Publishers (www.kendallhunt.com).

Experience is a hard teacher.
It gives the test first, and then the lesson.
—Vernon Sanders Law

Each of the activities in this book was chosen because of the unique teachable moments that present themselves during the completion of the activity or puzzle. The teachable moment in the arrowhead puzzle comes from realizing that even when there appears to be insufficient resources, if you use the resources you have creatively, you can often do more with less. By placing the four complete arrowheads in a 2x2 pattern, a fifth arrowhead magically appears in the space between the other arrowheads!

Let's take this concept a step further and consider what collaboration and synergy can mean to an organization. Imagine that you have one employee creating the training manuals for your organization. With the recent hiring of more employees, you are going to need more manuals very soon, so you hire nine additional employees to perform this task. You're good at math, so you calculate that if one employee can produce ten training manuals in a week, ten employees should be able to produce 100 training manuals in that same week. While the mathematics in this example are simple, the organizational culture is not. For some organizations a tenfold increase in manpower will yield a tenfold increase in output. For synergistic organizations that are efficient, a tenfold increase in manpower can yield greater than a tenfold increase in output. Unfortunately, this same concept works in reverse. For organizations that are struggling, a tenfold increase in manpower not only does not produce a tenfold increase in output, but the overall efficiency of the entire organization goes down with change.

The Arrowhead Puzzle is a great activity to help your team understand the value of synergy. Synergy can be described metaphorically as $1 + 1 = 3$. Synergy exists when the output of a team is greater than the combined output of each individual person. The scenario above demonstrates this point. If one team member can produce one unit of output and we hire nine additional team members, we expect to be able to produce a total output of ten units. If our team members work synergistically, they can actually produce more than ten units of output. Conversely, if our team members do not work synergistically or even worse, reduce each other's effectiveness, less than ten units of output will be produced. From this simple analysis you can see that teams operating synergistically have a substantial advantage over teams that do not.

Learning how to solve puzzles is not only a recreational pastime, but practice for real life as well. The skills required to solve challenges and puzzles translate to other parts of our lives. Patience, creativity, problem solving, determination, tenacity, working as a team—these are all useful skills that when practiced are likely to improve the quality of our lives and our value as a member of a team.

Within the solution to a challenging puzzle comes a key moment when the facts and realities of the puzzle become increasingly clear. This unique moment, sometimes referred to as the "aha!" effect, or even as a BFO (Blinding Flash of the Obvious), is the separation between challenge and solution, between a puzzle presented and a puzzle solved. Within this moment come lessons that last long after the puzzle has been forgotten. This is what we refer to as a "teachable moment."

To bring out the teachable moment from this puzzle, the facilitator can ask the team at the completion of this project, "Does this puzzle remind you of any other situations, and if so, what are they?" Or, "What other projects do you have limited resources with which to complete the task?" By exploring this line of discussion at the completion of the puzzle, participants are given the opportunity to transfer the skills learned from the activity back to their work environment. This approach sometimes helps a team member solve not only the puzzle of the day, but additional challenges they are facing as well. One of the most important questions you can ask is, "What skills have been gained from this experience that can help you solve other problems in the future?"

3-12 SEVEN FOLDS

How many times can you fold an index card in half?

Consider this challenge as a form of extreme origami. Take any standard index card (any size, shape or color), and fold it in half. That's one. Now fold it in half again. That's two. And again, and again, and again until you have made seven folds. Can you do it?

The simple task of folding an index card is easy at the start, but becomes more difficult with each additional fold. If practice makes perfect, why doesn't folding an index card get easier with each fold rather than more difficult? What happens between the fifth, sixth and seventh folds that is different than between the second, third and fourth folds? Does the thickness of the index card have anything to do with the difficulty of this challenge? Does the size of the index card matter? Would it be possible to fold the paper in half a different way, to make this task easier?

To make this activity more of a team challenge (rather than an individual challenge), try the following: Demonstrate folding an index card in half three consecutive times. Then ask your audience to estimate how many times they could fold a similar index card successfully. Write these estimates on a flip-chart or white board, calculate the numerical average and range, and ask the group to reach consensus on a goal for the total number of folds possible. Then pass out index cards and challenge your audience to meet their goal.

Most groups are capable of folding the index card five times. Some creative groups may even reach six folds. Seven folds are extremely difficult. Once your audience has completed this first team challenge, pass out a different size index card and invite the group to experiment with different techniques for folding the card in half multiple times. Then ask the group to set a goal for themselves. No doubt this time, their estimate will be much closer to their actual performance—thus illustrating that experience can be quite valuable when estimating future performance. Without experience, our estimates are often little more than random guesses.

Just to give you some idea of the magnitude of this challenge, the following data show the increase in thickness (and the reduction in area) for each fold of an index card.

Initial Thickness	Layers	Thickness	3x5 Card	5x8 Card
Plain Index Card	1 layer	0.007"	3.00 x 5.00	5.00 x 8.00
1 fold	2 layers	0.014"	2.50 x 3.00	4.00 x 5.00
2 folds	4 layers	0.028"	1.50 x 2.50	2.50 x 4.00
3 folds	8 layers	0.056"	1.12 x 1.50	2.00 x 2.50
4 folds	16 layers	0.112"	0.75 x 1.12	1.25 x 2.00
5 folds	32 layers	0.224"	0.56 x 0.75	1.00 x 1.25
6 folds	64 layers	0.448"	0.37 x 0.56	0.62 x 1.00
7 folds	128 layers	0.896"	0.28 x 0.37	0.50 x 0.62

According to www.listverse.com it is possible to fold a piece of paper seven times. By starting with an extremely thin piece of paper, multiple folds are possible. In 2002 Britney Gallivan folded a piece of gold leaf foil (approximately 0.00004 inch thick) more than seven times.

3-13 CONUNDRUM CARDS

Adventures in logic and reasoning.

If you enjoy logic and reasoning, you'll enjoy these two classic card conundrums. The challenge here is not so much in finding a solution to each conundrum, but in the discussion and exploration of each card. Chances are you'll learn more about the other members of your group (as you debate each card) than you will from the cards themselves. You can prepare for this activity by printing the information shown below on several index cards and sharing these with your audience.

The Card Paradox
(A Variation of the Liar's Paradox)

If you consider the statement on the front side of the card true, then the statement on the backside must also be true. But if the statement on the backside is true, then the statement on the front side is false. Hence if the statement on the front side of the card is true, then the statement on the front side of the card is false!

But if you consider the statement on the front side of the card false, then the statement on the backside of the card is also false, meaning that the statement on the front side is true. Proving that if the statement on the front side of the card is false, then the statement on the front side of the card is true!

How can such simple messages produce such a confounding situation?

Front Side of the Card

> # The statement on the other side of this card is true.

> # The statement on the other side of this card is false.

Back Side of the Card

The Error Card (A Contradiction or Not?)

At first glance, there doesn't appear to be any typographical error on the card. The words are spelled correctly. The punctuation is correct. Turning the card over only produces a side that is blank. What exactly is meant by "error"? If the statement is true, then there must be an error. Since the card itself is not erroneous, then perhaps the error lies within the message itself.

> # There is an error on this card.

Both of the above conundrums are variations of a classic riddle known as the Liar's Paradox. The first is a non-self-referential (or circular) variant constructed by Philip Edward Bertrand Jourdain (1879-1919). The second appears contradictory, but therein lies the answer!

3-14 THREE HOUSES AND THREE UTILITIES

Can you think both inside and outside the box?

The three houses shown in the illustration below have just been constructed. Each house needs to be connected to each of the three utilities (electricity, water, Internet), but local zoning laws prohibit any utility lines crossing each other and only direct connections (no branches or joints) are allowed. Can you figure out a way to connect each house to each utility (nine connections lines in total)?

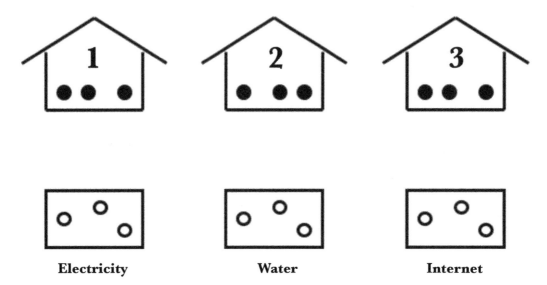

| Electricity | Water | Internet |

Draw lines that connect a black dot on each house to a white dot on each of the three utilities without crossing the path of any other utility line.

For this puzzle, you can copy the illustration shown above to a single index card and invite your audience to work out a solution with a pencil or use a single index card for each house and utility and provide your audience with short pieces of string to serve as the connection lines.

One of the techniques in many puzzles is to create one line of reasoning that seems to be working, only to have this technique fail at some point in the puzzle. And that is exactly what is happening here.

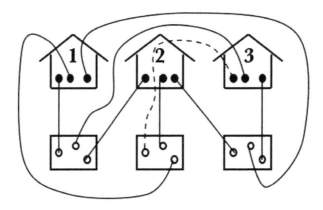

Solution: One (or more) of the connection lines must pass through one of the houses or one of the utilities.

3-15 DRAWING IN THE DARK

Creating a masterpiece with your eyes closed.

To prepare for this artistic endeavor, provide each member of your audience with a large blank index card and an artistic drawing tool, such as a pen, pencil, crayon or marker. Then ask everyone to close their eyes as you read one of the following narratives.

I'd like you to draw the following things on your index card. To begin, place your card in landscape position. Now draw a simple house in the center of the card. Place a door in the center of the house and two windows on the second floor. Don't forget to put a doorknob on the front door and curtains in the windows. Draw a chimney on right side of the roof. On the left side of the house, draw a tall tree with a bicycle leaning up against the lower trunk. Draw a sidewalk leading up to the front door, and smoke coming from the chimney. Finally, draw a bright sun over the house, with two birds flying nearby.

I'd like you to draw the following things on your index card. To begin, place your card in landscape position. Next, draw a typical bus, with lots of windows. Place a driver with a baseball cap in the front window of the bus. Write the name "Sullivan Tours" on the side of the bus. In the second window, show a curly-haired girl. Make sure your bus has one wheel in the front and two wheels in the back. In the last window, show a boy listening to music with headphones. In front of the bus, put a sign that reads "Chicago – 126 Miles."

When completed, invite your audience to share their drawings with each other.

_____

If you wish to add a bit more complexity to these drawings, you can include instructions for your audience to rotate the cards occasionally, to add a new feature, or switch their drawing tool to the other hand. You can also invite them to turn to card over and sign their name before returning to the front to continue adding new features. Every time the position of the card is reoriented, the artist loses some ability to remember exactly where previous features were positioned.

3-16 ALPHABETICALLY

Knowing the answers from A to Z.

For each of the categories listed below, challenge your audience to work together as a team to brainstorm answers, from A to Z, that fulfill each column completely.

	Cities	Animals	Songs	Food	Movies	Automobiles	TV Shows
A							
B							
C							
D							
E							
F							
G							
H							
I							
J							
K							
L							
M							
N							
O							
P							
Q							
R							
S							
T							
U							
V							
W							
X							
Y							
Z							

If you enjoy this style of word game, also try the 1920s era game Guggenheim. You can find more information about this game in classic games books such as *Family Fun & Games* (ISBN 978-0-8069-8776-6) by The Diagram Group.

3-17 CLOSE ALL THE DOORS

Finding the answer is only the first step in this challenge.
Fixing the problem is the ultimate goal.

This activity was created by Dr. Jim Cain for the book *Teambuilding Puzzles*, co-written with Jim's friends and colleagues Chris Cavert, Mike Anderson and Tom Heck. At the first publishing, Close All the Doors presented this simple question: Is it possible for a single person to walk through each doorway just once, locking the door behind them and ending up outside the building with all doors locked? Consider this possibility first, then a second component of this puzzle will be shared below.

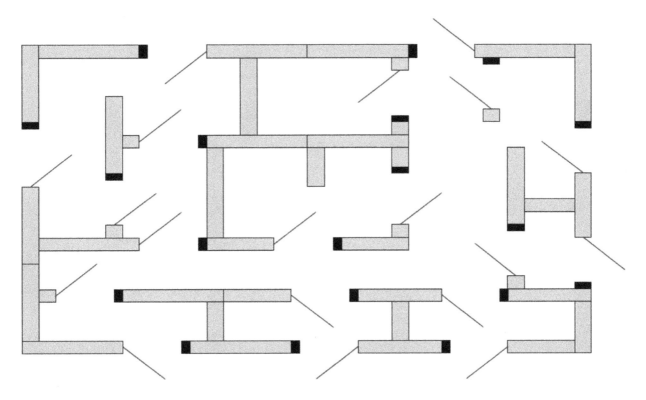

You'll soon discover that with the current architectural configuration, it is NOT possible to perform the task mentioned above (to close and lock all the doors by passing through each just once). Now comes the second challenge. What is the least number of modifications (in doors or walls or procedures) that must be made for the original task to be possible? For example, eliminating two doors in the upper left corner of the building is possible, but is there a way that requires less than two modifications? Another possibility is closing a door without walking through it. Can you think of other possible solutions?

———————————————

If you like this activity, see The Box Maze in Chapter 7 of this book, and for more puzzles that create teachable moments, see *Teambuilding Puzzles* by Jim Cain, Chris Cavert, Mike Anderson and Tom Heck (ISBN 978-0-7575-7040-7) available from Kendall/Hunt (www.kendallhunt.com). This book has recently become a valuable resource for the design of escape rooms and other teambuilding challenges.

3-18 TONGUE TWISTERS AND OTHER LINGUISTIC CHALLENGES

Linguistic challenges to amaze and amuse audiences.

You need New York, unique New York. You know you need unique New York.

The following Tongue Twisters are linguistic challenges that are sure to test your team's verbal skills. You can attempt to speak the following phrases by yourself or in unison with the other members of your team. Prepare for this activity by writing each one of the following phrases on a separate index card. Then shuffle this deck of cards and invite individual members of your audience to quickly say each phrase three times, without making a mistake.

A critical cricket critic	Does the wristwatch shop shut soon
A regal rural ruler	Fast Frank fries frankfurters and French fries
Peggy Babcock	I thought I thought of thinking of thanking you
Cheap ship trips	Eleven benevolent elephants
Rubber baby buggy bumpers	The sixth sheik's sixth sheep's sick
Six selfish shellfish	I slit a sheet, a sheet I slit, upon a slitted sheet I sit
Six thin thistle sticks	A proper cup of coffee from a proper copper coffee pot
Toy boat	Blame the big bleak black book
Truly rural	Old oily Ollie oils oily autos
Green Greek grapes	Popular people prefer properly prepared peppery pizzas
Real rock wall	William's real rear wheel
Aluminum - Linoleum	A box of biscuits, a box of mixed biscuits and a biscuit mixer
Mixed Biscuits	Red leather, yellow leather

It may seem odd to some participants that they can demonstrate proficiency with other challenges in this book and yet have so much difficulty when it comes to just talking. The good news is that verbal ability is a bit like physical ability—it improves when you exercise. Some keynote speakers, actors and professional TV and radio personalities use tongue twisters to warm up before a broadcast or performance. They are also a favorite of speech therapists.

THE TTTT CHALLENGE

In the Kendall/Hunt book *Teambuilding Puzzles*, Chris Cavert proposes this technique for using Tongue Twisters with groups of ten people:

Hand out ten index cards with a different Tongue Twister on each. The challenge is to go for the best (minimum) TTTT (Tongue Twister Total Time). Each Tongue Twister must be said three times, quickly in repetition, without mistakes, for time. The total time for all ten Tongue Twisters is the group's TTTT. It will be up to the group how they present each Tongue Twister. Each person can be responsible for one, or it can be a group effort. Good luck!

A FINAL LINGUISTIC CHALLENGE

During a recent workshop one of my participants shared a very interesting vocal warmup activity using the book *Fox in Socks* by Dr. Seuss (ISBN 978-0-394-80038-7). In our circle of about twenty people, he presented the book, and then handed it to the person next to him to begin reading. The challenge of this activity is for each person to begin reading aloud and continue until making a mistake, at which point the reader passes the book along to the next person. The goal is to finish the book before it is passed around the entire circle.

Tongue Twisters are a sequence of alliterative words that are difficult to quickly articulate. If you like such things, there is an amazing collection of tongue twisters (more than 3,600 entries in 118 languages) at www.uebersetzung.at.

You'll find this activity (and 99 more) in *Teambuilding Puzzles* (ISBN 978-0-7575-7040-7) by Mike Anderson, Jim Cain, Chris Cavert and Tom Heck, available from www.kendallhunt.com and www.amazon.com. This book has recently become one of the most requested books for people designing (and enjoying) escape rooms.

3-19 RIDDLE CARDS

Encouraging creative problem solving, often with a surprising twist.

For this activity, write the following riddles on one side of an index card and the answer to each riddle (in smaller text) on the other side. Then invite participants to solve as many as they can. Some of these riddles are classic, such as "Why can't a person living in North Dakota be buried in South Dakota? Because they are still alive!" Others require a variety of knowledge and skills to solve. Enjoy!

What gets wetter the more it dries?

A towel.

How do you make 7 even?

Take away the S.

Can you name ten body parts (in English) that have only three letters?

eye, ear, lip, jaw, gum
leg, arm, toe, hip, rib

Why are 1996 U.S. dimes worth almost $200.00 U.S. dollars?

Because one thousand nine hundred ninety-six dimes are worth $199.60!

How many marbles can you put into an empty bag?

One. After that it is no longer empty!

How can you put ten horses in nine stalls?

| T | E | N | H | O | R | S | E | S |

How many letters are there in the correct answer to this question?

Four

In writing the words for the numbers from one to ninety-nine (in English), ten letters of the alphabet are never used and one letter is only used twice. What letters are these?

ABCDJKMPQZ and L (eleven, twelve)

If you were in a footrace and you passed the person in second place, what place would you be in now?

Second place, not first!

How many letters are in "the alphabet"?

There are eleven letters in the phrase "the alphabet."

What number from one to ten, written as a word, would make the following statement true? *"In this quote, there are _____ e's."*

Seven

What word becomes shorter when you add two letters to it?

Short.

When you land at the Cincinnati airport, what state are you in?

Kentucky!
(the Cincinnati / Northern Kentucky Airport)

What did David Bradley create that is an essential part of our modern lives?

The key sequence <Ctrl> <Alt> <Del> that reboots personal computers.

In writing the words for the numbers from one to nine hundred ninety-nine (in English) how many times is the letter A used?

None!

What is the only number whose letter count is the same as the number itself?

Four.

Magic Squares – Can you create a magic square (where the addition of the numbers in any row, column or diagonal equals the same number) for a 3x3, 4x4 and 5x5 square?

8	3	4
1	5	9
6	7	2

16	3	2	13
5	10	11	8
9	6	7	12
4	15	14	1

17	24	1	8	15
5	7	14	16	23
4	6	13	20	22
10	12	19	21	3
11	18	25	2	9

*Magic Squares have been around for centuries. Draw a single number on each index card and rearrange each magic square until each row, column and diagonal add up to the same number. Incidentally, there are 880 ways to create a 4x4 magic square and a whopping 275,305,224 ways to create a 5x5 magic square.

Here is a classic riddle story. See if you can work out the answer. *As I was going to St. Ives, I met a man with seven wives. Every wife had seven sacks, and every sack had seven cats, and every cat had seven kits. Kits, cats, sacks and wives, how many were going to St. Ives?*

One! (as I was going to St. Ives)

Name a sport in which neither the spectators nor the participants officially know the score until the contest ends.

Boxing

Name a fruit that has its seeds on the outside.

Strawberries

In the cartoon series *Tom Terrific*, what was the name of Tom's dog and Tom's nemesis?

Mighty Manfred the Wonder Dog and Crabby Appleton.

How long did the Hundred Years War last?

116 years, from 1337 to 1453.

You have an empty 5-liter and a 3-liter container. How can you use these two containers to create exactly 4 liters?
Hint: create a 5-liter index card and a 3-liter index card.

Fill the 5-liter container and then empty 3 liters into the 3-liter container, then empty the 3-liter container. Pour the remaining two liters from the 5-liter container into the 3-liter container. Fill the 5-liter container again and pour 1 liter from it into the 3-liter container, leaving exactly 4 liters in the 5-liter container.

Which of the following letters is different than all the other letters, and why?

$$k \mid j$$
$$- - - \mid - - -$$
$$m \mid s$$

The letter t is different. It is drawn with a dashed instead of a solid line (like k, j, m and s).

A train one mile long is traveling at a rate of sixty miles per hour. The train enters a tunnel that is exactly one mile long. How long does it take the train to completely pass through the tunnel?

Two minutes. Sixty miles per hour is the same as one mile per minute. The first car of the train (the engine) reaches the beginning of the tunnel at time = zero. The last car of the train (the caboose) reaches the beginning of the tunnel at time = 1 minute, and it reaches the end of the tunnel one minute after that, for a total of two minutes.

What are the alter ego names, occupations, and first appearance dates of the following superheroes: Captain America, The Green Hornet, Captain Atom, Superman.

Captain America, Steve Rogers, Delivery Boy, 1941
The Green Hornet, Britt Reid, Publisher, 1936
Captain Atom, Dr. Rador, Australian Doctor, 1948
Superman, Clark Kent, Newspaper Reporter, 1938

Of all the lakes in the northeastern part of the United States, exactly six have been named as "great lakes." Can you name all six?

Erie, Huron, Ontario, Michigan, Superior and Lake Champlain (temporarily given "great lakes" status, but then quickly removed).

In the movie *The Day the Earth Stood Still*, what are the words that stop the robot?

Klaatu Barada Nikto

Name the three subtractive colors.

Cyan, yellow and magenta

In the history of the United States, only two foreign citizens have ever been given honorary U.S. citizenship. Name them.

Winston Churchill and Raoul Wallenberg

What organization was formed at the request of President Teddy Roosevelt in 1905 as a direct result of the numerous deaths from the college football flying wedge formation?

The National Collegiate Athletic Association (NCAA; www.ncaa.org)

In what month do Russians celebrate the October Revolution?

November

Which country makes Panama hats?

Ecuador

Can you compose a sentence that ends with the word *the*?

I just did!

The creative staff of YMCA Camp Greenville have a wonderful gameshow-like format for presenting riddles and questions like those shown here. An announcer reads one of the questions or riddles above, and then four members of the staff give their expert opinions to each conundrum. The audience (typically campers, school students and other youth) then vote which answer they believe is true. Points are awarded for correct guesses, and questions range from simple riddles and trivia, to difficult math problems, environmental education, science, foreign language translations, current events and other educational content. One day, I overhead tremendous shouting, table pounding and laughter as an audience of over one hundred campers screamed for their favorite answer to each question. It was one of the most engaging educational sessions I have ever witnessed.

3-20 ULTIMATE TIC-TAC-TOE

Raising the strategy level of a simple game to that of a chessboard!

If Tic-Tac-Toe were a sandwich, then Ultimate Tic-Tac-Toe would be a full course meal, with dessert! Prepare for this activity by drawing the ten-grid Tic-Tac-Toe system shown on the left side below, with one large grid and nine smaller ones. Two players then begin playing this multiple grid system, with the following rules:

One player (X) goes first, followed by the other player (O). The position played on any smaller Tic-Tac-Toe grid determines which grid the next player will use to place their mark. In the example below, when a player places a mark in the upper right corner of the upper left smaller grid, this directs the next player to place a mark somewhere in the smaller grid located in the upper right corner. Any player creating three in a row (horizontally, vertically or diagonally) on a smaller grid is invited to draw their own large mark (X or O) over that grid. Play continues until one player achieves three in a row on the large grid.

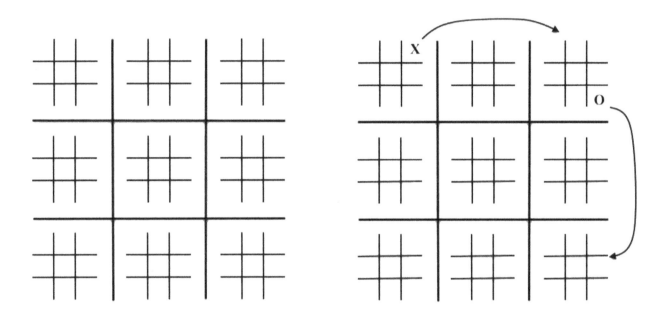

If a player makes a mark which sends their opponent to a smaller grid that has already been completed (marked with a large X or O), then that opponent is free to go to any location available to place their next mark.

I first learned of Ultimate Tic-Tac-Toe from my friend and camp director Joe Richards (www.yoyojoe. com). Joe mentioned that the time required to play a game of Ulimate Tic-Tac-Toe (on the back of a restaurant paper placemat) is about the same as the time between when you order your dinner and when it arrives at your table. A perfect activity for those with young children!

You can find several digital apps of Ultimate Tic-Tac-Toe to use on your smartphone or tablet, but I prefer the index card version shown here.

3-21 TRIPLETS

Can you add the perfect third?

The things listed on this page come in a collection of three. Place the first two things in each collection on the front side of an index card, and the third (in parenthesis) on the back side. Then invite your audience to see how many correct answers they can provide.

Hook, Line and _____ (Sinker)

The *Nina*, the *Pinta* and the _____ (*Santa Maria*)

Baubles, Bangles and _____ (Beads)

Life, Liberty and _____ (the Pursuit of Happiness)

Sugar and Spice and _____ (Everything Nice)

Butcher, Baker and _____ (Candlestick Maker)

Healthy, Wealthy and _____ (Wise)

Animal, Vegetable and _____ (Mineral)

Stop, Look and _____ (Listen)

Lock, Stock and _____ (Barrel)

Stop, Drop and _____ (Roll)

Rock, Paper and _____ (Scissors)

On Your Mark, Get Set, _____ (Go!)

The Good, the Bad and _____ (the Ugly)

The Truth, The Whole Truth and _____ (Nothing but the Truth)

Small, Medium and _____ (Large)

Ready, Aim, _____ (Fire!)

Friends, Romans and _____ (Countrymen)

If you want to grow your list of Triplets, invite the members of your audience to brainstorm even more interesting things that come in threes.

3-22 CARD TRICKS

Can you discover the secret?

Here is one of my favorite card tricks. Try this trick with your next audience and see if they can discover the secret. You'll need nine index or playing cards and an assistant for this trick.

Card Trick 1: Begin by placing nine cards onto a table in the 3x3 pattern shown here. Ask your assistant to step away from the table and invite a member of your audience to touch one of the cards on the table. Then invite your assistant to return and while pointing to various cards, ask "Is it this one?" Your assistant will say no until you select the correct card, at which point the assistant will reply, "Yes!" So how did the assistant know?

The solution to this card trick is that the facilitator points to the correct card position by where they touch the very first card. For example, if the facilitator asks, "Is it this one?" as they point to the upper right-hand corner of the lower left corner card, the assistant replies, "No" and continues to reply no until the facilitator points to the card in the upper right-hand corner of the 3x3 arrangement. If the first card the facilitator points to is the middle of the card in the middle of the 3x3 configuration, the assistant says "Yes!" immediately.

Card Trick 2: If your audience figures out the secret to the card trick above, you can switch to a different technique. Pick up the nine cards from the first round and shuffle them along with the remaining cards in the deck. Then place any nine cards in a 3x3 pattern and hold the remaining cards in your hand. Invite your assistant to depart and then ask a member of the audience to choose one of the nine cards by touching it. When your assistant returns, inform your audience that your assistant has an amazing sense of smell. Next, your assistant will sniff a few of the cards and immediately choose the correct card!

The trick in this version is that you place your thumb over the location of the correct card on the remaining cards you hold in your hand (as if there were a 3x3 grid of cards on the top card). If the middle card is chosen, you place a thumb in the middle of the top card you hold in your hand. When your assistant returns, they will immediately see the location of your thumb and know the correct card.

This card trick falls within the category of I'm In Games (games for which the facilitator is aware of the trick and audience members try to figure out exactly what is going on). You can find more than a dozen of these I'm In Games in the book *Find Something To Do!* (ISBN 978-0-9882046-0-7) and still more in the *Teamwork & Teamplay International Edition* (ISBN 978-0-9882046-3-8) featuring the dice version of Polar Bears and Ice Holes. Both books are by Jim Cain and available from www.healthylearning.com and www.training-wheels.com.

3-23 SPEED SPELLING

High speed word processing for teams

Speed Spelling is a fun way to get teams working and playing together. You can prepare for this activity by creating a deck of twenty-six index cards, with one letter of the alphabet on each card. You'll need one of these decks for each team of about ten players. Next, prepare a list of common or if you prefer, unusual words that can be spelled using only the letters available. Then, when all teams are ready, shout out

one of the words and see which team can assemble the appropriate letters to spell the word correctly in the least amount of time. Each letter of the word should be held by a different member of the team. Bonus points for spelling difficult words correctly.

Be sure to include words with some of the less frequently used letters of the alphabet, like X, J, Q and Z. If you would like to increase the difficulty of this game, write one letter on the front side of each index card and a different letter on the backside. Then check to make sure your word list can be made from the cards available in each set of letters.

The challenge of this game comes from the speed of assembling the correct letters and organizing them in the proper order. This is not a spelling bee, so your choice of words should generally be familiar and simple. But if you happen to have a talented audience, you might consider throwing in a few more challenging words, scientific terms, foreign language words, medical terminology, legal-ese, technobabble or some other unusual text.

For youth groups and summer camps, I like to change the format of this activity, by asking participants to fasten letters to the bottoms of their shoes (with looped masking tape), so that when a word is given, players roll into position on the ground, spelling out the word. This is a hilarious variation for those with agility and flexibility.

If you are curious, the letter used most frequently in the English dictionary is the letter E, followed by A, R and I. The least used letter is Q, followed by J, Z and X. The complete list, from E to Q is: E, A, R, I, O, T, N, S, L, C, U, D, P, M, H, G, B, F, Y, W, K, V, X, Z, J, Q. For comparison, the frequency of letter usage in the English language in general is E, T, A, O I, N, S, R, H, L, D, C, U, M, F, P, G, W, Y, B, V, K, X, J, Q, Z.

3-24 THE WALKABOUT CHALLENGE

How far can you travel with an index card on your head?

The Walkabout Challenge is a fun way of determining who has the most poise and grace as your entire audience moves about with an index card on their head. You can play this game of balance and awareness for a set period of time, or until a majority of your audience has dropped their card. For a higher level of challenge, you can ask your audience to perform additional tasks, such as holding a paper cup filled with water, or signing their name on a piece of paper, or shaking hands with others they meet or dancing a popular line dance while keeping the index card in place on the top of their head. Juggling, jogging, jumping rope, yoga, eating lunch, standing up and sitting down are other interesting challenges.

In some parts of the world, carrying objects on your head is a perfectly normal way to transport them from point A to point B, and many of those objects are considerably heavier than an index card.

As an alternative to the Walkabout Challenge mentioned above, you might try placing the index card on your foot. This version incorporates some of the basic philosophy of mindfulness, as participants carefully move about, while focusing their attention on the index card they are transporting with their foot.

3-25 MAKING STUFF UP

A word, a definition and a poem.

For this artistic activity, you'll need an index card for each player, seated around a table. You can also supply a variety of creative and colorful writing tools.

The activity begins by inviting everyone to invent a new word, and write it prominently at the top of an index cards. When everyone has finished, the cards are shuffled and redistributed (or simply passed three people to the left) and the second component is added. This time, a definition is required for the word printed on the card. Cards are then shuffled or redistributed for the final component, creating a poem using the defined word.

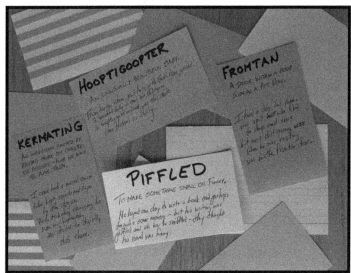

More than a decade ago I traveled to Roanoke, Virginia, to work with the staff of an outdoor education program. After dinner one evening, a member of the staff shared a version of Making Stuff Up, which he had given the made-up name of Uüb. When playing with the college age staff, the results were sometimes amazing, generally humorous, and occasionally inappropriate!

I thought the game was uniquely original. Or at least I did until I discovered a book in a foreign language with a very similar game. Roughly translated as Drawing Conclusions, this after-dinner game has four components. The first contributor writes a descriptive sentence on one side of an index card, such as, "It was indeed a beautiful sunrise for a Wednesday." The next person turns the card over and draws a picture based upon the sentence description. The third person (without reading the original sentence) draws a caption below the illustration. The fourth and final person views both sides of the card and assigns a grade (A+ for example) and commentary to the project (on the sentence side), such as "Illegible penmanship, outstanding artwork and surprisingly succinct captioning" and then returns the card to the original sentence author. No doubt these artistic cards will become refrigerator art somewhere very soon!

———

If you think that Making Stuff Up isn't necessarily a good career decision, consider what happened to Theodor Geisel. One of the reviews on his early works included the phrase, "You can't just go around making up words!" But Theodor Geisel, better known as Dr. Seuss, made a lifetime of doing just that!

3-26 DIRECTIONALLY CHALLENGED

Follow the leader, or not!

> *The illiterate of the future will not be those who cannot read and write,*
> *but those who cannot learn, unlearn and relearn.*
> —Alvin Toffler

This activity is an interesting way to illustrate our ability (or lack thereof) to "rewire" our brains to meet the needs of a changing environment. Each of the four situations below are presented so that participants can monitor their own ability to adapt, and all that is needed is one large index card per person, with a large arrow drawn on each card.

In each of the four stages, the facilitator will face in the same direction as the audience and hold a large index card (with a clearly visible arrow) over their head while inviting the audience to replicate the actions being performed (with some interesting variations). Typical actions include orienting the card so that the arrow points upward, downward, to the left or to the right, while saying these various directions.

Stage I: Audience members are invited to do what the facilitator does and say what the facilitator says. This is generally an easy task and one that most individuals will have no difficulty replicating. Left (left), Up (up), Right (right), Down (down).

Stage II: Audience members are next invited to do what the facilitator does but say the opposite. That is, when the facilitator shows the arrow pointing upward and says "Up," the audience orient their arrow cards pointing upward but say "Down." Left (right), Up (down), Right (left), Down (up). Some confusion and laughter may result in this round, as audience members struggle to complete the task.

Stage III: Audience members do the opposite of what the facilitator does but say the same. So, for this stage, when the facilitator shows the arrow pointing down and says "Down," the audience orient their arrow cards pointing upward and say "Down." Again, more confusion is likely in this stage.

Stage IV: In this final stage, audience members do the opposite of what the facilitator does and say the opposite, too. When the facilitator orients the arrow card to the right and says "Right," the audience point their cards to the left and say "Left."

One variation of this activity (without index card arrows) invites the audience to jump forwards, backwards, to the left and to the right, following the four stages above. For this kinesthetic version of the activity, be sure participants stand with adequate space between each other (so they don't jump into another person during the activity).

When we are instructed to do the opposite of what we observe our leader doing, there is a disconnect. Leaders are often regarded as role models. We emulate them and attempt to be like them. When we are asked to produce a result that is contrary to those demonstrated by our leader, we struggle. We hesitate. We fail. As John Maxwell would say, we need our leaders to "know the way, show the way and go the way." We need our leaders to be positive role models with actions that we can replicate.

There is a simple definition of the word *integrity* that I appreciate. If what persons say and what they do align, they are said to have integrity. In stages II, III, and IV above, there is a lack of integrity between what audience members and their leaders say and do, and this lack of integrity is the cause of confusion and poor performance in the completion of the task. This topic is worthy of more discussion with your audience, after completing all four stages of this activity.

3-27 WHAT ARE WE YELLING?

A burst of language with significant meaning.

This is yet another noisy activity. Prepare for this activity by writing several popular or familiar phrases (of about ten words or less) onto separate index cards. Then shuffle this deck of cards and deal them out to each team of approximately ten people present. This activity can be used with as few as two teams, and as many as six.

The challenge of this activity is for each team to present the complete phrase written on their index card, by having team members each say one word from that phrase, at the same time. So the words in the phrase "To be or knot to be" are all simultaneously spoken (yelled) at the same time, in one short burst of language (but all the information is there). Other teams try to guess what the complete phrase is. For extremely challenging phrases, teams can repeat their phrase a second time, if requested.

When two teams are present, one team shouts their phrase and the second team tries to translate their burst of language into a familiar phrase. When three or more teams are present, one team shouts their phrase and other teams race to be the first to translate the phrase correctly (adding an element of urgency to the task).

If you happen to be working with a corporation or organization, try using a familiar phrase or sentence from the company's website or mission statement. For younger audiences, try using the words from a familiar song, movie or TV show. For a higher challenge, shout out the words from a song, movie or book and then ask the other teams to guess which song, movie or book has that phrase.

3-28 SHERLOCK HOLMES

Investigation is elementary, my dear Watson!

To prepare for this activity, insert some unique (and durable) objects (about the size of a tennis ball) into a drawstring stuff sack and tightly close the sack. Then pass the sack around the group, just once, allowing everyone to feel the various shapes inside the sack. Next, ask the group to identify as many of the objects as they can and as a team, write down their guesses on an index card.

Durable objects can include such things as a golf ball, hockey puck, wooden spoon, paperback book, deck of cards, plastic drinking cup, squishy toy, action figure, belt, set of keys, apple, empty water bottle, shoe, pair of gloves, candy bar, spatula, cloth napkin, can of sardines and other similar things.

There is a unique variation of this activity that does not require a sack at all. Simply invite your group to form a circle with everyone facing inward. Then ask each person to place their hands behind their back and pass each item around the circle in this manner. Participants can feel each object, but not see them. After each item has been passed just once around the circle, invite each participant to individually list as many of the items as they can on an index card. Then invite small groups of four people to form and using each of their individual lists attempt to create a master list that is as accurate as possible. When each group has finished, display all the various objects and provide a prize to the group with the most accurate inventory list.

In this "pass it around" version of Sherlock Holmes, you can also ask each group of four to identify some key features of these objects, including: Which object is the biggest? Which object is the heaviest? Which object costs the most? How many objects are in the sack? Which item is the smallest? Which items are edible? Which object would you most want to possess?

For a more acoustic version of this activity, instead of passing each item around the circle, drop each item onto a large metal cookie sheet, metal pan or metal bucket. Invite your audience to guess the identity of each object by the sound it makes when dropped and write this guess on an index card. Choose appropriate objects with significantly different acoustic results, such as a set of keys, block of wood, several dice, pencil or pen, tennis ball, metal spoon, wooden spoon, shoe, paperback book, screwdriver, pair of scissors, necklace or bracelet, several nails or screws, coins, unpopped popcorn, marbles, ice cubes, metal coat hanger and anything else you have in your junk drawer at home.

As a variation of this activity, instead of selecting objects at random, invite your participants to each bring a durable object with them and place these into the sack. In this version of Sherlock Holmes, in addition to identifying the object, participants must also try to guess the identity of the person in their group who owns the object.

3-29 THE INTERNET SHOPPING NETWORK

You can buy almost anything online.

In this modern version of a scavenger hunt, teams of ten people are asked to produce a variety of common (and occasionally not so common) objects currently in their possession. You can prepare for this activity with a creative list of objects by writing one object per index card. Then shuffle these cards and let the fun begin.

The activity leader (or Internet Shopping Network host) turns over the top card from the deck and boldly mentions the object written there. Teams quickly try to locate that object among the members of the team and then bring this object to the host.

I like to break my audience into smaller, equal sized teams and let them compete to produce each item mentioned as quickly as possible. The first team to produce an object wins 5 points, followed by 4 points for the second team, 3 points for the third team, 2 points for the fourth team and 1 point for any other team. I find that competition raises the energy of this activity tremendously.

You can include some of these common items in your Internet Shopping Network deck of index cards: a wristwatch with a large face, a photo ID card, a two-dollar bill, coins totaling forty-one cents, shoelaces (but no shoes), a belt with a shiny buckle, eyeglasses, two socks that don't match, a leather bracelet, a collection of keys, a hair ornament, one large earring, a cell phone with less than 50% battery life, a comb, a pen, foreign currency (paper money from another country), a store coupon, any card that has expired, a business card, a toy, lipstick, a leather wallet, a button, something with a battery, something worth less than $1, an index card!

Here are a few items that are a bit more challenging for participants to produce: a yoyo, a fidget spinner toy, a flash drive, a coin with a date before 1990, a library card with no bar code, a photograph more than ten years old, a personal check, a toothbrush, any kind of map, a paperback book, a thermometer, a compass, a pair of scissors, a spoon or fork, any kind of ball.

Over the years, I've heard this activity called by several different names, including Human Scavenger Hunt and Department Store. But some of those titles go back fifty years or more, so I decided to use a more modern title in this book.

––––––––––––––––––

The Human Scavenger Hunt is a variation of the Internet Shopping Network where instead of requesting objects, human features are mentioned, such as someone with blue eyes, the tallest person in the room, someone who is a twin, anyone under five feet tall, two people whose combined age adds up to more than fifty years, someone wearing sandals, someone wearing socks that don't match, someone with lots of jewelry, someone with freckles, anyone wearing glasses, someone with heterochromia iridium (two different color eyes), someone with a visible tattoo, someone with fingernails painted different colors, someone with braces on their teeth, someone wearing a wrist watch, someone not wearing a belt, etc.

3-30 THE WHOLE STORY

From an old-fashioned parlor game to a modern storytelling technique.

The Whole Story is a variation of a classic after-dinner game from over a century ago. To play this story game, first distribute a large index card to every person seated around a large table. Then begin building the story, one line at a time. The first person writes the adjective for a man near the top of the index card and then folds this portion of the card over, so the next person cannot see it. Then the card is passed one person to the right. The second person adds a man's name. This process of writing and folding continues until all elements of the story are complete, at which point someone unfolds the card and reads the story aloud for all to hear.

To play, enter the following information:

An adjective for a man	What the woman is doing
A man's name	What the weather was like
What the man is wearing	Where they met
What the man is doing	What he said to her
An adjective for a woman	What she said to him
A woman's name	The consequences of meeting
What the woman is wearing	What the world said

Then the story is read aloud, for example:

> *Bookworm Ted*, wearing his favorite *Superhero T-shirt*, was *visiting the Shopping Mall* when he met *Triathlete Samantha*, wearing *an 1890s swimming costume*. It was *exceedingly stormy* that day in *the elevator*. He said, *"Have you read Be My Enemy by my favorite author Christopher Brookmyre?"* She said, *"I don't typically eat guacamole."* Because of this exchange, they decided to *start a company and write apps for smartphones*. And the world *continued spinning, though with some trepidation.*

Long before word games such as Mad-libs were first published (1958), there were parlor games known by the names Consequences and The Purple Door, where audiences supplied random names, adjectives, nouns, verbs, and other words, which were added to the basic elements of a story. After filling in all the necessary words, a narrator read the finished story to the audience, often with hilarious results. There is even a picture version of the game, called The Exquisite Corpse (credited to Andre Breton, the surrealist artist) where participants took turns adding not words but drawings of various body parts, to create a final artistic masterpiece.

If you think that writing in this style doesn't produce a coherent work, then visit your library and take out a copy of the book *Naked Came the Manatee* (ISBN 978-0-3991-4198-8) which has thirteen chapters written in sequence by thirteen different Miami, Florida, writers, including Dave Barry, Paul Levine, Brian Antoni and Carl Hiassen. The title of this book is based upon one of the most famous literary hoaxes of all times, the book *Naked Came the Stranger*, credited to Penelope Ashe, but in fact written by a group of twenty-four journalists, led by columnist Mike McGrady. This 1969 novel went on to become a bestseller, and sales continued even after the hoax was revealed.

3-31 VERBOSE VERBIAGE

A game of words where simplicity is the key.

Verbose – *using more words than necessary to convey information.*
Verbiage – *an excessive amount of words.*

OK, so the title of this activity is a little redundant, but in reality, quite accurate in describing the elements of the game. See if you can work out what each of the following phrases are trying to express.

Begin by writing the verbose text on one side on an index card and the simplification of that phrase on the other side. Then provide each group with a collection of twenty cards and see if they can work out a simple translation for each complicated and excessively worded (but often familiar) phrase.

Verbose Verbiage	Simplified Phrase
Under no circumstances should you compute the quantity of your barnyard fowl previous to their incubation.	Don't count your chickens before they are hatched.
Surveillance should precede saltation.	Look before you leap.
Gramineous organisms are perpetually more verdant when located on an adjacent surface.	The grass is always greener on the other side.
It is futile to attempt to indoctrinate a superannuated canine with innovative maneuvers.	You can't teach an old dog new tricks.
The greatest of need is the maternal parent of the art of original contrivance.	Necessity is the Mother of invention.
Abstention from any aleatory undertaking precludes a potential escalation of a lucrative nature.	Nothing ventured, nothing gained.
A revolving lithic conglomerate accrues no lichen.	A rolling stone gathers no moss.
The temperature of the aqueous content of a metallic receptacle under unremitting surveillance does not attain its level of evaporation.	A watched pot never boils.
Members of an avian species of identical plumage congregate.	Birds of a feather flock together.
The stylus is more potent than the claymore.	The pen is mightier than the sword.
Where there are visible emissions from carbonaceous materials, there exists conflagration.	Where there's smoke, there's fire.

Verbose Verbiage	Simplified Phrase
Similar sire, similar scion.	Like father, like son.
Pulchritude reposes within the optic parameters of the perceiver.	Beauty is in the eye of the beholder.
Male cadavers are incapable of yielding any testimony.	Dead men tell no tales.
Integrity is the superlative strategy.	Honesty is the best policy.
A plethora of individuals with expertise in culinary techniques vitiates the potable concoction.	Too many cooks spoil the broth.
All articles that coruscate with resplendence are not, ipso factor, auriferous.	All the glitters is not gold.
Consolidated we maintain ourselves erect; bifurcated we plummet.	United we stand; divided we fall.
A feathered biped in the terminal part of the arm equals the value of a brace of such creatures in densely branched shrubbery.	A bird in the hand is worth two in the bush.
Individuals who make their abode in vitreous edifices of patent frangibility are advised to refrain from catapulting petrous projectiles.	People who live in glass houses shouldn't throw stones.
A single graphic facsimile is appraised in excess of myriad articulations.	A picture is worth a thousand words.
A precipitate avian ensnares the vermiculate creature.	The early bird catches the worm.
Rectitude does not attach itself to binary transgressions.	Two wrongs do not make a right.
You cannot estimate the value of a bound narrative from its exterior vesture.	You cannot judge a book by its cover.
A single pyrus malus per diem restrains the arrival of the Hippocratic apostle.	An apple a day keeps the doctor away.
Although it is within the realm of possibility to escort equus caballus to a location providing a potable mixture of hydrogen and oxygen, one cannot coerce said mammal to imbibe.	You can lead a horse to water, but you cannot make it drink.

3-32 SEVEN DOTS

The beginning of something artistic.

This artistic group activity has two parts. First, participants each take an index card and place seven dots randomly around the face of the card. Then they trade cards with another person in the group and draw something on the card that incorporates each of the seven dots.

If you like, you can prepare a theme for each round of this activity, such as people playing sports, a nature scene, wild animals, faces, tall buildings, stick people, signs, advertisements, food, etc.

When everyone has finished, display the card for all to see, and invite commentary from the audience on the content of each card, including the artist's ability to incorporate each of the seven dots.

For centuries, we have assigned images to clusters of stars visible at night from our earth. If you like, you can preprint star constellations on each index card and invite your audience to incorporate these stars (dots) into their own interpretation of the heavens. Then compare your modern artists' renditions to that of ancient artists and mariners.

3-33 REFRIGERATOR ART

Creativity and artistic expression.

You can prepare for this artistic activity by supplying your audience with a wide variety of creative (and quick drying) art supplies and a pile of index cards. Place the index cards (of various sizes, colors and patterns) in the center of a table, surrounded by the art supplies. Then invite your audience to create whatever inspires them on an index card. The images can be abstract or something with more form and shape. When artists are satisfied with their creation, they sign it (with a bold marker so their signature is easily visible) and place it in a second pile on the table, and then choose a new index card as they continue creating. When all index cards have been used, the creativity moves from artistic expression to choosing a caption for each creation. This can be an individual contribution (as players take a card at random and assign a caption to it) or a group process (where everyone contributes their ideas and the group decides on the final caption together). Write these captions on the backside of each image.

You might be truly surprised with the artistic ability of the members of your group, both with the visual artwork and the literary captions.

If you wish to continue this activity further, consider a third round where an esteemed panel of judges (your audience members) evaluate each work of art and write their impression on the back of each image, such as "This work of art expresses the way I feel after a long winter when spring has finally arrived!"

At the conclusion of this activity, invite artists to take a few of their own creations and share a few more with others in the group. Then invite everyone to go home and decorate the front of their refrigerators with this collection of artwork.

The artwork displayed here was created by Emma and Bente, the children of Ester Hoefsloot of the Netherlands. Ester created the Dutch translations for my book, *The Teamwork & Teamplay International Edition* (ISBN 978-0-9882046-3-8) and her daughters fill the front of her refrigerator with artwork on a regular basis.

3-34 WHY? BECAUSE!

Gathering advice.

Why? Because! is a unique game of questions and answers. To begin this activity, invite your audience to take two index cards. On one card, they write a question and on the second card, the answer. Then add both of these cards facedown to the appropriate stack of question or answer cards near the middle of the table. When all cards have been collected, shuffle each stack of index cards. Next, invite individuals to select one question card and one answer card, and to share the information printed there with the entire audience.

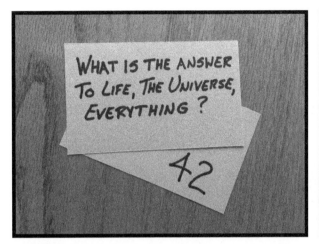
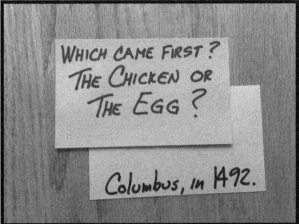

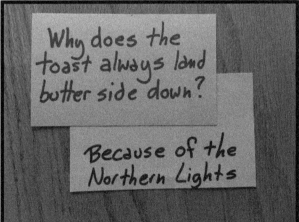

When all questions and answers have been read, it is time for phase two of the activity. See if you can pair a question card with the intended answer card for each of the cards present.

While most of the pairings of questions and answers in this activity are likely to be somewhat silly, every once and a while some really profound combinations occur. Enjoy this activity, but don't take the answers, or yourself, too seriously!

3-35 BOARD GAMES

Board games from around the world—on cards.

You can construct each of the board games below by drawing the pattern shown on a large index card and using coins or small stones as the game pieces. If you laminate each card, including instructions and collect a variety of game pieces, you can create a convenient game box. These are perfect for those rainy days at camp, a long bus trip or after lunch at school.

Place the playing surface on the front side of each card, and the instructions for play on the backside, including a list of any additional equipment (dice, pencils, markers, etc.) required to play.

Achi (a version of tic-tac-toe from Ghana, Africa)

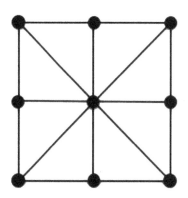

This two-player game requires four game pieces for each player. The object of the game is to be the first player to achieve three pieces in a row. Players begin by taking turns placing pieces on the board. Once all eight pieces are on the board, players take turns moving (sliding) one of their pieces along a line into an empty location (no jumping is allowed). The first player to get three of their pieces in a row (horizontally, vertically or diagonally), wins. You can also play another version of this game, called Picaria, with just three game pieces for each player.

One vs. Many (from Egypt and Spain)

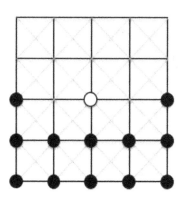

One vs. Many is a classic game of a single player trying to defeat multiple opponents. A board of twenty-five locations is created. One player has a single white stone, while their opponent has a total of twelve black stones. The starting position for the game is shown here. The white stone can jump over any black stone, removing it from the board. Black stones cannot jump, but simply slide one space along a line to any open space. The objective for the black stone player is to confine the white stone so that it cannot move. Any stone can move vertically, horizontally or diagonally to another open space. The single stone player moves first.

Pen the Pig

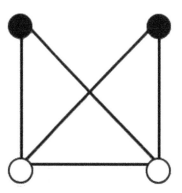

I first learned this simple board game from the craft instructor at 4-H Camp Ohio, in St. Louisville, OH. Two players with two stones each begin in the starting positions shown. Players can slide their stones along a line to any open position (no jumping). There are five positions on this board. The four starting positions plus the center (X) position. The player that confines their opponent from moving, wins!

Len Choa
(a hunting game from Thailand and a variation of One vs. Many)

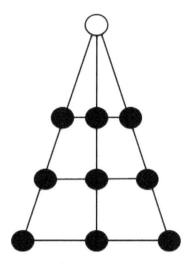

Play begins for this two-person game with an empty board. One player possesses a single white stone (the tiger) and places this stone at the top of the triangular board. The other player has six black stones (the leopards) and can place a single stone anywhere on the board during each turn but cannot move one of these stones until all six leopards (black stones) are on the board. The tiger can jump over a leopard (removing it from the board). The leopards attempt to corner the tiger so that it cannot move. Each move must land on one of the ten positions on the board.

Roman Draughts
(a greatly simplified version of checkers for two players, from Italy)

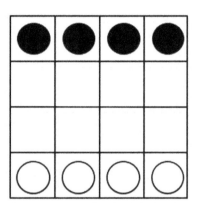

Players can only move their stones straight or diagonally forward, one space at a time. Jumping over an opponent's stone removes it from the board. Once stones reach the opposite side, they are allowed to move forwards, backwards and diagonally (but not horizontally) to any open space. To win, capture all your opponent's stones or corner your opponent to prevent him or her from making a move.

Up the Ladder

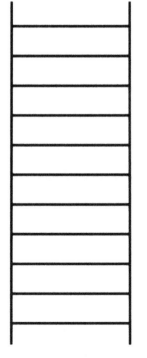

The first thing to do for this board game is to draw a simple graphic for a ladder, with as many rungs as you like. You can change the number of rungs from game to game.

    Players take turns placing three markers (coins or stones) on the ladder. One on each rung, all three on one rung, or any combination they choose, starting with the bottom rung. The goal is to be the first player to put a marker on the highest rung (the top of the ladder).

Five Field Kono (a board game from Korea)

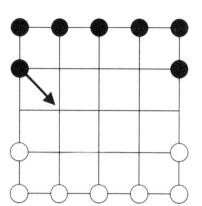

The authentic way to play Five Field Kono requires moving (sliding) pieces diagonally across the board spaces. Five Field Kono is a race to move your playing pieces (stones or coins) to the opposite side of the board. First player to accomplish this task is the winner. No jumping is allowed in this game, but players can move their pieces forwards or backwards.

Four Field Kono (Nothing like Five Field Kono!)

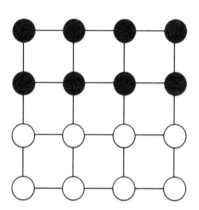

Four Field Kono is a strategy game unlike Five Field Kono. In this version of the game, all spaces on the board are filled. Players remove their opponent's markers from the board by first jumping over one of their own pieces and landing on their opponent's stone. Stones can be moved by sliding or jumping. Play is over when all of one player's stones are captured or when no additional moves are possible (gridlock).

Board games exist for almost every culture in the world. Game boards have been found in Egyptian pyramids, on the stone tile roofs of ancient buildings and on tile floors in public places throughout the world. As an example, I recently discovered the tic-tac-toe style game scratched into the stone floor of the Great Wall of China on the west side of an area known as the Water Gate. Some of the board games featured here have been played for over one hundred years!

3-36 THE JIGSAW HUNT

A treasure hunt with index cards.

For this treasure hunt activity, you'll need plenty of index cards with different colors, sizes, patterns and styles. Before cutting each card into four unique pieces, add some important information to that card (such as words, illustrations, messages and clues). Then cut each card into four pieces using the creative scissors found in craft stores (that produce wavy, interesting lines). Present one piece from each puzzle to individuals in your audience and hide the other three pieces. Then invite everyone in your audience to find the other pieces that will complete their card. Once everyone has found their card and completely reassembled it, invite them to use the information on each card for the next challenge.

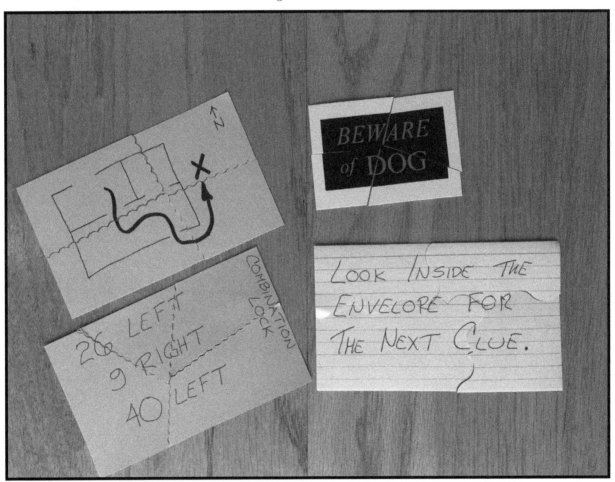

The content printed on each index card in this activity can be as creative as you are. Index cards can contain illustrations (such as a treasure map!) or words (such as song lyrics or words from the activity Quotes In Order, also in this book), or directions to the next clue (for escape rooms and team challenges). Index cards can also contain additional puzzles to be solved, clues to a mystery (such as 13 Clues, in this book), photographs used during a debriefing session (such as traffic signs), passwords, the numbers that open a combination lock, titles of books in the room, where additional clues can be found and many, many more.

3-37 TEAM ORIGAMI

Paper folding on a giant scale.

The Japanese art of paper folding is known as origami. Most designs start with a square piece of paper, but a large (5x8 inch) index card will work fine for our purposes.

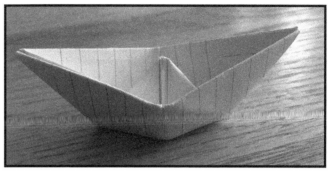

The first step in Team Origami is for individuals to learn how to fold a simple paper hat from a large index card. You can find dozens on Internet sites with origami instructions, including www.kidspressmagazine.com.

The goal of Team Origami is to create a large-scale version of an origami design as a team. In this case, after perfecting the paper hat design individually, the entire team (four to eight people) attempt to fold a large tarp into this same shape, using the skills they learned individually. The only additional constraint is that team members all grasp the tarp at the beginning of the activity and must continue to be in contact with the tarp throughout the folding process, until they are wearing the giant hat together at the completion of the activity.

I've always felt that teamwork is not easier. It is better, but not easier. Learning a skill individually (as in the paper folding hat that begins this activity) is one level of competency. But using that skill as part of a team is quite a different thing. Participants will realize this fact when they attempt to create the team-size hat required in this activity.

> *Coming together is a beginning.*
> *Keeping together is progress.*
> *Working together is success.*
> —Henry Ford

3-38 NUMERIC LOGIC PUZZLES

A new style of logic puzzle, called Suguru.

There are many styles of logic puzzles these days. The London newspaper carries two full pages of number and letter logic puzzles in the Sunday edition, including Suguru puzzles, invented by Naoki Inaba of Japan. Jim Bumgardner has created a truly amazing (and exhaustive) collection of Suguru puzzles that you can download for free online at www.krazydad.com.

A Suguru puzzle consists of "containers." A container with one cell will have exactly one number in it, the number 1. A three-cell container will have the numbers 1, 2 and 3. A five-cell container will contain 1, 2, 3, 4 and 5. Adjacent cells (those that touch each other) may never contain the same number and this includes vertical, horizontal and diagonal connections. The example shown on the left below shows a typical starting pattern for a Suguru puzzle. The solution to this puzzle is shown on the right. On the following page, you'll find one of Jim's Stupendous Suguru puzzles.

One easy way to hand-draw these puzzles onto index cards is to find an index card with a grid pattern printed on it. Then simply sketch the 6x6 grid pattern, darken in the cell lines and draw in a few numbers (clues). Or you can print directly onto paper or index cards from the amazing collection of numeric logic puzzles available at www.krazydad.com. Happy puzzling!

There are many types of number puzzles available to amuse the members of your audience. Sudoku, KenKen, Futoshiki and Kakuro are just a few possibilities. Each of these puzzles has unique rules. The Suguru cell puzzle introduced here is also known as a Tectonics or Number Block puzzle. Introduce the members of your audience to each style starting with an easy puzzle and gradually working up to more difficult and challenging ones. One of the best websites (with free printable puzzles and solutions) is www. krazydad.com, which has a wide variety of puzzles, mazes and logic challenges, for beginners, intermediates, and experts. You can also purchase *Stupendous Suguru—Volume I* by Jim Bumgardner at www.amazon.com.

In case you are wondering, it can be quite challenging to create your own numeric puzzles. But if you want to try, Gerard Butters, Frederick Henle, James Henle and Colleen McGaughey of Smith College have written the paper "Creating Clueless Puzzles" and posted it on the web at www.math.smith.edu.

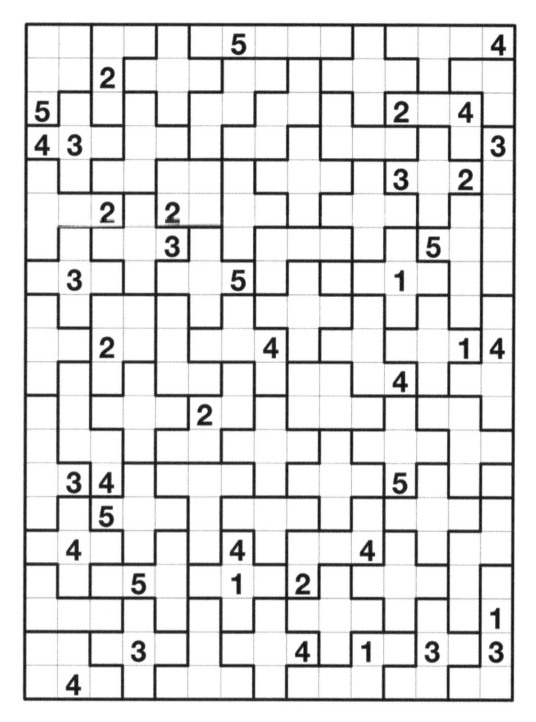

The Stupendous Suguru puzzle featured on this page is from the creative mind of Jim Bumgardner, who describes himself as a programmer, musician, composer, author, artist, puzzle maker and teacher. You can find many, many more of Jim's puzzles at www.krazydad.com.

While some Suguru puzzles are small in size (5x5 or 6x6 cells) and perfectly suited for a single person to complete, the 15x20 full-page puzzle on this page lends itself to teamwork, with multiple contributors attempting to complete the puzzle together. Two (or more) hands (and minds) are better than one, in this case. Good luck!

3-39 SQUIGGLES

Creative drawing.

Here is the perfect activity for occupying your audience for a while. Begin this activity with a pile of blank index cards, several permanent black markers and a variety of other colorful writing instruments such as colored pencils, crayons, various color pens and markers.

Next, invite everyone to take a blank index card and a black permanent marker and quickly draw a squiggly line or two on the card. Then pass this card one or two people to the left and invite that artist to "complete" the drawing by incorporating the dark line squiggle into the final work of art. Invite the artist to choose a pencil, pen or crayon that is a different color than the original squiggle.

If needed, you can prepare a large quantity of index cards with black squiggle marks on them, and then invite your audience to take a card from the pile and turn the squiggle into something artistic.

3-40 NURSERY RHYME HEADLINES

A linguistic challenge from childhood.

Write down each of the following nursery rhyme headlines on one side of an index card and the actual title on the opposite side. Then shuffle the deck and invite your audience to see how many they can correctly identify.

Nursery Rhyme Headline (A Brief Synopsis)	The Actual Nursery Rhyme
Sheep relentlessly follows young girl.	Mary Had a Little Lamb
Farmer's spouse attacked by rodents	Three Blind Mice
Infant falls from tree.	Rock-a-Bye Baby
Married couple never eat same food.	Jack Sprat
Wool supply assured, inquiry reveals.	Baa Baa Black Sheep
Fast, agile boy jumps wax decoration.	Jack Be Nimble
Rodent ascends then descends at 1300 hours.	Hickory Dickory Dock
Girl frightened by arachnoid while eating dairy products.	Little Miss Muffett
Three violinists perform for royalty.	Old King Cole
Numerous children reside in footwear.	The Old Woman Who Lived in a Shoe
Entire royal brigade cannot reassemble eggman.	Humpty Dumpty
Missing livestock returns home.	Little Bo Peep
Sleeping shepherd allows livestock to wander.	Little Boy Blue
Morning oatmeal still good after a week and two days.	Pease Porridge Hot
Man lives his whole life in just one week.	Solomon Grundy
Man with scoliosis finds money on fence.	There Was a Crooked Man
Agriculturist's canine's name diminishing.	B-I-N-G-O
Siblings injured while attempting to transport liquid.	Jack and Jill
Elderly male unable to get up after weather event.	It's Raining, It's Pouring
My offspring sleeps with pants and one shoe.	Diddle, Diddle, Dumpling, My Son John
Friar oversleeps, neglects morning duties.	Frere Jacques (Are You Sleeping?)
Arachnoid perseveres in quest for altitude despite inclement weather.	The Itsy-Bitsy Spider

---

As a variation of the index card technique presented above, you can also verbally inform your audience of each headline and either invite them to write down the answer on an index card or shout out the answer as soon as they know it.

3-40½ NURSERY RHYME MYSTERIES

How many can you remember?

Write down each of the following mysteries on one side of an index card and the answer on the opposite side. Then shuffle the deck and invite your audience to see how many they can solve.

Nursery Rhyme Mystery	Answers
Who increased enormously in size with a single drink?	Alice (in Wonderland)
Name all nine of Santa's reindeer.	Dasher, Dancer, Prancer, Vixen, Comet Cupid, Donner, Blitzen and Rudolph
Whose life was spared 1001 nights because of the stories she told?	Scheherazade, the Vizier's daughter
Where did the old women with many children live?	In a shoe
What five things did King Cole want?	Pipe, bowl and fiddlers three
Who tried to put Humpty Dumpty together again?	All the King's horses and all the King's men
What children attempted to eat a house?	Hansel and Gretel
When Jack fell down and broke his crown, what was used to fix him up again?	Vinegar and brown paper (in the second verse!)
What is the magic password in Ali Baba?	Open Sesame
All for one and one for all was pledged by whom?	The Three Musketeers
Who were the three men in a tub?	Butcher, baker and candlestick maker
When this old man played three, where did he play it?	On his knee.
If that looking glass is broke, what will Mama buy?	A billy goat.
In One, Two Buckle My Shoe, what happens at Five, Six?	Pick up sticks.

While many people know the more familiar nursery rhymes, only a few know the content beyond the first verse. A few of the questions above come from the second or even third verses of these nursery rhymes and children's stories.

As a variation of the index card technique presented above, you can also verbally inform your audience of each mystery above and either invite them to write down the answer on an index card or shout out the answer as soon as they know it.

3-41 OBSCURED

Artistic pattern recognition.

I wish I could explain how I created this activity. In fact, I wish I could replicate that creativity over and over again, but alas, the idea came to me while reading a book on an airplane, that oddly enough had absolutely nothing to do with art!

According to the dictionary, the verb *obscure* refers to a variety of ways to conceal something or keep it from being seen, and that is exactly what is happening in this activity.

Start with a photograph or graphic image that is familiar to most people, such as the Eiffel Tower. Then, using a variety of index cards, cover up about 90% of the picture and invite your audience to see if they can identify the object in the photograph, based only upon the 10% or so that they can see.

The goal is to obscure the details of an image so that very few people can accurately identify what the complete image reveals.

You can play Obscured as a contest. Collect ten familiar images and cover 90% of each image with index cards. Then invite your audience to guess the identity of each obscured image. Give a prize to the player with the most correct guesses.

For extremely difficult images, you can write a hint or two on the index cards used to obscure the photograph. For the image on the right side of this page, one potential hint might be a Pink Floyd album.

To prepare for this activity you will want to collect images of familiar people, places and things (such as the Eiffel Tower, The Colosseum in Rome, The Great Pyramids of Giza, The Parthenon, Niagara Falls, *The Mona Lisa*, The Taj Mahal, The Statue of Liberty, a famous musician, a classic painting, sheet music for a popular song, traffic signs, sport superstars, movie stars, etc.). You can even include photographs of people in your audience. For photographs of architectural marvels, see the book *Wonders of the World* (ISBN 978-1-4351-3732-5) edited by Francesco Boccia.

3-42 SNAP WORDS

More answers from A to Z.

You can prepare for this game by creating a double deck of alphabet index cards (fifty-two cards in total). Each card should contain one letter of the alphabet written in large, block capital letters. Shuffle this deck of cards and you are ready to begin.

The dealer calls out one of the categories listed below and turns over the top card in the deck so that everyone in the group can see it. The first player to shout out an answer (by mentioning an object that begins with the letter shown on the card), wins the card. If no one responds within five seconds, the card is returned to the bottom of the deck and play continues. The player that collects the most cards during the game, wins!

Categories for Snap Words can include such things as movies, songs, automobiles, sport teams, books, TV shows, famous people, cities, food, animals, kitchen utensils, things you find in a garage, countries, cartoon characters, super heroes, parts of a computer, words in foreign languages, things you can buy in a discount store, articles of clothing, toys and even card games.

You can play a slightly more competitive version of Snap Words by splitting a group in half and inviting each half to form a line. The first two people in each line race to identify an object that begins with the letter turned over by the facilitator. You can modify the activity so that objects are associated with something specific, such as things you can buy in a hardware store. After each round, the first two people in each line move to the end of their line and two new players arrive at the front. The winning team gets to keep the card. The first team to collect twenty cards, wins!

3-43 THE SECRET WORD

Some words have consequences.

Here is a silly game that you can play with your family and friends. Start with a collection of twenty index cards and write one commonly used word on each card in big letters. Then shuffle these cards and place the deck face up in the middle of a table. Next, invite your friends to gather around the table and have a conversation about anything at all. Whenever someone mentions the secret word (written on the topmost card) everyone touches their index finger to the side of their nose, and the conversation continues. The last person to touch their nose (i.e., the last person to notice that someone has said the secret word) has to stand up and turn a 360 while singing the "I'm Sorry" song.*

In the early part of the 1900s social recreation books often had entire pages of "forfeits" or tasks that must be performed by a person losing a game or contest. You can find free electronic book formats of these historical (and sometimes hysterical) publications at www.archive.org. While performing a forfeit was a time-honored tradition of the past, I'm not really comfortable with it in the present. So, for this activity and any other game where someone occasionally goofs up, I'd recommend a fun alternative to performing a forfeit (like the "I'm Sorry" song), or no consequences at all. Games should be fun and if

your choice of consequences for making a mistake lessens the likelihood that participants ever want to play the game again, then you might want to rethink the reason you played the game in the first place.

---

*In my family, the "I'm Sorry" song is a fun way of expressing regret for having messed up, usually for something silly and non-life threatening. The song goes (to no particular tune): "I'm sorry, I knew it, I'm sorry, I blew it, I'm really, really, really very sorry."

3-44 PIRATE'S TREASURE

Communication under pressure.

This is one of the more hilarious and physical activities in this book. Two teams of four players are required for each match.

Team 1 has a blindfolded *Seeker* that is on their hands and knees trying to find an index card which has been placed somewhere on the floor or ground. Team 1 also has two *Lookers* who can see the *Seeker* but cannot speak, and one *Communicator* who can speak and who can see the *Lookers* but has their back to the *Seeker* so they cannot see the *Seeker*. The *Lookers* watch the *Seeker* and (using hand gestures) inform the *Communicator* where to tell the *Seeker* to move to find the index card.

Team 2 has a blindfolded *Whomper* who wields a long foam pool noodle and tries to contact (Whomp!) the *Seeker*. There are also two *Lookers* and one *Communicator* on Team 2.

Each team is trying to be the first to complete their task. The *Seeker* is trying to find the index card (although other objects can be used, such as a tennis ball, stuffed animal or even a cowbell). The *Whomper* is trying to contact the *Seeker* with the foam noodle. The *Lookers* are giving hand motion instructions to the *Communicator* who is shouting directions to the *Seeker* (or *Whomper*). The first team to accomplish their task twice, wins! After each match, invite the players within a team to rotate responsibilities and play again, or to change roles for each team, from *Seeker* to *Whomper*.

I first witnessed this activity at an outdoor education center in central Pennsylvania. The school-aged participants would play this game for hours!

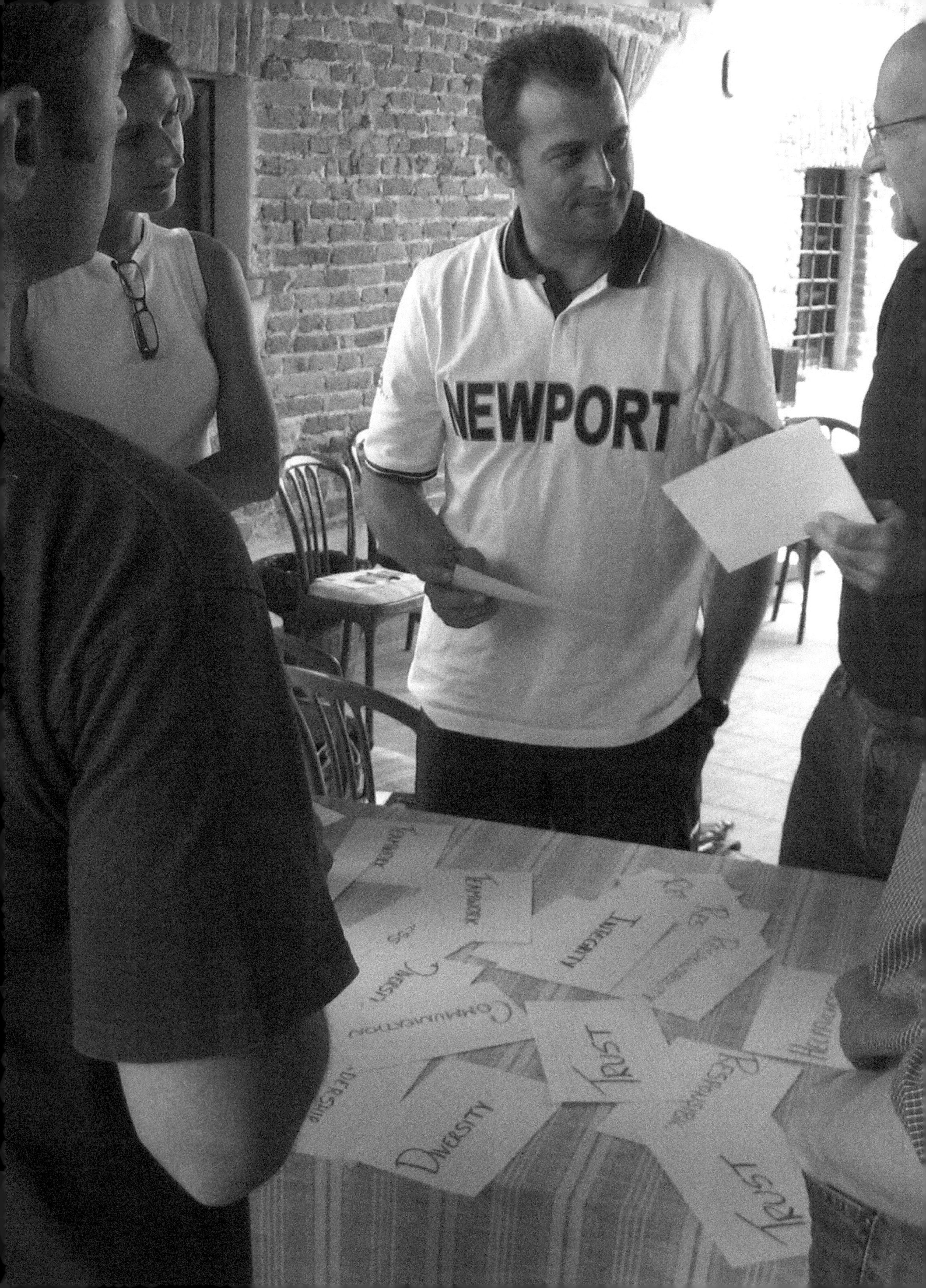
NEWPORT
INTEGRITY
COMMUNICATION
TRUST
DIVERSITY
TRUST

REVIEWING, REFLECTION, AND CLOSING ACTIVITIES

CHAPTER FOUR

This fourth chapter is a filled with activities for processing, debriefing, reviewing and reflection plus several closing activities.

NO.	ACTIVITY NAME	TEACHABLE MOMENT	IDEAL GROUP SIZE
4-1	Thumbprints	Team Evaluation	6–15 people
4-2	Fortune Cookies	Reviewing Activity	Any
4-3	Pillow Talk	Final Debrief of the Day	2 or more people
4-4	The Free Pass	A Wild Card Technique	Any group
4-5	End of the Day Questions	Self-Generated Debrief	Any group
4-6	Watch 4 It	Observation	Any group
4-7	DIY Debriefing Questions	DIY Reviewing Technique	Any group
4-8	Worms	A Visual Review Technique	5 or more people
4-9	The One Ball That Does It All	Active Debriefing	Any
4-10	Message in a Bottle	Min. Words – Max. Impact	Any
4-11	Post Card Debrief	A Visual Review Technique	Any
4-12	One for the Road	Summarizing the Experience	Any
4-13	Consensus Cards	A Way to See Consensus	Any
4-14	Evaluation Cards	Lightning Fast Evaluations	Any group
4-15	Thank You Cards	Gratitude	Any
4-16	Five F's / Share Something	Reviewing Techniques	Any
4-17	Action Pak Cards	Reviewing Technique	Any
4-18	The Final Word	Inspiration	Any
4-19	Bingo Debriefing Cards	A Game Format Debrief	Any
4-20	The Toss of a Coin	Random Debrief Technique	5 or more people

4-1 THUMBPRINTS

A treasure hunt to begin a class, meeting or event.

Thumbprints is a visual debriefing tool that illustrates a full range of team performance. The circular people (thumbprints) on these cards transcend culture, ethnicity and race with familiar imagery related to how teams function. You can enlarge the images on this page to make your own set of Thumbprint debriefing cards.

At the completion of an activity or program, place these images so that they are visible to all the members of your audience. Then invite participants to interact with these images while discussing the following questions:

1. Place these images in order from best (ideal) team behavior to worst (poorest team behavior).
2. Which images illustrate positive team behavior and which are negative?
3. Which image most accurately illustrates the present nature of this group right now?
4. Which image is most like this group when things are going well?
5. Which image represents this group under pressure or experiencing conflict?
6. Which thumbprint (circle person) do you most identify with in any given illustration? Why?

The Thumbprints found here and on the Teamwork & Teamplay Training Cards were created by Dave Knobbe. These cards are available from www.healthylearning.com, www.trainerswarehouse.com and www.training-wheels.com. Together with Clare Marie Hannon and Jim Cain, Dave Knobbe is the author of *Essential Staff Training Activities* (ISBN 978-0-7575-6167-2) available from www.kendallhunt.com and www.amazon.com.

There are in fact many visual debriefing cards available. The *Images of Organizations Toolbox* of cards is available from www.rsvpdesign.co.uk and is one of the best collections of such cards in the world. *Soularium* cards with a Christian focus are available from www.CruPress.com. *Chiji Processing Cards* by Steve Simpson were some of the original visual debriefing cards and now there is the *Chiji Guidebook* (ISBN 978-2-8854-7384-4) available from www.training-wheels.com. *Stones have feelings too!* is a collection of fifty-two cards with instructions for talking about and reflecting upon feelings, from Innovative Resources (ISBN 0-9578-2319-3). *Picture This* includes seventy-five color images for conversation and reflection (ISBN 978-1-9209-4527-5) also from www.innovativeresources.org. A complete set of Thumbprints can be found on the Teamwork & Teamplay Training Cards (ISBN 978-0-9882046-2-1). For more information about these cards visit www.teamworkandteamplay.com or www.trainerswarehouse.com.

4-2 FORTUNE COOKIES

A unique (and edible) way to review.

Fortune Cookies can become a new prop for your processing, debriefing, reviewing and reflection activities, with just a few modifications. First, you'll need to obtain enough fortune cookies for your next group. If you get the edible variety, you can pull out the fortunes that come with each cookie and replace them with printed debriefing questions. Then, when your participants complete an activity, invite them to find a partner, enjoy their cookie, and ask their partner the question found inside. If you decide to use (and reuse) the fabric variety of fortune cookies, you can place a debriefing question inside (and perhaps a piece of candy too).

The fortune cookie technique mentioned here is actually a kind of random number generator for reviewing and debriefing conversation. Participants randomly choose a fortune cookie and then discuss the question inside. You simply need to fill your fortune cookies with questions for reviewing and reflection. You can find many more processing, debriefing, reviewing and reflection activities in the book *A Teachable Moment* (ISBN 978-0-7575-1782-2) by Jim Cain, Michelle Cummings and Jennifer Stanchfield, available from www.kendallhunt.com and www.training-wheels.com. You can also purchase a collection of fabric fortune cookies from www.training-wheels.com or create your own with instructions available on the Internet. There are dozens of craft (and cooking) websites with information on how to make your own fabric (and edible) fortune cookies.

Did you know that the fortune cookie is an American invention? The San Francisco bakery Benkyodo is credited with the creation of a cookie which features a piece of paper on which a prophecy or aphorism is written.

In Japanese temples a different form of fortune is available. By making a donation and then randomly shaking loose a numbered stick from a sealed box, an Omikuji fortune is revealed.

4-3 PILLOW TALK

A wonderful way to end the day.

This activity was originally created for an end of the day closing activity for resident summer camps, sometimes referred to as "cabin chat" time. It is a great idea to have some wind down time after a long day at camp, and conversation is a brilliant way to do just that. It also is a good idea to have the last thought on a camper's mind each night be a positive one.

During the evening hours of your program, while most of your participants are busy with other activities, visit the cabin (sleeping area, tent, dorm room, hotel suite, etc.) and place one index card beneath the pillow of each of your campers (or program participants). On each card, write an interesting question and invite the reader to reflect on the answer, or share the answer with someone else that evening.

Here are a few examples of some questions you might consider for your version of Pillow Talk:

What challenged you today? How far did you hike today? How many different kinds of food did you taste today? What was your favorite moment of the day? Did you make a new friend today? What was your favorite activity today? What groups were you a part of today? What staff member encouraged you today? What did you discover today? What did you learn today? Who did you meet today? Did you create anything today? What part of today would you like to repeat again? What was your favorite song (or dance) today? Did you see any animals today? Describe the sunrise or sunset today. Describe today in just one word. What surprised you today?

My first experience using Pillow Talk came in the middle of a rainy week at summer camp. For two days campers had been slogging around in the mud and dampness and many spent the final hours in the cabin each evening complaining about the weather. Rather than have their last moment of the day focus on something negative (which we really couldn't do much about), I decided to have them focus on something (anything!) positive. That's when the idea for Pillow Talk came about. I grabbed a sack of index cards, and the next evening, while it continued to rain, I snuck back into our cabin and placed one index card beneath the pillow of my campers. When they arrived that evening for bedtime, tired and damp, they found something positive beneath their pillow. Chatter quickly began as everyone searched to see if they too had a card. Then campers began to read their card and discuss the content there. Finally, a positive ending to what (for many of my campers) was yet another soggy day. I told other counselors about the positive outcome and by the next evening, every cabin was using the Pillow Talk activity as their final closing activity of the day.

You can find this activity and fifty more in the *Teamwork & Teamplay International Edition* by Jim Cain (ISBN 978-0-9882046-3-8) available from www.training-wheels.com. This book not only contains fifty-one of my favorite team activities, it also contains translations in sixteen different languages from around the world. All in one book!

4-4 THE FREE PASS

And other important cards.

My guess is that if you look in your wallet or purse right now, you'll find plenty of cards: credit cards, library cards, loyalty program cards, identification, insurance, AAA cards and more. The game of Monopoly has many cards, including a "Get out of jail free" card, that can be very helpful. If you ask your audience about the cards currently in their possession, you will probably find they have dozens of cards.

But even with this wide variety of cards, there are three unique cards that you should consider presenting to each and every group you facilitate, and those cards are a Free Pass, a Help Card, and the unusual S&WTCH (pronounced Sand Witch) Card.

The Free Pass gives the group holding the card control of their fate. With a Free Pass, a group might choose to skip a particular activity, or remove a consequence, or allow a person with a limitation to pass by a particular station or element. The Free Pass allows an individual or group to make a decision that directly affects the situation. But mostly the Free Pass gives power and choice to those using it.

The Help Card is exactly what it says, a card that when presented can be used to obtain assistance. Such a card can be used to receive more information about an activity or challenge, or provide assistance in the completion of a task, or to receive additional equipment or props. With a puzzle or challenge, the Help Card might be used to obtain a helpful hint or clue.

The S&WTCH Card or the "Strange & Wonderful Things Can Happen" card is a bit of a wild card. When presented by an individual or group, something strange or something wonderful could happen. Such an event could include losing a critical piece of equipment needed for a task or gaining more time to complete a challenge. A strange thing could be asking the group to transport a five-gallon bucket of water during the completion of their challenge or turning the lights out halfway through a task. A wonderful thing might include a snack for everyone in the group or a hint where to find a needed piece of equipment to complete a task. The important thing is that the group cannot know for sure whether the card will produce something strange or wonderful.

The true value of a Free Pass, a Help Card or the S&WTCH Card mentioned here is their ability to give your audience a choice! In many teaching, training and facilitation situations, participants are required to follow a set curriculum, with surprisingly few opportunities for empowerment, decision making and choice. Whether or not your audience uses one of these cards is less important than the fact they have one. They have a choice. They are empowered to make decisions that affect them personally. They have that ability and right. And that opportunity is typically sufficient to engage most audiences at a higher level. So, if you want to empower your audience, give them a choice. Offer them one (or more) of the cards mentioned here.

4-5 END OF THE DAY QUESTIONS

An invitation for your audience to create their own debriefing questions.

As a facilitator, I like to find the perfect closing activity or final debriefing technique for any particular group. Recently I invented this new debriefing technique that has proven to be outstanding. Instead of randomly choosing one of my favorite closing activities or preparing general reviewing questions in advance, I simply ask a group at the start of the program what questions they would like to ask themselves at the end of the day.

Sometimes I pass out index cards and pencils to every participant and ask them to write down one or two questions for their own private review. Other times I stand at the front of the group with a flipchart and record three or four questions. I keep this list visible throughout the day, so that participants are reminded that we will discuss these questions at the end of the day.

End of the day questions might include:

What do you want to see happen as we continue to build relationships with each other in the workplace? How can we continue to do this, and why should we?

What are some current barriers to this happening?

List something positive that you learned about yourself today.

What do you want to tell your leaders about today?

Did anyone in your group do a particularly great job today? Tell us about them.

List the top three insights you'll take away from today's experience.
1.
2.
3.

You are welcome to replicate the closing questions (above) for your next group or invite your audience to create their own unique end of the day questions. For many corporate groups, I share the information collected on these documents with the group managers or leaders at the end of the program—a valuable feedback technique, indeed.

4-6 WATCH 4 IT

Recognizing character when you see it.

People often find what they are looking for. Watch 4 It is an activity where everyone in the audience is given one specific behavior, skill, character trait or attitude and encouraged to watch for situations where this particular theme appears.

This activity can be used during a single teambuilding activity, an entire training day, or even throughout a semester's worth of classes and events. The underlying idea for this activity is to help participants identify when and where specific attributes manifest themselves, and then to bring this to the attention of the group so that everyone becomes aware of this occurrence.

You can use one or more of the twenty-six different character words on the *Teamwork & Teamplay Training Cards* for this activity. These cards include such themes as Leadership, Trust, Teamwork, Authenticity, Social Responsibility, Grit, Patience, Flexibility, Balance, Empathy, Accountability, Creativity, Positive Attitude, Gratitude, Respect, Appreciating Diversity, Helpfulness, Integrity, Honesty, Humor and many more. Or create your own collection of words, especially those that you would most like for your audience to observe and report.

Watch 4 It cards are a simple way to help groups identify when they have accomplished something significant. By identifying a specific behavior, talent or skill, participants become more focused on identifying when and where these things take place during the completion of a group challenge.

Prepare a collection of Watch 4 It cards, using words that are custom designed for the team. Here are a few examples of words that you might include:

> Balance • Creativity • Courage • Empathy • Kindness • Flexibility • Common Sense • Honor
> Teamwork • Honesty • Respect • Appreciating Diversity • Character • Integrity • Helpfulness
> Positive Attitude • Leadership • Responsibility • Communication • Trust • Grit • Cooperation
> Tenacity • Wisdom • Skill • Perseverance • Clarity • Resourcefulness • Inclusion • Friendliness

Before presenting a teambuilding challenge to your group, pass out a Watch 4 It card to each member of the team and ask them to look for moments when the word on their card becomes obvious within the group. Then introduce a challenging activity of your choice to the team. When the activity is completed, invite everyone to pull out their Watch 4 It card and share when and where they observed this word in action.

You'll find a collection of several decks of cards in the reference section of this book that are perfect for the Watch 4 It activity mentioned here, including *T&T Training Cards* and also *Strength Cards* and *Choosing Strengths* cards from Innovative Resources. Or make your own cards based upon the mission, vision, values, strengths or beliefs of your audience. The more relevant the words are to your audience, the greater the opportunity for them to identify and relate to these topics.

4-7 DIY DEBRIEFING QUESTIONS

A do-it-yourself debriefing technique for capable groups.

When you are working with a high-performing group, consider allowing them to run their own debriefing session after an activity. To provide a little structure to that process, introduce the group to the following "do-it-yourself" or self-debriefing questions.

Below you will find a collection of DIY debriefing questions that you can share with your next high-performing group. Write these questions onto separate index cards and distribute them to the members of your group. If you like, invite the group to write down their answers to each question on the back of each card (for you to review after the event) or simply to share answers aloud. There are also questions for individual comments, opinions, recommendations and suggestions.

Was each member of the group given an opportunity to contribute to the success of the group? Did a leader emerge during the activity? Who demonstrated leadership capabilities? What did they do that demonstrated leadership? If you had the opportunity to perform this task again, what would you do differently? If you were to hire a new employee to complete this task, what skills would you want them to possess? List five things that you learned during this activity? On a scale of 1 to 10, with 1 being low and 10 being high, how would you rate your team's performance? Complete the following comment: I was surprised that... How many ideas were considered during the early stages of the activity? Was each idea given an opportunity to be heard or tried? Was the success of the group due more to careful planning or luck? Did the group change course during the activity? Was there a breakthrough moment during the completion of this project? Draw a graph showing the progress made by the group during the completion of the activity. Complete this sentence: I never thought… Which was more important to the group, taking care of everyone in the group or completing the task? If you were asked to give advice to a new team trying to accomplish this assignment, what information would you share with them to help them be more successful? What would have made this activity better? What valuable skill(s) did you learn during the completion of this activity? How did your group define success for this activity? Was each member of the group engaged throughout the activity? What distracted your group from the completion of the task?

THE REVIEWING CUBE

A slightly more kinesthetic variation of this activity involves a foam-filled six-sided cube with a clear plastic pocket on each face. Six of the questions mentioned above can be placed into these pockets, and the dice (cube) can be rolled to discover the next question for the group to consider. You can find these oversized dice at stores that carry teacher supplies. You can even create a digital version of the reviewing cube on your smartphone with the Make Dice app.

I use this style of self-debriefing along with some STEM (Science, Technology, Engineering and Math) activities I've been creating. You can find several STEM activities on the T&T website at www.teamworkandteamplay.com. Click on the Downloads button to find teambuilding and STEM activities that you can download for free. Try the one I titled "My Favorite STEM Activity."

You can find DIY Debriefing Questions, The Cube and over one hundred more reviewing activities in the book *A Teachable Moment* (ISBN 978-0-7575-1782-2) by Jim Cain, Michelle Cummings and Jennifer Stanchfield, available from www.kendallhunt.com and www.amazon.com.

4-8 WORMS

A nonverbal reviewing activity.

One of the most unusual things about this particular debriefing activity is that it can be performed without your audience ever having to say a single word!

Worms, and the photographs and images that go along with them, are a truly unique combination. Worms are short segments of rope, about 4 inches (10 cm) long, that are dropped onto a photograph or image, registering the opinion or vote of a participant. The photographs presented to the audience can be a wide variety of images, including traffic signs, weather patterns, post cards, magazine clippings, emoticons and the thumbprint images found earlier in this chapter.

After a particularly insightful activity or event, a facilitator will display (typically on the ground or a central table) images and photographs with significance to the group. The facilitator may also frame this part of the reviewing process with a question, such as "Which of the following images best describes how this group performed in the last activity?"

Participants are then invited to take a worm and, after analyzing the images available, place their rope worm on the image that best reflects their opinion or vote. It can be helpful in some groups to have all participants drop their (identical) worms at the same time, to protect the identify of which worm belongs to which person.

If you like the worm idea, but lack the necessary rope, you can still use this concept with other tokens such as coins, stones, poker chips, paperclips and even plastic worms from your local fisherman sports store or museum/nature center. For photographs and images, search for illustrations that will have meaning to your audience, or have your audience create their own images on index cards at the start of the program, and then use these images during one of the debriefing opportunities.

David Knobbe created this activity so that teens who joined his adventure program could participate in the reviewing and debriefing segment, without ever having to speak a single word. David also created the Thumbprint images shown above as a way for groups to analyze their performance. He often uses these two techniques together.

The traffic sign cards shown above (top) were purchased at an educational supply store. The Thumbprints (middle) are included in the T&T Training Cards (ISBN 978-0-9882046-2-1) and the Action Pak debriefing cards (bottom) are a collection of one hundred colorful cards, spanning the range of human emotion with images and words, created by Craig Rider. For more information about any of these cards contact Jim Cain at jimcain@teamworkandteamplay.com.

You can find this debriefing activity in the book *Rope Games* (ISBN 978-0-9882046-1-4) by Jim Cain and in the book *A Teachable Moment* (ISBN 978-0-7575-1782-2) by Jim Cain, Michelle Cummings and Jennifer Stanchfield.

4-9 THE ONE BALL THAT DOES IT ALL

A simple way to make one tool work many different ways.

For this debriefing activity, all you need is a spiral-bound collection of index cards and a ball (roughly the size of a soccer ball). Begin by writing a sequential series of numbers (from 1 to 10), randomly located on the surface of the ball with a permanent marker. Then select various themes for your debriefing sessions, such as leadership, general debriefing questions, group dynamics, icebreakers, get-acquainted questions, teambuilding and any other themes you like. Brainstorm a series of ten questions for each theme and write these questions and themes on index cards.

Then toss the ball to various participants in your group. The person catching the ball identifies the number closest to their right index finger and then answers the question associated with this number from the index card list.

The index card questions should be prepared in advance, and can be for a variety of topics, from leadership to teamwork to communication to debriefing or reviewing, such as: *What leadership talents do you find most helpful in a group setting? or How did you define success in this activity? or List three things that could have made your group more effective in this activity.* A spiral-bound set of index cards is a simple way to keep track of your multiple-theme question cards. You can invite participants to read these questions, empowering the group to control their own reviewing session.

If transporting a soccer ball is inconvenient, you can substitute a round balloon for the ball in this activity and inflate it once you have arrived.

You can find this activity and many more in the *Teamwork & Teamplay International Edition* (ISBN 978-0-9882046-3-8) by Jim Cain, available from www.training-wheels.com and www.healthylearning.com. This unique book contains 51 of Jim's favorite activities, translated into sixteen languages, including Chinese, Japanese, Thai, Mongolian, Russian, Turkish, German, Italian, French, Spanish, Portuguese, Greek, Danish, Dutch, Hebrew and English. All in one book!

You'll find 130 more ideas for processing, debriefing, reviewing and reflection in the book *A Teachable Moment* (ISBN 978-0-7575-1782-2) by Jim Cain, Michelle Cummings and Jennifer Stanchfield, available from www.healthylearning.com and www.kendallhunt.com.

Another similar debriefing tool is known as a Thumball™ produced by the company Answers in Motion. Thumballs™ is the award-winning creation of Gregg Pembleton. These creative products come in a variety of sizes, content and languages, including icebreakers, leadership, communication, conflict resolution, movement, the alphabet, numbers and creative debriefing questions. You can even customize your own design. Visit www.thumball.com for more information.

4-10 MESSAGE IN A BOTTLE

Maximum expression from minimum words.

This unique debriefing technique comes with two potential themes. The Message in a Bottle activity can take on the traditional shipwreck-themed rescue note or the significantly more valuable treasure map variety.

For this activity (which occurs at the completion of a teambuilding challenge or task), present your audience with a pencil and a single index card, plus the required clear glass bottle and a cork stopper. Instruct your group to compose a brief message using one of the themes below and place this message inside the bottle and seal it with a cork.

The rescue note variety of a Message in a Bottle focuses on the difficulties experienced by the group as they attempted to complete the challenge as presented. The group critiques their performance, expressing sorrow for their shortcomings, praising those that tried their best and identifying critical skills or abilities that they lacked but which they hope future adventurers will use to their advantage. This style of message is appropriate for groups that may have fallen short of their own expectations while completing a specific challenge or task.

The hidden treasure variety of Message in a Bottle focuses on the valuable things that a group experienced as they completed a challenge. The group is invited to list skills, talents, abilities and other useful or valuable behaviors that resulted in the successful completion of a task. This version is best when groups successfully complete a challenge or task and especially when they can identify the critical skills and talents that resulted in their success.

You can find this activity and many more processing, debriefing, reviewing and reflection activities in the book *A Teachable Moment* by Jim Cain, Michelle Cummings and Jennifer Stanchfield (ISBN 978-0-7575-1782-2) available from www.kendallhunt.com.

4-11 POST CARD DEBRIEF

Inspiring meaningful reflection and conversation from unique images.

Here is a popular way to start off a class, training program or teambuilding event with style and a visually impactful way to reflect and celebrate the strengths and achievements of individuals and groups at the end of an event.

Begin with a large collection of post cards and display these cards in a manner accessible to everyone in your audience. As a beginning activity, ask participants to choose a card that represents a goal they have for the program, or their expectations for the day, or a unique perspective they bring to the group. Then ask everyone to share why they selected that particular card.

As a tool for individual reflection, invite the members of your audience to select a card that represents their role in the most recent task or challenge, or a personal strength that they shared with the group. Individual reflection does not require participants to share their insights aloud.

To stimulate group dialogue, invite your audience to agree on a single card that best represents what they have accomplished today, or three cards that tell the story of the group's journey from where they began to where they finished today, to where they hope to be in the future.

The photos show the Pick a Postcard™ Kit from Jennifer Stanchfield (on the left) and a rather significant collection of postcards that I've collected since I was a child (on the right). If you have a collection of images or postcards, you can create your own version of this activity.

The *Pick a Postcard Conversation Starter and Reflection Tool* was created by Jennifer Stanchfield, one of my coauthors for the book *A Teachable Moment* (ISBN 978-0-7575-1782-2) from www.kendallhunt.com and used here with her permission. Jen is also the author of two other books of merit, *Tips & Tools—The Art of Experiential Group Facilitation* (ISBN 978-1-885473-71-4) and *Inspired Educator Inspired Learner* (ISBN 978-1-939019-13-4). To order a Pick a Postcard™ Kit and other valuable reviewing and reflection resources, visit www.experientialtools.com.

4-12 ONE FOR THE ROAD

Walking away with a single significant insight.

No doubt most audiences are exposed to plenty of valuable things during your teaching and training programs. Unfortunately, it is unlikely that they will be able to remember everything you have presented. One for the Road is an attempt to have each person focus on a single significant, valuable insight from the day by writing this insight on a colorful index card and then placing this card in a highly visible location after the conclusion of the program.

At the end of your program, pass out index cards and pens to your audience and allow each person to write down one significant thing they have learned from the day. Then invite each person to find a partner or form a small group and share the one thing written on their card. Next, invite each person to share how they plan to use this information in the future. These simple techniques increase the probability that your participants will take the valuable information you have shared during your program and transfer it to their own world.

According to Edgar Dale's *Cone of Learning,* the greater the interaction of the learner with the material, the greater the retention of that information. By writing, reading, sharing and discussing the One for the Road insights, each participant increases the probability of remembering that valuable lesson.

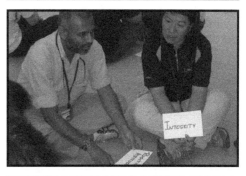

Index cards are a creative and inexpensive way for you to provide a memento for your audience members to take with them after the completion of your program. By writing a single significant insight on an index card, the value of that card increases greatly, especially to the owner of the card. Be sure to provide colorful writing tools and index cards with interesting colors, patterns and shapes. The more creative and unusual the index card, the greater the probability that the message contained there will be cherished and remembered.

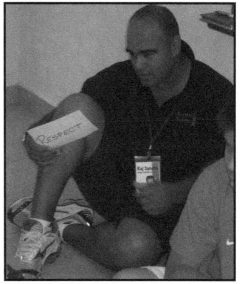

4-13 CONSENSUS CARDS

I see what you mean.

There are times during a discussion when it is helpful to know whether or not the other members of the group are in agreement on a particular topic, from something as simple as where to go for lunch, to something as complicated as how to solve a problem. Consensus Cards are a useful tool for just this purpose. They provide immediate feedback, even while the proposal is being made. They also enable every voice in the group to be heard. But one of the best features of Consensus Cards is that they help create a true consensus when making a decision, not just a simple majority rules.

Below you will find two examples of Consensus Cards. The three-color card, featuring red, yellow and green dots (rather like a traffic light), allows for three levels of feedback. *Green—I agree. This option is my first choice. I support this decision. Yellow—I have a question before proceeding or I need more information. I am undecided or uncertain about this information. Red—I do not agree. I cannot support this option.* These cards work well in small groups where everyone can see and hear each other.

The second style of Consensus Card works well with very large groups of people, such as an auditorium full of conference attendees. The three cards in this collection are color-coded green, yellow and red as well, and have bold letters on each color stating that intention (agree, uncertain and disagree).

Two of the more unique qualities of a discussion using Consensus Cards is that speakers get immediate feedback on the buy-in from their audience and participants are not required to wait until a vote to voice their opinion. These can be powerful tools, especially when achieving true consensus in a timely fashion is desired.

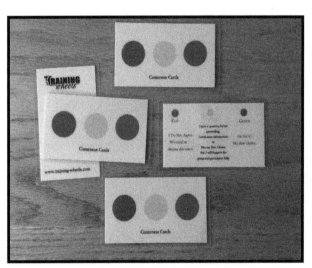 

You can create your own style of consensus cards simply by providing your audience with three index cards (red, yellow and green) and instructing them how to voice their opinions using the cards.

You can find this activity and many more in the processing, debriefing, reviewing and reflection book *A Teachable Moment* by Jim Cain, Michelle Cummings and Jennifer Stanchfield (ISBN 978-0-7575-1782-2) available from www.kendallhunt.com. You can make your own Consensus Cards or obtain them from www.training-wheels.com.

4-14 EVALUATION CARDS

See all the data at a single glance.

While evaluations can be helpful, the evaluation process is sometimes overly complicated. Here is a very simple way to gather information and quickly review the data collected. If you happen to run back-to-back classes, workshops or programs, this technique will allow you to quickly scan the data received after one class and refine your content as necessary before the next one.

Evaluation Cards are the size of 3x5 index cards, made from heavy card stock and printed with scales along the edges. Each index card contains four edges on two sides, for a total of eight potential scales. Add to this the interior space on both sides of the card and you have a total of ten unique areas with which to solicit feedback from your audience.

Participants are invited to darken in the circle, space or number that corresponds with their evaluation of that metric. Once collected, these evaluation cards form a compact deck of cards. To review the information provided by your audience, you can quickly riffle the edge of the deck of cards and allow your eyes to record the areas shaded for each metric. For simplicity, I recommend that each scale on your evaluation card consist of no more than five unique numbers.

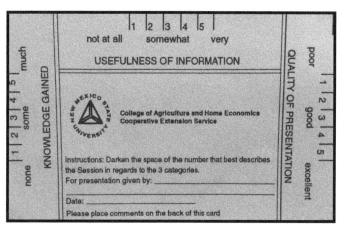

Here is a template that you can use to create your own evaluation cards and an example of an evaluation card of this style from a training workshop.

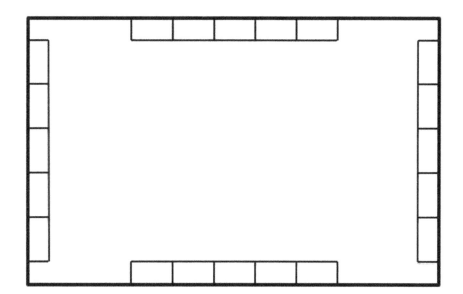

With the advent of smartphones and other computerized technology, many conferences elect to conduct their evaluations online. But for smaller events or workshops where internet access isn't easily available, this old-school pencil and paper technique provides quick and useful feedback.

4-15 THANK YOU CARDS

Gratitude—the quality of being thankful.

Gratitude affects not only the person receiving it, but the person giving it as well. By simply reflecting on gratitude in your life, the positive effects of this reflection can last for days. Leave time at the end of your next program for participants to express their gratitude to each other, to the event organizers, to anyone they would like. This gratitude can be expressed verbally or written down on index cards or in dozens of creative ways of your choosing. Visit Pinterest for some truly amazing and artistic ways to express thankfulness and gratitude.

In the book *59 Seconds*, Richard Wiseman reveals that having people list three things that they are grateful for in their life or to reflect on three events that have gone especially well recently can significantly increase their level of happiness for about a month. This, in turn, can cause them to be more optimistic about the future and can improve their physical health.

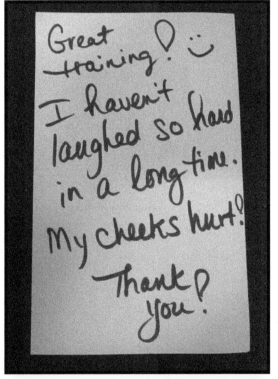

I have had the opportunity to visit more than thirty countries so far and one of the first things I try to learn when I visit a new country is how to say hello and thank you in the local dialect. With only these two phrases, you'd be surprised how easy it is to connect with people around the world. Next time you travel to a foreign country, try learning these two phrases before you arrive.

In the corner of my office there is a box that I have filled with thank you cards over the years. Some are treasured keepsakes. Some are hastily written on scraps of paper, maps, receipts and other simple things. A few are even written on index cards (see the accompanying photos). But each of these messages is a reminder of wonderful people, places and events. It really doesn't matter how much the card costs or the penmanship of the author; what matters most (to me) is the words themselves. So, the next time you want to thank someone, don't be afraid to write a quick note on an index card and place it in a convenient place where it will be found, and treasured!

4-16 FIVE F'S / SHARE SOMETHING

Debriefing techniques with index or playing cards.

FIVE F'S

To use this debriefing technique, select the four aces from a standard deck of cards, plus one of the jokers. These five cards represent: Facts (Diamonds), Feelings (Hearts), Findings (Spades), Future (Clubs) and Freedom (the wildcard or Joker). Alternatively, you can write down these five words beginning with the letter F on five index cards (as shown in the photo).

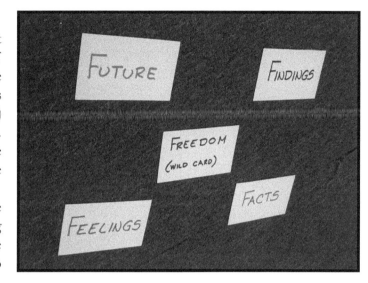

Participants can select any one of the four aces to discuss specific themes during the final debrief of the day or select the wildcard (Joker) giving them the freedom to discuss anything at all.

You can display these cards, so that anyone is free to select them, or pass out multiples of these cards to everyone in the group and allow them to select the theme they like the most.

Consider using very large cards for this activity, so that participants can easily see what is displayed on each card selected.

SHARE SOMETHING

This playing card processing technique invites a facilitator to randomly deal out cards of each suit, one card per participant. Then ask each person to reflect on the events of the day, using the suit of their card as a theme. For example:

♥ **Hearts** Share something from the heart—something that you feel inside.

♣ **Clubs** Share something that needs to grow—something that happened that has planted a seed of hope for the future.

♦ **Diamonds** Share something of great value that you learned today.

♠ **Spades** Share something you dug up during the program—something surprising or something you really had to dig for.

———————

You can find these activities and many, many more processing, debriefing, reviewing and reflection activities in the book *A Teachable Moment* by Jim Cain, Michelle Cummings and Jennifer Stanchfield (ISBN 978-0-7575-1782-2) and on Roger Greenaway's outstanding reviewing website (www.reviewing.co.uk).

4-17 ACTION PAK CARDS

A creative deck of 100 cards, for debriefing and more.

The Action Pak Cards, created by Craig and Pat Rider, are a collection of 100 cards filled with words and images that cover the full range of the emotional spectrum. With these cards you can facilitate a variety of team activities.

Trading Cards (an opening activity with the opportunity to read the mood of the group). Pass out several cards to each participant and invite all participants to trade cards with others in the room until they have just two cards that accurately describe their present mood or state of mind. In addition to the cards circulating within the group, place any additional cards face-up on a central table and invite participants to trade cards at this location as well. When all participants have chosen their two cards, create groups of six people and invite everyone to share why the two cards in their possession accurately describe their present mood or state of mind.

Creative Sentences (a lesson in creativity and teamwork). Pass out ten cards to each group of six people and ask them to construct a sentence using all the words on their cards.

Insight (connecting a single word to the team). Hand-select sufficient cards with positive words, pass out a single card to each participant and ask participants to take a few minutes to think how this word relates to the group (or the organization, or the company, or the team, or the school…).

The Memory Game. You can use a double deck of Action Pak cards to play a version of the memory game, where participants turn over cards hoping to find a match. When all cards have been turned over, invite participants to choose a card with a word they believe is important. Then ask each group to turn over some cards but leaving just five cards face-up containing the five words they believe are most powerful to their group.

Opposites. Ask participants to choose their favorite and least favorite cards from the collection and then explain what is good about their least favorite card, and what is not good about their favorite card.

3-2-1 Go! Spread out all the Action Pak cards and as a final debriefing activity invite each participant to choose three cards that describe what the team did well, two cards that describe what individuals did well and one card the describes something the team needs to continue working on for the future.

Corporate Inventories and Instruments. To create subject matter reviewing cards, some facilitators take the Action Pak collection of image cards and modify them with labels (for such instruments as MBTI, Disc, StrengthFinders, True Colors and other corporate diagnostic tools).

This is Me. Invite each person in your audience to take five Action Pak cards at random and place these cards in order from "most like me" to "least like me." Then invite everyone to discuss their cards with a partner. This debriefing technique incorporates private (internal) processing before sharing (external processing) with a partner.

If you like the idea of a colorful collection of reviewing cards, the Action Pak Cards mentioned here are just one of many decks currently available. You'll find a comprehensive list of reviewing cards in the References and Resources chapter of this book, but some are worth mentioning here:

Images of Organizations Toolbox (www.rsvpdesign.co.uk) is one of the best collections of corporate reviewing cards in the world.

Soularium Cards (ISBN 978-1-5733-4062-6) are discussion cards with a Christian focus (www.CruPress.com).

Chiji Processing Cards (www.wnbpub.com) by Steve Simpson were one of the original visual debriefing cards and now there is the *Chiji Guidebook* (ISBN 978-2-8854-7384-4).

Stones Have Feelings Too! (ISBN 0-9578-2319-3) is a collection of fifty-two cards with instructions for talking about and reflecting upon feelings, from Innovative Resources (www.innovativeresources.org).

The Teamwork & Teamplay Training Cards (ISBN 978-0-9882046-2-1) by Jim Cain contain seventeen team activities, plus a dozen images of team performance, perfect for debriefing with youth and/or adults.

Picture This (ISBN 978-1-9209-4527-5) includes seventy-five color images for conversation and reflection (www.innovativeresources.org).

I first met Craig Rider at the National Challenge Course Practitioner's Symposium in Boulder, Colorado more than a decade ago, and we became fast friends. Craig does an amazing job with leadership training, as does his wife Pat. Together they created The Action Pak. When Craig and his wife moved to Hilton Head Island (and had to downsize their possessions) I became the recipient of over 200 decks of Action Pak cards. If you are interested in obtaining a deck or two (or more!) please contact me at jimcain@teamworkandteamplay.com for more information. And soon you'll be able to purchase a dual-language deck of Action Pak cards combined with Kerfuffle cards from FangMa International Education and Culture Company, LTD of Beijing, China.

One of the things I like about the Action Pak collection of cards is that there is room for translations on each card, for those moments when I happen to have an audience that speaks more than one language, or a different language than English. You can use some of the convenient internet language sites (or apps) to translate these simple words into other languages as needed.

4-18 THE FINAL WORD

An inspiration to take away.

At the completion of an event, program or meeting, invite everyone to write a single, inspirational word on an index card, for a specific person in the group (such as the person currently sitting to their right). On the back of this card, the author can provide additional information or inspiration.

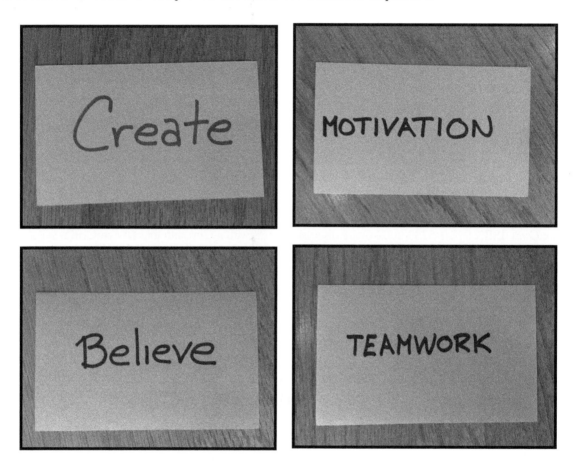

A variation of this activity (and one that does not involve writing) would be to supply index cards with prewritten inspirational words on them and then invite participants to choose a card for a specific person in the group and present them with this card. Then encourage participants to explain why they chose this particular word. Some of my favorite words include:

Believe • Dream • Connect • Community • Well Done • Tenacity • Perseverance • Hope • Wonder
Teamwork • Respect • Courage • Creativity • Understanding • Reflection • Unity • Knowledge

---

Many events conclude with no tangible takeaway for participants. The Final Word is an inexpensive way to extend the event in a private, personal, tangible and inspirational manner. Encourage participants to post this index card on their refrigerator, dashboard or office wall and to reflect on it from time to time.

4-19 BINGO DEBRIEFING CARDS

Pick five in a row to win!

In the United States, bingo cards have been around since the late 1920s. Instead of numbers for our modified bingo card, we'll create a 5x5 grid and fill these spaces with events that your audience is likely to have experienced during the course of the program.

Pass out one Bingo Debriefing Card to all participants and invite them to reflect on their experiences that day. Then ask them to be prepared to discuss the contents of any five boxes in a row (vertically, horizontally or diagonally).

For example, you can discuss five separate events during today's experience where you may have listened to someone (tell about it), tried something new (what was this new thing?), considered a different point of view (share it with the group), played outside your comfort zone (what event put you there?), and offered someone encouragement (who, and what was happening?).

Laughed	Changed Something	Offered a Suggestion	Developed a New Skill	Listened to Someone
Use My Problem Solving Skills	Said Thank You	Was Glad to Be Part of This Team	Tried Something New	Assisted Someone
Saw Something Amazing	Cheered	Considered a Different Point of View	Made an Improvement	Sacrificed My Personal Goals for the Good of the Group
Tried but Just Couldn't Do It	Played Outside My Comfort Zone	Applauded	Learned Something New	Expanding My Personal Boundaries
Encouraged Someone	Played a Different Role	Used Talents that I Possess	Felt Challenged	Asked Someone for Help

Bingo as we know it today is based upon *Lo Giuoco del Lotto d'Italia* which originated in the early 1500s. Toy salesman Edwin S. Lowe initially presented the game in Atlanta, Georgia in 1929 by the name Beano, but renamed it when he overhead a winner yelling "Bingo" instead!

4-20 THE TOSS OF A COIN

A random debriefing technique.

For many adventure-based learning activities, facilitators prepare a convenient list of suitable questions to debrief the activity. Here is a random way of empowering your group to select and answer their own debriefing questions, and all you'll need are a dozen index cards and a large coin.

Begin by writing a series of debriefing questions on large index cards, one question per card. At the conclusion of an activity, place these cards face-down in the center of your debriefing circle and provide your group with a large coin. Invite each member of your group to toss the coin toward the cards, select the card that is closest to the final resting position of the coin and instruct the person that tossed the coin to read the card aloud. You'll find examples of additional questions on the next page.

You can find 130 unique and creative ways to process, debrief, review and reflect in *A Teachable Moment* (ISBN 978-0-7575-1782-2) by Michelle Cummings, Jim Cain and Jennifer Stanchfield, available from www.kendallhunt.com, www.amazon.com and www.training-wheels.com.

Here are a few examples of debriefing questions that you can use with any activity:

Who took a leadership role for this activity? What did this person do to show good leadership?

If you had to do this activity over again, what would you change the second time through?
If you had to hire new employees to do this task, what skills would be helpful for them to have?

Was the quality of your final result up to your own professional standards?

Was there a breakthrough moment in this activity? What changed at that moment?

How much time did you spend planning versus doing in this activity?

If you could make recommendations to another group, what would you tell them to help them be successful in the completion of this task?

What are three things (teachable moments) you can take away from this activity?

How did you contribute to the group? What did you do that made a difference?

CREATIVE THINGS TO DO WITH PLAYING CARDS

CHAPTER
FIVE

This chapter switches over from index cards to some very creative things you can do with playing cards, other than simply playing cards! Here you'll find puzzles, activities, icebreakers, team challenges and more. After playing these games, you'll never look at a deck of cards in the same way again.

NO.	ACTIVITY NAME	TEACHABLE MOMENT	IDEAL GROUP SIZE
5-1	Search and Rescue	Treasure Hunt, Teamwork	Multiple small groups
5-2	Pass the Deck	Prob. Solving, Teamwork	Multiple teams of 4–10
5-3	I Doubt It	Trust Building	3–6 players
5-4	Press Ten	Prob. Solving, Teamwork	Multiple small teams
5-5	The Four Card Challenge	Problem Solving	Individual challenge
5-6	The Sixteen Card Challenge	Teamwork	Multiple small teams
5-7	The Ten Card Square Puzzle	Problem Solving	Multiple small teams
5-8	The Twelve Card Puzzle	Problem Solving	Multiple small teams
5-9	Stack the Deck	Prob. Solving, Teamwork	Multiple small teams
5-10	Playing Card Icebreaker	Icebreaker Activity	8 or more players
5-11	Never!	Discovery	Teams of four
5-12	The Hunt	A Quick Search	Any
5-13	The Poison King	Problem Solving	Any
5-14	The Extra Card	Problem Solving	Any
5-15	Four of a Kind	Action, Teamwork	Multiple small groups
5-16	Action / Reaction	Quick Reflexes	4 players

5-1 SEARCH AND RESCUE

A treasure hunt to begin a class, meeting or event.

For this activity, you'll need two identical decks of playing cards. Before your audience arrives, take one deck of cards and hide each card randomly around your program space (under a chair, partially sticking out of a bookcase, behind a picture frame, on the branches of a tree, etc.). When your audience arrives, invite them to take a card from the second deck and then go searching for the matching card located somewhere in the program space. When found, bring both cards back to the starting position and select another card. You can include clues for finding the matching cards, if you like.

If you would like to add an element of teamwork to this activity, you can organize teams of two to four people and have them search together for a specific card. Teams can scatter to cover the program space as quickly as possible, or you can require each group to stay in constant contact with each other throughout each mission.

As a variation of this activity, you can require your audience to collect and return each of the cards in a specific order. For example: hearts, spades, clubs and diamonds, starting with the 2 and finishing with the ace of each suit.

There are many different styles of playing cards available, including round cards, very big and very small cards, transparent cards, international cards, etc. If you want to challenge your audience at a higher level, create a complete deck of playing cards using a variety of sizes, shapes, colors and designs. One of the more unusual playing card decks I've discovered is available from Dear Adam (www.dearadamobjects.com) and was designed by Adam Farbiarz and Adam Thompson. This hand-illustrated deck of playing cards is called *Fine Line* and is as unique as it is interesting. It's perfect if you want to really challenge your audience.

If you happen to only have a single deck of cards available, you can just hide this single deck and invite your audience to find them all, in any order. But be sure to remember where you have concealed all the cards or your deck is likely to become incomplete if your audience does not find them all!

One of the more unusual variations of this activity was created by an organization that didn't have an abundance of hiding places in their available program space—a large gymnasium. Instead of concealing the first deck of playing cards, they simply scattered them about the floor and then turned off the lights. Then they provided each team of four people with one very small, dimly-lit flashlight and required each team to stay connected with each other as they searched for a specific card. This resulted in a unique and rather spooky variation that worked well for the group, given the program space available.

5-2 PASS THE DECK

A fast-paced problem-solving challenge.

This simple challenge is sure to create high energy in your group, especially if you invite two (or more) teams to compete at the same time.

Begin this activity (for each team) by placing a deck of fifty-two ordinary playing cards in a stack on a table, then invite the team to line up from this table to another one nearby. The challenge is to individually pass each card in the deck from the first table to the second, as fast as possible, so that each card comes in contact with each person and no cards touch each other during the transfer process (until they are piled together on the second table). Time begins when the first card on the first table is touched and ends when the final card is placed down on the second table.

Take a few minutes after explaining this activity to allow each group to strategize how they will complete the task in a minimal amount of time. After the first round, invite each team to experiment with different passing techniques and to look for opportunities to improve their time.

Two of the most common errors in this activity are dropping a card somewhere between the two tables and allowing two cards to touch each other along the journey from table one to table two. Personally, I prefer not to ask a group to start over (which can substantially reduce the energy of the team) but instead assign a five-second penalty for any card-to-card contact and no penalty for a dropped card (just pick it up and continue the journey).

If you want your group to focus on the problem-solving process allow them a first attempt at Pass the Deck, and then invite them to think of ways to improve their card passing techniques. Then inform them they will have two more attempts to dramatically improve their time in this activity. Focus more on the technique of problem solving than actually passing cards.

If passing all fifty-two cards takes longer than you would like, or you happen to have extremely large teams with fifteen or more participants, consider passing just the thirteen cards from a single suit.

———————————————

You can find this activity and sixteen more on the *Teamwork & Teamplay Training Cards* (ISBN 978-0-9882046-2-1), available from www.training-wheels.com, www.trainerswarehouse.com and www.healthylearning.com. This large format (5" x 8") full-color deck contains some of the very best activities from this book, with instructions.

5-3 I DOUBT IT

A card game that is all about trust.

For this hilarious card game, you'll need a standard deck of fifty-two playing cards for up to ten players. After shuffling the deck, the dealer deals out all the cards. It is not necessary for all players to have the same number of cards. Play begins in an ascending order from ace up to king and then repeats.

After the deal, the player to the left of the dealer begins the game by declaring that they have a specific number of aces, while laying that number of cards face-down in the center of the table. The number this player declares could be true or false. The next person then declares a specific number of twos, while laying down that number of cards. The game continues with players declaring threes, fours and up to kings, before starting over again with aces.

If at any time another player wishes to make a challenge, they simply say, "I Doubt It," as a player lays down their cards. The person laying the cards down on the table must then show the cards played. If they are indeed the cards declared, the challenger must pick up ALL the cards currently on the table. If they are not as declared, the player laying down these cards must pick up ALL of the cards currently on the table. The first person to get rid of all their cards is the winner.

The strategy in this game is to be able to declare even a false number of cards with a straight face. As the game progresses, more and more players will be bluffing, especially the second or third time through the deck.

I Doubt It is also known by the card game name Cheat. But I prefer the slightly more honesty invoking name used here.

5-4 PRESS TEN

A fun way to use a deck of cards as a teambuilding tool.

Here is a fast-paced, high-energy activity that only requires a deck of cards and a long (50–100 feet [15–30 meters]) piece of rope. Begin by creating a large rectangle with the rope. Divide your audience into two teams of six to twelve people per team. Provide each team with ten cards of the same suit (ace through ten) face-down in random order. The goal is for each team to turn over the ten cards, one at a time, in ascending order.

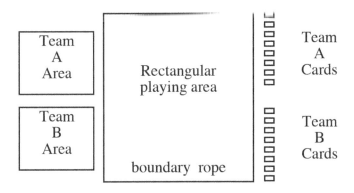

Each team is allowed to send one player at a time to turn over a single card. If it is not the next card in order, the player must turn the card face down and return to the group. The first team to sequentially turn over all ten cards wins.

Immediately after the first round, reshuffle the cards and begin round two. After round two, allow each team five minutes to plan a strategy for round three.

Thanks to Dr. Preston Cline, Director of Wharton Leadership Ventures, for creating and sharing this activity. Preston was pressed for time and had limited props and resources for a teambuilding event. He quickly came up with this rather unique teambuilding activity, using just a single deck of playing cards and the long rope he had available.

5-5 THE FOUR CARD CHALLENGE

A logic puzzle about playing cards.

Here is a logic puzzle featuring four playing cards, in the style of Einstein's Riddle (Activity 2-15½) featured earlier in this book. The challenge is to determine the value and suit for each of the four cards shown below, using the following information:

1. There are exactly one King, one Jack, one Queen and one Ace.
2. The Heart is farther to the left than the Jack.
3. The Diamond is farther to the left than the Queen.
4. The Spade is farther to the right than the Jack.
5. The Club is farther to the right than the Queen.
6. The Ace is farther to the right than the Spade.

You can make this activity a purely theoretical investigation, but I prefer to actually place the four cards face down on the table, so that when individuals or teams have solved the puzzle, they can immediately confirm their guesses.

For future reference, the solution to the Four Card Challenge is secretly within the original clues. The order, from left to right is King, Jack, Queen and Ace, and the suits are (again from left to right) Hearts, Diamonds, Spades and Clubs.

If you enjoy this style of puzzles with playing cards, you can find even more ideas in these books: *Games and Fun with Playing Cards* by Joseph Leeming (ISBN 978-0-4862-3977-2), *Tricks and Stunts with Playing Cards* by Joseph Leeming, *Deal Me In! The Use of Playing Cards in Teaching and Learning* by Margie Golick (ISBN 978-0-8843-2253-X), *Mindgames* by Laura Parsons (ISBN 978-1-4452-4969-8), *Playing with a Full Deck* by Michelle Cummings (ISBN 978-0-7575-4094-3) and the rare *25 Card Puzzles for a Rainy Afternoon* by Joseph Leeming (ISBN 978-1-4465-2438-1).

5-6 THE SIXTEEN CARD CHALLENGE

A challenging playing card puzzle.

With a standard deck of playing cards, you have sufficient cards for three sixteen-card puzzles. Begin with all four suits of four different value cards. For example: Aces, Kings, Queens and Jacks. Place these cards face up, in a 4x4 pattern. The challenge is now to rearrange these cards so that no two cards in any row or column have the same face value or suit (diagonal similarities are okay). One example of a workable solution is shown on the left below.

For a higher level of challenge, using these same cards, rearrange them so that no two cards in any straight line of four cards (horizontally, vertically or diagonally) are the same suit or face value. One possible solution is shown on the right below.

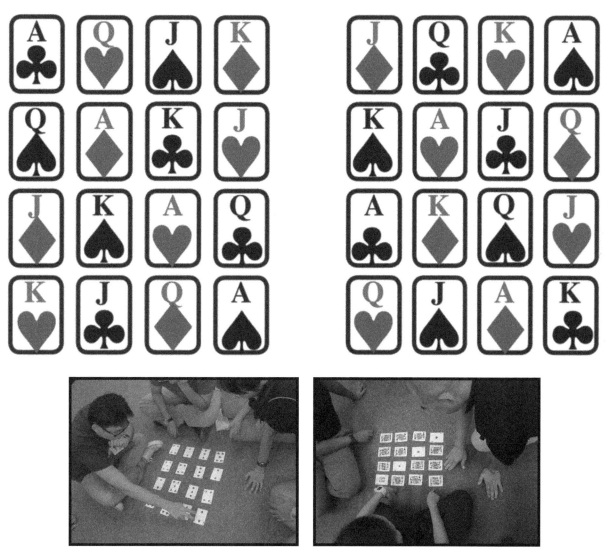

You'll find this particular playing card challenge and sixteen more activities in the *Teamwork & Training Training Cards* by Jim Cain (ISBN 978-0-9882-0462-1).

5-7 THE TEN CARD SQUARE PUZZLE

A puzzle with playing cards.

Take ten cards from any single suit (Ace, 2, 3, 4, 5, 6, 7, 8, 9, 10) and place them in the square pattern shown here. Next, rearrange the cards so that the total value (sum) of cards on each of the four sides of the square equals the same number.

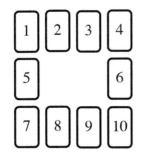

You can provide the total value (sum) for each side of the square, but part of the challenge in this activity is figuring out what that sum should be. Some teams may find the solution completely by accident. Some teams may estimate the possibilities, reducing the total number of attempts required to produce a workable solution. Below you will find several ways to estimate (or bound) the total value of cards for each side of the square. Spending a little time at the beginning of the activity (estimating the range of possibilities for the total value on each side of the square) will save you time later (by eliminating sums that are simply not possible).

One question raised by the Ten Card Square Puzzle challenge is, "What should the sum on each side of the square be?" Here are three approximations that can be used to identify reasonable values for the sum. You'll still need to place the ten cards in the proper order but knowing the total value of cards on each side of the square is a giant step toward finding the solution to this puzzle.

The maximum value for any three cards in a row would be 10 + 9 + 8 = 27. The minimum value for four cards in a row would be 1 + 2 + 3 + 4 = 10. So, we know that the sum of card values on each side of the square must be a whole number between 10 and 27, reducing the range of possibilities here. The average of these two limits is 18.5, making a value of 18 or 19 a reasonable place to start.

As a second approximation divide the total value of the cards (1 + 2 + 3 + 4 + 5 + 6 + 7 + 8 + 9 + 10 = 55) by the total number of cards (10), to get the average card value of 5.5. The sum for three cards would be 16.5 and the sum for four cards would be 22. The average of these two limits is 19.25.

If we average the maximum value for three cards (10 + 9 + 8 = 27 and 7 + 6 + 5 = 18) we get the value of 22.5. If we average the minimum value for four cards (1 + 2 + 3 + 4 = 10 and 5 + 6 + 7 + 8 = 26) we get the value of 18, which leads us to the conclusion that the total sum is likely to be a whole number between 18 and 22.5. With just five possible integers (18, 19, 20, 21 and 22) to consider, it is reasonable to try working out a solution with the cards for one of these values. The actual value, for the solution shown, is a sum of 18 for each side of the square.

Such estimation (or bounding) of solutions actually has a name. It is known as a Fermi Problem, names after Enrico Fermi and involves some rather simple (back of the envelope) calculations for approximating the solution of what might be considered some rather complex challenges (such as How many piano tuners are in Chicago?).

You can find this activity and sixteen more on the *Teamwork & Teamplay Training Cards* (ISBN 978-0-9882046-2-1) available from www.training-wheels.com and www.healthylearning.com. This large format full-color deck contains some of the very best activities from this book, with instructions.

5-8 THE TWELVE CARD PUZZLE

A challenging playing card puzzle.

For this puzzle, choose all the cards from any single suit in a deck, except for the queen, for a total of twelve cards. The challenge is to place these twelve cards into a square pattern so that the sum in any row or column of four cards is exactly twenty-three. The value of each card is shown below:

Ace	=	1	Five	=	5	Nine	=	9
Two	=	2	Six	=	6	Ten	=	10
Three	=	3	Seven	=	7	Jack	=	11
Four	=	4	Eight	=	8	King	=	13

Here is one solution to this problem. Are there others?

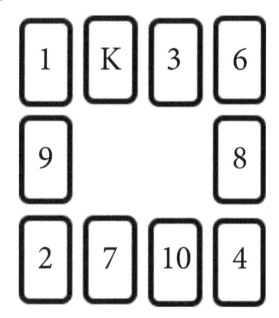

For a more challenging version of this activity, invite your audience to create the twelve-card racetrack configuration shown here, but do not tell them the value for each side of the square. The Fermi techniques for approximating suitable values, mentioned in the previous activity (5-7) will suggest a value between 18 and 35, and an average of 26. Which is close to the value of 23, but not exact by any means.

What happens if you replace the king (with a value of 13) with a queen (with a value of 12) for this activity? Is it still possible to create the square pattern with each side of equal value? What will the value of each side be?

You'll find this particular playing card challenge within the deck of *Teamwork & Teamplay Training Cards* (ISBN 978-0-9882046-2-1) by Jim Cain, available from www.trainerswarehouse.com and www.training-wheels.com. These cards are now available in a dual-language deck (English and Chinese) from FangMa International Education and Culture Company, LTD of Beijing, China. Visit the Teamwork & Teamplay website at www.teamworkandteamplay.com for more information.

5-9 STACK THE DECK

A fast-moving team activity.

This fast-paced sorting activity is simple and fun. Begin by shuffling any standard deck of fifty-two playing cards. Then hand this deck to each team of approximately four to six people and invite them to sort the deck into each of the four suits, placing the cards in order (2, 3, 4, 5, 6, 7, 8, 9, 10, J, Q, K, A) and then restacking these four suit piles into a single stack. The time required to complete this task is the team score.

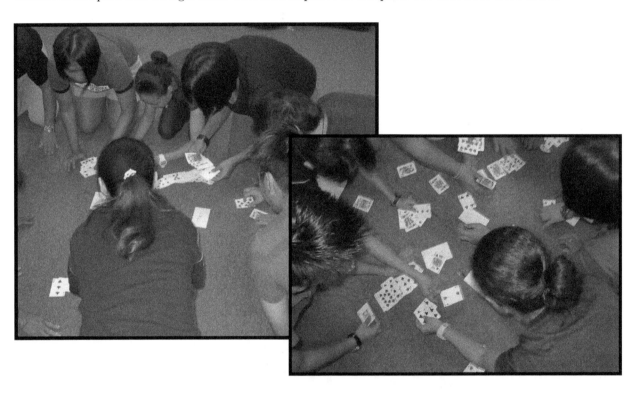

The best time I've seen for the completion of this activity, by a team of six people, is eighteen seconds! Most teams identify opportunities for improvement from the very start of the activity.

I've noticed that teams are more likely to repeat an activity (and try again) when the duration of the activity is short (under a minute in this case). So, having a few quick activities on hand is a great idea, especially if you wish to keep the energy of the group high during the program.

For many years Karl Rohnke and his college roommate Adrian Kissler held an event in California called The Centurian. I happened to attend this event one summer and enjoyed a full week of playful fun with Adrian and Karl. One of Karl's amazing talents is his ability to take ordinary objects (such as a rubber band, a plastic teaspoon or deck of playing cards) and repurpose them to do something even more fun than their original intended use. Stack the Deck, as shared here, is a variation of an activity that Karl shared with us that summer. You can find many of Karl's books online (at websites like www.kendallhunt.com or www.allbookstores.com). My favorite is the 25th anniversary edition of *Silver Bullets* (ISBN 978-0-7575-6532-8) available from Kendall Hunt Publishers.

5-10 PLAYING CARD ICEBREAKER

A deck of playing cards can be a valuable tool for icebreakers.

For this get-acquainted activity, participants use playing cards to identify the number of interesting things they tell their partner about themselves. You'll need multiple decks of playing cards, but only the cards showing an ace, 2, 3, 4, 5 or 6. Using these twenty-four cards from each deck, shuffle and ask each member of your audience to take one card. Then invite everyone to find a partner and introduce themselves.

Pip – the small symbols on the front side of playing cards that denote the suit and rank of that card. Pip cards are numbered one (ace) through ten, and do not include the three face cards (jack, queen and king).

Partners are invited to share as many facts about themselves as the number of pips they have showing on the playing card they possess. After both partners have spoken, they exchange cards, raise their new card high above their head, and go looking for a new partner (who also has their card above their head), and the icebreaker continues.

At any time, a participant may exchange the card they are holding for one of the multiple cards being held by the facilitator. This can be helpful if someone is holding a card with a large number of pips.

With all the pip cards (ace through ten), you can perform this activity, but the time required for each round will increase, especially for those players holding a card with seven or more pips.

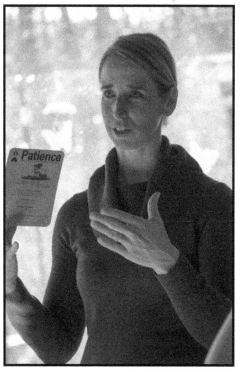

You can also perform this icebreaking activity with dominoes rather than playing cards. Players share the number of facts with their partners as the number of dots (also known as pips) showing on both ends of the domino they hold.

You can perform this activity and many more with the *Teamwork & Teamplay Training Cards* (ISBN 978-0-9882046-2-1) by Jim Cain, available from www.training-wheels.com. This unique deck of large format (5" x 8") full-color cards includes instructions for seventeen team and community building activities that explore such topics as leadership, teamwork, problem solving, communication, trust, icebreakers, character building, creative debriefing techniques and other valuable group skills.

5-11 NEVER!

A game of discovery and deprivation.

To begin this interesting card game of discovery, deal out five cards to each player. Any player begins by making a statement, such as "I have never been to Singapore." Each player that has been to Singapore must give one of their cards to the person who has never been to Singapore, along with a respectable amount of "Awe, poor you!" and "There, there" commentary.

Then the next player makes a remark, such as "I have never eaten brussel sprouts," and the players who have eaten them must pass this player one of their cards.

Play continues until someone wins all the cards or one player runs out of cards completely.

Even a simple game like this can provide some opportunities for group discussion and discovery. "Really?!? You have never eaten Thai food?" Or perhaps, "You have never seen a sunrise over the ocean?!?" The amount of disclosure to the group is also a measure of the security and trust present in the group. Players typically begin with statements that do not require significant personal disclosure, but as they become more acquainted and trusting with the group, their level of disclosure increases as well.

———————————

In Chapter 1 of this book, the game Have You Ever? was presented. This get-acquainted activity is an active version of the game presented on this page. But instead of celebrating all the things we have in common with each other, Never! attempts to discover the things that make us unique and that are different from others in the group.

5-12 THE HUNT

How quickly can you find a specific card?

For this game, every participant has a deck of cards. Begin by asking everyone to shuffle their deck of cards multiple times. Then select one player to be "the caller." The caller places their deck of cards face-down on a table and when ready, turns over the top card (face up) and announces the identity of that card, such as "queen of clubs." The first player to find the queen of clubs and show it to the caller wins that round. The first person to win ten rounds, wins the game. After each round, all players (except the caller) return the card randomly to their deck of cards, and the game continues.

You can add a physical element to this activity by requiring players to run from a starting position to a nearby table, find the card of choice, and run back with that card to the caller. You can also incorporate an element of teamwork to this game by requiring two players from each team to approach a table and work together to find the card as quickly as they can, before running back with it.

You can modify this activity to make it easier for players by allowing cards to be spread out face up, for quicker identification of the selected card. Teams could even place cards in order by suit and value to make identification as quick and easy as possible.

For a higher level of challenge, require players or teams to return each collection of cards to a stacked deck after the removal of the required card. Or try playing in reduced lighting with flashlights.

5-13 THE POISON KING

Here is an amusing game for two players using the thirteen cards from any suit in a standard playing card deck. Begin by laying all thirteen cards in order (from ace to king). For each turn, players remove cards, beginning with the ace. Each player can remove one, two or three cards per turn. The goal is NOT to take the final card (the "poison" king).

The key to controlling the outcome of the game is to obtain card number eight. The way to guarantee that a player gets card number eight is for them to obtain card number four. If a player controls card number four and eight, the other player will most likely have to take the final card (the king).

One of the teachable moments in this game is for players to strategize how to win. Players quickly learn that they will have to take the poison king if the other player controls card number eight. Then the opportunity is for them to decide what card they need to control to get card number eight every time. This discovery comes by engaging some problem-solving methodology. What if I do this? What if I take this card? How many cards should I take here? What is the right number of cards to take at the beginning of the game?

This playing card activity is a variation of the two-person game The 15th Object, which can be found in Chapter 2 of this book and also in the book *Teambuilding Puzzles* by Jim Cain, Chris Cavert, Mike Anderson and Tom Heck (ISBN 978-0-7575-7040-7) available from Kendall Hunt Publishers (www.kendallhunt.com).

5-14 THE EXTRA CARD

How quickly can you find the fifty-third card?

To prepare for this activity, take an ordinary deck of playing cards and slide one additional card (similar but not necessarily identical) into the deck, now shuffle this deck. Next, challenge your audience to brainstorm ideas for the quickest method of identifying the additional (duplicate) card. Then hand them the deck of fifty-three cards and time them as they work to find the duplicate card.

For a higher level of difficulty, make sure the card you insert into the deck is identical (the same brand with the same back-of-the-card artwork) to the other fifty-two cards.

Some of the more interesting techniques include fanning the cards out face-down and looking for a card with a different pattern on the back side; or sorting each of the four card suits and then focusing on the suit with fourteen cards. Or, one person deals out all the cards, one at a time, face up and the rest of the team looks for duplicates.

While there is no official world record for this activity (yet!), groups can often determine the duplicate card in fifteen seconds or less.

Does the amount of time required to find the duplicate card change if the group knows the identity of the duplicate card in advance?

———————————————

An interesting variation of this activity is rather than adding a card, remove one card from the deck and then hand your audience the deck of fifty-one cards and see how quickly they can identify the missing card.

5-15 FOUR OF A KIND

One of the most active card games ever!

For this active card game, you will need a complete deck of (52) playing cards (well shuffled) and a long rope (50 feet). Create a rope circle on the floor with the long rope and place all the cards face down, in random order, inside the circle. Around this central circle of cards, you'll also need one smaller rope circle (about the size of a card table) for each team of four players. This smaller rope circle becomes the home base of each team.

When play begins, one person from each team can enter the card circle and pick up any single card. This card is then transported back to their home base. Neither the person collecting the card nor anyone on their team can look at the card until it is placed face up in the home base. The team must then decide to keep the card or return it to the circle. Any player can return a card to the circle (face down) and/or collect a new card during their turn.

The goal of this game is for every team to collect four cards that are of the same rank (four kings, for example, or four tens). The game is not over until every team has four of a kind.

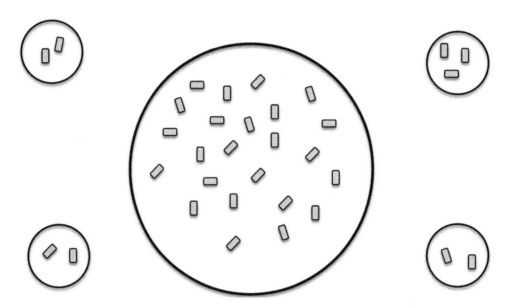

Games like this often create a competitive atmosphere. Teams often try to beat each other to the finish, especially if you choose to time the event with a stopwatch. But after the first round or two, teams begin to consider collaboration. For example, no rule states that a player from another team cannot look at a card chosen by another runner. And no rule states that a runner cannot name the card they are returning to the central circle. These possibilities make the game much more interesting and potentially collaborative rather than competitive.

This unique playing card activity was created by Chris Cavert, author of such books as *Affordable Portables* (ISBN 978-1-885473-40-0) and *Portable Teambuilding Activities* (ISBN 978-1-939019-14-1). You can find more information about Chris at www.fundoing.com.

5-16 ACTION / REACTION

A quick memory and fast reflexes!

You'll need a full deck of ordinary playing cards for this frantic game of memory and actions. Begin by shuffling and then dealing out all fifty-two cards to the four players present (thirteen cards per person). Place these cards in a pile, face down, directly in front of each player. When everyone is ready, have all four players simultaneously turn over their top card and drop it near the center of the table.

If three (or four) of the cards are the same face value (such as sevens or kings), everyone touches the top of their head with their hand. If three (or four) of the cards are either black suits (clubs or spades), players touch the table. If three (or four) of the cards are either red suits (diamonds or hearts), players show a thumbs-up sign. If three (or four) of the cards have the same face value AND three (or four) of the cards are red or black, then players perform BOTH signals. The last player to correctly perform the signal(s) required inherits all of the cards in the center of the table. Play continues until one player runs completely out of cards.

Action / Reaction Card Game

If three or more cards have the same face value (7's) players touch the top of their head.

If three or more cards have either black suit (clubs or spades) players touch the table.

If three or more cards have either red suit (diamonds or hearts) players show thumbs-up.

If none of the above results occur, play continues (until it does).

If you like, you can list the basic rules for the game on an index card and place this card so that all players can easily see it. You can also change the signals required from round to round if you like.

I discovered the original description for this activity in a 1950s resource notebook from the Buckeye Leadership Workshop, held annually each spring in Ohio. Sometimes games are so old they become new again! You can find out more information about rec labs and specifically the Buckeye event at www.buckeyeleadership.com.

For a more modern variation of this game, check out the video of the Happy Salmon card game by Ken Gruhl and Quentin Weir, from North Star Games (www.northstargames.com).

SPECIAL ACTIVITIES FOR TEACHERS, TRAINERS, AND FACILITATORS

CHAPTER SIX

This sixth chapter presents activities that are particularly powerful in educational settings.

NO.	ACTIVITY NAME	TEACHABLE MOMENT	IDEAL GROUP SIZE
6-1	Match Cards	Active Learning	Multiple small groups
6-2	Six-Word Stories	Concise Writing	Any
6-3	Ecological Sudoku	Playful Ways to Learn	Any
6-3½	The Sudoku Square Technique	A New Way to Play	Any
6-4	One Long Line/Just Passing Through	Creativity	Any
6-5	The Top Ten List	Educational Categories	Multiple small groups
6-6	The Creativity Slam	Creativity and Innovation	Multiple small groups
6-7	Goal Setting	Setting Achievable Goals	Any
6-8	Searching for the Answers	An Alphabetical Challenge	Any
6-9	Almost Lost in Translation	International Linguistics	Any
6-10	Unique Debriefing Cards	Content and Closure	Any
6-11	Camouflage	Artistic Hide and Seek	5 or more people
6-12	Line Up	Identify the Correct Order	Any
6-13	Scenarios and Simulations	Setting Priorities	Any
6-14	The Big Answer	Seeking Advice	5 or more people
6-15	Kaboom!	Explosively Fun Learning	3 or more students
6-16	The Value of an Education	Teachable Moment	Any
6-17	The Welcome Mat	Messages and Directions	Any
6-18	A Literary Scavenger Hunt	Using Books for Fun	Any
6-19	Creative Group Formation	Subject Matter Groups	Large groups
6-20	Hey Buddy, Can't You Read the Sign?	Exploring Diversity	Any

6-1 MATCH CARDS

The Match Cards activity mentioned in Chapter 2 utilized words of character. A valuable teachable moment for sure, but this card game can be expanded to teach many different things depending on the content written on each card. For example, instead of finding matching words, your collection of match cards could contain any of the following:

A Historical Date in History	and	The Event that Happened on that Day
A Mathematical Equation	and	The Answer to that Equation
A Familiar Word	and	The Definition for that World
Any Word	and	The Opposite Word
Any Word	and	A Translation of that Word in Another Language
A Photo or Illustration	and	A Slightly Different View of that Same Image

Match Cards are a variation of the memory game. Twelve different word pairs are written on twenty-four index cards and these cards are randomly placed face-down on a table. You will need one collection of these cards for each group. At the beginning of the activity, one team member approaches their table and turns over any two cards, revealing the words. If the words match, the cards are placed in their original position face-up. If the words do not match, the cards are turned face-down. Then the second person repeats this process. The first team to turn over all twenty-four cards is the winner.

After turning over the cards in the first part of this activity, you can use these same cards (and the information they contain) as a teaching and debriefing tool. Invite every member of your group to take one of the cards and reflect on the information contained there. If it is a photograph or image, ask your audience to see if they can identify the location of that image or form a connection to the picture. If historical events are present, ask your audience to expand on the significance of the dates shown on each card.

 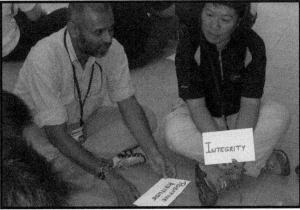

The *Teamwork & Teamplay Training Cards* have twenty-six different words of character that you can use for this activity (and sixteen more activities, too!). You can purchase these cards from Healthy Learning (www.healthylearning.com) and Training Wheels, Inc. (www.training-wheels.com). These cards are now available in a Chinese/English dual-language version from FangMa International Education and Culture Company, LTD of Beijing, China. Visit the Teamwork & Teamplay website at www.teamworkandteamplay.com for more information about these dual-language cards.

6-2 SIX-WORD STORIES

A whole novel in just six words.

Most students are less than excited about writing projects, so here is one that is short and sweet. Six Word Stories is a concise collection of prose that some describe as so few words, so much meaning! To prepare for this writing experience, you might try searching the internet for "six-word stories" and providing your students with some examples. One ideal source is the website www.sixwordstories. net, which features this 2014 post by Newtonswig, "Torched the haystack. Found the needle."

After reading dozens of six-word stories, I discovered that many are dramatic, occasionally sad and sometimes depressing. "Bachelor party, YouTube video, wedding cancelled." But I found a few that were funny, inspirational and creative. "Finding you was like coming home." Happy searching!

So, pass an index card to each of your students and invite them to craft their own six-word stories. You may be surprised at the content they create. Or, if you happen to conduct this activity after a teambuilding program or event, you might challenge your participants to write their final comments as six-word stories. A fairly interesting and concise way of completing your day together, indeed.

The "original" six-word story was penned by Ernest Hemmingway, "For Sale: baby shoes, never worn." In the song, "A Better Place To Be," Harry Chapin sings about a chance encounter where "she left a six-word letter, saying 'it's time that I moved on.'"

If you'd like to read a whole book full of such unique works, see the book *Not Quite What I Was Planning—Six-Word Memoirs* by Famous and Obscure Writers (ISBN 978-0-0613-7405-0) edited by Rachel Fershleiser and Larry Smith of *Smith Magazine*.

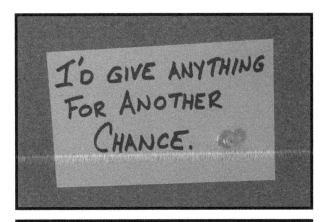

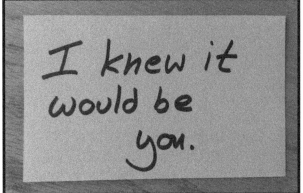

6-3 ECOLOGICAL SUDOKU

Creating teachable moments with puzzles.

This environmentally themed Sudoku-like puzzle was created by Shawn Moriarty to acquaint students with the stages of the food chain. Shawn began with an "easy" Sudoku puzzle drawn onto a tarp and substituted the numbers one through nine for the following terms, with each term printed on a different color card stock. Students were then challenged to complete the grid, using standard Sudoku rules.

1 The Sun	4 Secondary	7 Decomposer
2 Food/Energy	5 Primary	8 Waste
3 Tertiary	6 Producer	9 Quaternary

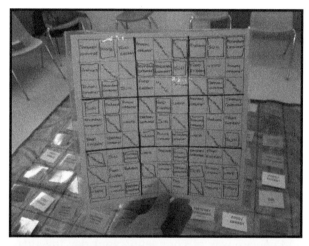

You can use this concept to teach a wide variety of subject matter. You can download a set of Ecodoku cards that cover eleven different ecological topics (thanks to Shawn) at www.asinglefootstep.com.

The subject matter you print on each card can be presented with words or pictures. It can be helpful to provide a list of all nine terms you plan to use. You can also include, in the case of environmentally themed puzzles, specific animals, plants or organisms that qualify for each term.

Ecological Sudoku or Ecodoku was created by my colleague and friend Shawn Moriarty and featured in his Kendall/Hunt book, *The Ropes of Ecology* (ISBN 978-1-5249-6264-7). Shawn finds amazing ways to bring outdoor education, ecology, environmental and earth sciences to life with rope course activities that are both engaging and educational.

6-3½ THE SUDOKU SQUARE TECHNIQUE

A new way to play Sudoku created by Dr. Jim Cain

I've been playing Sudoku for a few years now, and recently I noticed something. The level of interest in any particular puzzle is highest as the puzzle is being solved, but rapidly decreases to zero once the puzzle is completed. I wanted to find an interesting way to increase the enjoyment of these wonderful puzzles, and here is my first idea, the Sudoku Square Technique (SST).

The basic idea is to complete the entire perimeter of the Sudoku puzzle (a square comprised of nine numbers on each side) before entering any numbers within the interior of the puzzle. This technique invites two moments of interest in every Sudoku puzzle. One when the square is complete, and the traditional second when the entire grid has been completely filled.

For example, start with the Sudoku puzzle on the left (rated easy) and see if you can fill in the entire perimeter (outside square) with numbers before entering any numbers to the interior blocks of the puzzle. The solution is given at the right.

		8			5		3	
6	5			1	3	9		
9					6	5	4	
		5		2				1
2								6
1				3		5		
5	2	6						9
		4	1	8			6	5
	1		5			4		

4	7	8	6	9	5	1	3	2
6	5			1	3	9		7
9					6	5	4	4
3		5		2				1
2								6
1				3		5		8
5	2	6						9
7		4	1	8			6	5
8	1	9	5	6	2	4	7	3

The Sudoku Square Technique is not only applicable to easy Sudoku puzzles. Even some of the most difficult Sudoku puzzles can be attacked using SST. So now, each time you solve a Sudoku puzzle, you can experience two moments of victory. First by completing the Sudoku Square, and second by completing the entire puzzle. Good luck!

Dr. Jim Cain invented the Sudoku Square Technique (SST) in November 2016. He is a teambuilding guru and author with over a dozen best-selling team and community building activity books, including *Teamwork & Teamplay*, *Essential Staff Training Activities*, *A Teachable Moment* and this book, *Teambuilding with Index Cards*. You can find out more about Jim and his work at www.teamworkandteamplay.com.

6-4 ONE LONG LINE / JUST PASSING THROUGH

Here are two index card challenges for your next audience.
Grab a pair of scissors and good luck!

The Longest Line

In a world of diminishing resources, doing more with less is not only less expensive, it is environmentally responsible. Consider that as you challenge your next audience to create the longest continuous line possible by creatively cutting a single index card. With a standard 3x5 index card and some creative scissor work, you can easily create a continuous strip of paper 10 feet long, or more.

Once your audience has created the longest line they can from a single index card, you can increase the challenge by inviting them to write a story on an index card and then cut this story into the longest line they can (and still be readable).

Just Passing Through

One of the classic problem-solving activities using an index card (or even a business card) is to creatively cut the card with a pair of scissors creating a hole large enough for an entire person to pass through. There are many techniques that work for this activity, including the two shown here. Just cut an index card along these lines and gently pull the card outward to form a large paper circle.

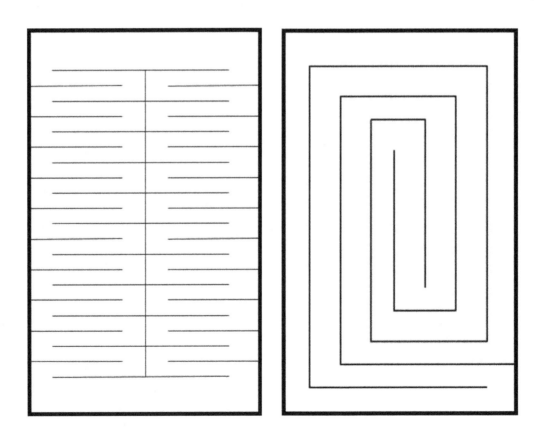

6-5 THE TOP TEN LIST

An educational challenge of categories.

Here is an educational technique for inviting your audience to think critically about various categories. Let's begin with the subject of fast-food restaurant chains. Ask your audience to brainstorm a list of fast-food chains and place each restaurant on a separate index card. Then ask your audience to guess which of these restaurants make the top ten lists for largest fast-food restaurant chains in the world and within the United States. By asking your audience to brainstorm and create the list themselves, you engage them at a higher level than just simply inviting them to sequence a collection of preprinted cards. The most recent list (I could find) declares that the largest fast-food restaurant chains are:

Top Ten Largest Fast-Food Restaurant Chains

In the World	In the United States
1. McDonalds	1. McDonalds
2. KFC	2. Subway
3. Subway	3. Burger King
4. Pizza Hut	4. Wendy's
5. Starbucks	5. Starbucks
6. Burger King	6. Taco Bell
7. Domino's Pizza	7. Dunkin' Donuts
8. Dunkin' Donuts	8. Pizza Hut
9. Dairy Queen	9. KFC
10. Papa John's Pizza	10. Sonic

The next challenge is to identify the Top Ten Christmas Toys in the United States from 1950. Again, have your audience brainstorm a collection of at least twenty items and then place ten of them in order. According to internet sources, the top ten Christmas toys of 1950 were: 10. Barbie, 9. Hula Hoop, 8. Pogo Stick, 7. Corn Popper (push toy), 6. Play-Doh, 5. Gumby, 4. Matchbox Cars, 3. Mr. Potato Head (with real potato!), 2. Colorforms, 1. Fisher Price Little People.

Finally, let's add a bit more educational content to this activity. Invite your audience to create a list of significant world events and rather than placing them in Top Ten order, ask them to place them in chronological order in history. For example, here are the dates of some significant world-changing events and when they occurred: The French Revolution 1789-1794, The October Revolution (Russia) 1917, The Invention of the Gutenberg Press 1440, The American Revolution 1765-1783, The Protestant Reformation 1517-1750, The Fall of Constantinople 1453, The Battle of Hastings 1066, Pax Romana (Roman Peace—200 years of relative peace) 27BC-180AD, The Black Plague 1346-1353, The Fall of the Roman Empire 1453, New Zealand is the first country to give Women the Right to Vote 1893.

Additional Top Ten lists can include: Junk foods, vehicles, sports teams, spoken languages, websites, gas stations, breakfast cereals, hotel chains, Civil War battles, video games, athletic shoes, ….

If you want to create your own educational Top Ten lists, you can find dozens of websites devoted to such things on the internet. In addition, you might want to borrow the following books from your library: *The Ultimate Book of Top 10 Lists* by Jamie Frater and *The Top 10 of Everything* by Paul Terry.

6-6 THE CREATIVITY SLAM

A fun way to be creative.

The Creativity Slam is a noisy, interactive and fun way to innovate. Start the process by inviting members of your audience to gather around round tables, filled with a pile of various size index cards, plus as many creative writing tools (pencils, pens, markers, crayons, etc.) as you can conveniently gather. Next, invite everyone to take an index card and a writing tool. Then explain the following guidelines for this activity:

> *Welcome to the Creativity Slam. In a minute, I'll suggest a topic. Your job is to take an index card and write a single idea based on the topic presented. Add any information you like to this idea, such as words, pictures, sketches, equations, you name it. After ten seconds, pass your card to the right, slamming it down loudly on the table. Then, either pick up the card passed to you on your left (and expound on what is already written there) or select a new card from the center and add another new idea to the mix. Change writing tools, be creative, think big and slam often!*

The Creativity Slam is an excellent way to build upon the ideas of others. Other thinkers can inspire us, challenge us, motivate us to consider new possibilities. Each time you slam an index card down on the table, it has the effect of startling others nearby. Once they recover and return to the task at hand, they come at it from a slightly different frame of mind, which can invoke some additional creativity. If you happen to have multiple tables in your Creativity Slam, occasionally transfer completed cards between tables to cross-pollinate ideas.

At the end of your Creativity Slam session, you are likely to have dozens of ideas for nearly any topic you choose. Some will be outrageous. Some will be hilarious. Some technologically impossible. Some may defy the current laws of physics, but a few may be in fact just what you are looking for!

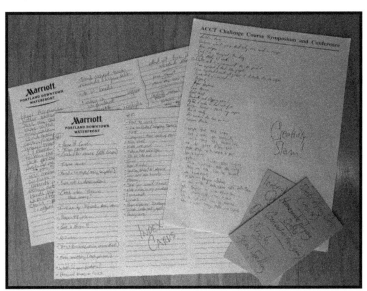

I presented the Creativity Slam at both the National Challenge Course Practitioner's Symposium (NCCPS) in Boulder, Colorado and at the Association for Challenge Course Technology (ACCT) conference in Portland, Oregon a few years ago, specifically with the topic of what to do with index cards. Some of the activities in this book came from the creative suggestions I received during those workshops.

6-7 GOAL SETTING

A fun way to share your goals.

To begin this goal-setting activity, invite everyone to write down a goal they have for the future on an index card. Goals can be focused on a particular theme, such as school-related goals, fitness goals, project goals or personal goals.

When all goals have been written down, invite everyone to find a partner and work together on the second part of this activity. First, partners should share their individual goals with each other. Then partner 1 hands their card to partner 2 and watches as partner 2 walks slowly away, while partner 1 remains stationary. When partner 2 has reached a reasonable distance, partner 1 instructs partner 2 to drop the goal card to the ground. With eyes closed, partner 1 then walks forward. When partner 1 believes they have reached the location where their index card lies, partner 1 bends over and attempts to pick up their goal card, and then open their eyes.

Reaching down and picking up their goal card (with their eyes closed) is metaphorically like achieving their goal. The question now is whether the placement of the card (the goal) was too easy, too difficult or just right. After partner 1 has attempted to reach their goal card, partners switch roles and partner 2 attempts to reach their goal as well.

After completing the task, partners can discuss what progress they are making toward reaching their goal—what skills they possess that will help them and which skills they still need to improve to successfully reach their goal.

One of the reasons for performing this goal setting activity with a partner is that many people succeed in achieving their goals when they share them with a partner!

One of the most well-known criteria for goal setting is to set SMART goals for yourself. SMART goals are specific, measurable, achievable, relevant and timely.

In the *Teamwork & Teamplay International Edition* by Jim Cain (ISBN 978-0-9882046-3-8) you'll find an interesting variation of this goal-setting activity that replaces index cards with shoes! Participants each toss one of their shoes a short, medium or long distance in front of them, and then close their eyes. Their personal challenge is to walk forward toward their shoe and reach down when they believe they are in a position to pick up their shoe. Was their goal too easy, too difficult or just right? The *Teamwork & Teamplay International Edition* features fifty-one of author Jim Cain's favorite team activities translated into sixteen different languages, including English, Spanish, Portuguese, Italian, German, Russian, Chinese, Japanese, Greek, Hebrew, Thai, Mongolian, Dutch, Danish, French and Turkish.

6-8 SEARCHING FOR THE ANSWERS

Finding the Answers in the Alphabet.

According to Edgar Dale's *Cone of Learning*, the greater the intensity of the learning experience, the greater the retention of that information by the student. The following activity uses this theory to increase the intensity of the learning experience. This technique can be used for nearly any word-based learning situation. As an example, consider this simple statement (which is foundational in the Teamwork & Teamplay philosophy):

The three essential ingredients for a high-performing team are: (a worthy) task,
(a chance for) growth and (the opportunity to build positive) relationships.

You might present such information to your students in a lecture, or with a fill-in-the-blank worksheet, or from a reading assignment, or by visiting a website, or by using computer presentation software, but consider using three index cards (of similar size and color) with the following content:

Card 1:   The three essential ingredients for a high-performing

team are _____, _____ and relationships.

Card 2:   A B C D E F G H I J K L M N O P Q R S U V W X Y Z   ____
Z Y X W V U T S R Q P O N M L K J I H G F E D C B   ____
Q W E R T Y U I O P A D F G H J K L Z X C V B N M   ____
Z A Q X S W C D E V F R B G T N H Y M J U I L O P   ____

Card 3:   Q A Z S X E D C F V B Y N U J M I K L P   __ __ __ __ __ __

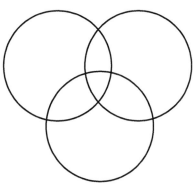

Card 1 delivers the basic question to be answered. Card 2 requires the student to find which letter of the alphabet is missing and write that letter in the space provided. You can see that the first two lines of capital letters is in alphabetical and reverse alphabetical order, which makes this version rather simple. If you randomize the placement of letters in each line of Card 2 (as shown in the last two lines), you can further increase the challenge of finding the missing letter. Card 3 requires students to identify the six missing letters from the string of capital letters and then to reorganize these six letters to form the answer (growth).

For even further stimulation during the learning process, include this graphic along with the commentary on Card 1. The three-component Venn diagram provides yet another "hook" to help students visualize and remember the content.

You can read more about the Task, Growth, Relationships model used by Teamwork & Teamplay in the books *Essential Staff Training Activities* (ISBN 978-0-7575-6167-2), *The Big Book of Low Cost Training Games* (ISBN 978-0-0717-7437-6) and *100 Activities That Build Unity, Community and Connection* (ISBN 978-1-6067-9374-9).

6-9 ALMOST LOST IN TRANSLATION

Words that endure.

Here is an international and unique way to play with words. Begin with any simple sentence, quote, motto or saying. Write this phrase on an index card. Then, using one of the freely available internet translation programs, translate the phrase from the original language to another language. Continue this process again, and again, and again, writing each translation down on a new index card. Then translate the final version back to the original language and compare this result to the original message.

Advertisers sometimes perform this task to ensure that their slogans are correctly translated into other languages. A message that can be translated multiple times and still maintain its integrity is indeed well worded. Consider the two examples presented below.

Early to bed and early to rise makes a man healthy, wealthy and wise.

Temprano a la cama y al levantarse temprano hace que un hombre saludable, rico y sabio.

早睡早起时能让男人健康，丰富而明智。

Un sommeil précoce et une ascension précoce peuvent rendre les hommes sains, riches et sages.

Früher Schlaf und früher Aufstieg können Männer gesund, wohlhabend und weise machen.

Early sleep and early advancement can make men healthy, prosperous and wise.

For the example shown, the phrase "Early to bed and early to rise, makes a man healthy, wealthy and wise," has been translated from English to Spanish to Chinese to French to German and then back to English. The final translation is similar to the original message. But for the second example below, the Thomas A. Edison quote "To invent, you need a good imagination and a pile of junk," translated from English to Russian to Arabic to Japanese and then back to English is somewhat distorted.

To invent, you need a good imagination and a pile of junk.

Чтобы изобрести, вам нужно хорошее воображение и куча мусора.

لابتكار ، تحتاج إلى خيال جيد وكثير من القمامة.

革新のためには、想像力とたくさんのゴミが必要です。

For innovation, imagination and lots of garbage are needed.

6-10 UNIQUE DEBRIEFING CARDS

Using familiar icons and imagery for outstanding reviewing results.

One of the best ways to engage your audience in the reviewing and debriefing process is to incorporate content that is familiar and interesting to them. Nearly every organization has some easily recognizable content, such as a mission statement, vision statement, corporate logos, icons and images. In my youth, for example, I was a member of 4-H, known for their four-leaf clover symbol with four H's designating head, heart, hand and health. I can picture dozens of card images depicting various forms of heads (with hats, various styles of hair, cultural hairstyles), hearts (valentines), hands (working gloves, shaking hands, hands of various colors and sizes) and tons of medical images for health. The YMCA has four core values: respect, responsibility, honesty and caring. These, too, can be easily turned into images.

Imagine an organization that is heavily into accounting and numbers. Create a set of debriefing cards for these folks, filled with what they know best: numbers, mathematical symbols, spreadsheet terminology, percentages, etc. If you happen to have computer programmers, borrow some code words from their programming language, plus pictures of their computers, hardware, software, apps and other computer-related images.

Most organizations maintain a website where you can find information and images familiar to that organization. Create your own, organization specific (and unique!) debriefing cards, filled with words (from their mission or vision statement, core beliefs or values) and images (company logos, products, services, and other familiar graphics).

Some of the most unique debriefing cards I've encountered are custom-made products from a creative facilitator. I've seen debriefing cards filled with images (such as the Chiji cards that originally started the revolution in image-based debriefing methods), postcards (see the Post Card Debrief from Jennifer Stanchfield in Chapter 4), emoji faces, mathematical symbols (for a group of computer programmers), Chinese characters, playing cards (thanks to Roger Greenaway's 5 F's debriefing technique, also in Chapter 4), hand and power tools (from Michelle Cummings, Training Wheels, Inc.), photographs (such as the Emotion Cards from Metalog Training Tools), Samurai warriors with strong visible emotions (on a deck of playing cards), abstract and incomplete art (from the Shiruranai Cards of Project Adventure Japan), Christian and other religiously focused cards (such as the Soularium Cards from CRU Press), artistic cards (such as the Climer Cards created by creativity guru Amy Climer) and even cartoon images (such as the popular Images of Organizations cards from RSVP Design).

If you would like to create your own set of unique debriefing cards you only need to know the subject matter or theme of the group you are facilitating. Start by visiting the website of the organization before the program begins. This will likely provide helpful information about their mission, vision, values and initiatives. You can create your cards using standard index cards, but for a more finished look, find blank playing cards (with rounded corners) from your local education/teacher supply store.

Be aware however, some organizations have copyright limitations on how and where their logos and other corporate graphics can be displayed. Check with your legal department before proceeding!

The *Teamwork & Teamplay Training Cards* have a dozen images of team performance that you can use for debriefing, plus sixteen more activities too! You can purchase these cards from Healthy Learning (www.healthylearning.com), Trainer's Warehouse (www.trainerwarehouse.com) and Training Wheels, Inc. (www.training-wheels.com).

6-11 CAMOUFLAGE

An artistic game of hide and seek.

This activity is a unique game of hide and seek, with an artistic flair. You can play this game inside or out. To begin, you'll need one index card for each person and marker or crayons with colors that match the local environment. The challenge of this activity is for participants to each color their card with colors and patterns that blend in with the local scenery and then place this card within the room, or a defined space if you happen to be outdoors.

When all cards have been secretly placed by their artist, it is time for everyone to try and find all the other cards.

There are four major components to this activity: first, studying the surrounding environment or habitat; second, creating the camouflage card; third, hiding the card; and fourth, searching and finding all of the other cards.

In addition to colorful markers or crayons, encourage your audience to use natural things to transform the color of their index card when they are in the great outdoors, such as water, mud, ashes, and other natural or organic things.

The challenge of finding every index card will be increased if you allow participants to bend, fold, and trim the size and shape of their index card. Spotting an index card leaf that is the same size, shape and color as a natural leaf will be a real challenge.

As a variation of the above activity, pass out a random selection of index cards in different colors and ask your students to find something in nature containing this color. Or have them hide their card (without any artistic camouflage) somewhere in your classroom and see if others can find it.

While you can find a variety of index card sizes, shapes and styles in office supply stores around the world, some very interesting index card stock can also be found at craft stores like Hobby Lobby (www.hobbylobby.com). The collection of colorful card stock shown here has dozens of different colors in 4x6 size. Perfect for this activity!

If you enjoy mixing adventure-based learning and the natural environment, you can find more activities in the book, *The Ropes of Ecology* by Shawn Moriarty from Kendall/Hunt Publishers (ISBN 978-1-5249-6264-7).

6-12 LINE UP

Learning from the order of things.

For this educational activity, you'll need to write each of the following items on an index card and invite your audience to place these cards in the correct order. You can use this page as a solution key for each category or simply write the numeric order or value on the back side of each card. Five unique collections are presented here. Can you think of more for your class?

The eight known planets in order starting nearest the Sun (plus Pluto, although now classified as one of five dwarf planets currently in our solar system) are Mercury, Venus, Earth, Mars, Jupiter, Saturn, Uranus, Neptune and Pluto, which can be remembered using the mnemonic "many very elderly men just sit upon neat pillows."

The Mohs Hardness scale for minerals (from softest to hardest) includes talc, gypsum, calcite, fluorite, apatite, orthoclase, quartz, topaz, corundum and diamond.

The twelve astrological signs of the zodiac, in order starting with Aquarius include Aquarius, Pisces, Aries, Taurus, Gemini, Cancer, Leo, Virgo, Libra, Scorpio, Sagittarius and Capricorn.

The decomposition rates for familiar items in a landfill include: plastic bottles 450 years, paper towels 4 weeks, foam plastic cup 50 years, cardboard 2 months, a tin can 50 years, leather shoes 40-50 years, thread 3-4 months, nylon clothes 40 years, diapers 500 years, glass bottle 1 million years, monofilament fishing line 600 years, and an aluminum can 200 years.

Ten significant events in history include: The French Revolution 1789-1794, The October Revolution (Russia) 1917, The Invention of the Gutenberg Press 1440, The American Revolution 1765-1783, The Protestant Reformation 1517-1750, The Fall of Constantinople 1453, The Battle of Hastings 1066, Pax Romana (Roman Peace—200 years of relative peace) 27BC-180AD, The Black Plague 1346-1353, The Fall of the Roman Empire 1453, and New Zealand becomes the first country to give women the right to vote 1893.

If you like this collection of educational rankings, you might also enjoy activity 6-5 in this book, The Top Ten List, featuring the ranking of interesting topics from around the world. The Top Ten List requires participants to generate their own lists and then rank them in order, while Line Up presents your audience with the information up front and then invites participants to rank these items accordingly. Two different activities requiring two different levels of participation.

6-13 SCENARIOS AND SIMULATIONS

Creating immersive simulations for group decision making.

A teambuilding scenario or simulation is an invitation for a group to discuss a survival situation and make decisions based upon the knowledge available. Some situations are based on historically accurate information or real-life scenarios.

To prepare for your teambuilding simulation, transfer the critical elements of your scenario to index cards. This includes a synopsis of the situation, personnel by name, various possessions, instruments, tools and resources, and a few wild card situations (such as changing weather, depletion of key resources, and other possibilities). Invite participants to read these cards, discuss the situation, rank priorities and make critical decisions about their situation. In historically accurate scenarios, you can assign your participants specific identities and incorporate actual events into the decision-making process, and then compare the decisions of your audience with the decisions of the actual personnel.

As with many scenarios, the correct prioritization or ranking of the available inventory is typically less important than the discussion of the situation itself. The ability of the team to work together, make decisions and survive is critical.

There are dozens of useful scenarios available for this activity. When discussing character and values, one of the classic scenarios is Alligator River, which can be found in the book *Values Clarification* (ISBN 978-0-4466-7095-2) by Sidney Simon, Leland Howe and Howard Kirschenbaum.

Two additional scenarios are available from the National Aeronautics and Space Administration (NASA) at www.nasa.gov/pdf/166504main_Survival.pdf. *Survival at Jamestown* is a historical recreation of life in Jamestown in 1607. *Survival on the Moon* is a futuristic adventure on the surface of the moon in 2025. Both scenarios are available for free on the web and include supplemental content for teachers and trainers to use, including expert rankings by professionals familiar with each situation.

A recent web search of "team building simulations" revealed dozens of additional possibilities, including Lost at Sea, an ocean-going survival scenario for small teams available at www.insight.typepad.co.uk/insight/2009/02/lost-at-sea-a-team-building-game.html.

As part of a leadership program, I visited the site of the 1949 Mann Gulch fire. This event is one of the most significant (and unfortunate) leadership events of the past century and is detailed in the book *Young Men and Fire* (ISBN 978-0-2265-0062-4) by Norman Maclean and critically evaluated in the book *The Leadership Moment* (ISBN 978-0-8129-3230-7) by Michael Useem.

But one of the most compelling scenarios is the historically accurate (and amazing) story of Sir Ernest Shackleton's Imperial Trans-Antarctic Expedition of 1914-1917, which resulted in their ship, the Endurance, being frozen and eventually crushed in the ice, hundreds of miles from safety. Here, at the hundred-year anniversary of this event, much of the information (including photographs taken by expedition photographer Frank Hurley) is easily accessible on the web, including copies of the book *South* by Shackleton (available at www.archives.org), expedition logs by the captain Frank Worsley and more. And best of all, this historic tale has a happy ending! All members of the *Endurance*, including stowaway Perce Blackborrow, were safely rescued and returned to civilization.

For slightly more modern events, consider using the TV series LOST or the movie and book *The Martian* (ISBN 978-1-1019-0500-5) by Andy Weir as epic situations worthy of a scenario discussion.

> *People never realize when they are in an epic situation that they are in an epic situation. That realization only comes later. Much, much later.*
>
> —Jim Cain

6-14 THE BIG ANSWER

A creative way to solicit advice from your peers.

Here is a very simple way for team members to solicit advice from other participants. You are welcome to make photocopies of the following page for each member of your group. Then instruct your participants to write one of their current challenges in the space provided (one question or challenge per page).

At this point, there are several ways to complete this activity. First, if participants are seated at a table, invite them to pass their Big Answer document one person to their right, and continue this process until everyone has seen and written some advice on each page. A second method is to place all the Big Answer documents on a table or wall and allow participants to read and write their recommendations throughout the day, during breaks. A third technique is to have participants mingle, trading papers each time they meet a new person and writing their own comments whenever appropriate. Finally, and most simply, just ask your participants to clearly write a current problem or situation they are struggling with on a large index card. Then pass this card around and invite participants to read each index card and provide helpful advice.

Of all the activities in this book, The Big Answer has the potential to be one of the most powerful! Finding the answer to help someone with a personal challenge can be a life-altering event. Just imagine how you would feel if someone offered a viable solution to the problem that has been plaguing you for a long time. That is the potential of this activity.

For a number of years, I've been using The Big Question as one of my favorite icebreakers. During a corporate teambuilding event, one manager remarked, "We already have enough big questions, what we need are big answers!" So, after lunch that day, I created a document (very much like the one shown on the opposite page) and shared it with the group. That day, everybody went home with some suggestions and recommendations on how to solve their biggest challenges at work, and now, you can too.

The Big Answer was originally published in the book *Essential Staff Training Activities* (ISBN 978-0-7575-6167-2) by Jim Cain, Clare Marie Hannon and David Knobbe, and is available from www.kendallhunt.com and www.amazon.com.

THE BIG ANSWER

We all have questions, for which we are constantly looking for answers. Write your choice of question in the space below and let's see if we can help you generate some appropriate answers, or at least some food for thought.

My question or challenge is:

For those of you receiving this page, your task is to carefully consider the question above, and write your best advice, answer or comment in one of the spaces below.

6-15 KABOOM!

Making learning explosively fun.

Here is an interesting way to make education fun. Create a stack of question cards and place these cards face-down on a desk or table. You'll need one deck of these cards for every four to six students. You can include questions on any subject you are currently studying in the classroom. You should also create two cards that have the word KABOOM! on them and insert these into the deck of question cards.

Students take turns turning over one card at a time from the stack. If they answer correctly, they keep the card. If their answer is incorrect, the card is returned to the bottom of the stack.

Play continues with each player answering questions and trying to collect as many cards as possible. If players select the KABOOM! card from the central pile, they must return ALL of their own cards to the stack. Continue playing for a specific time period, or until someone has collected ten cards.

The card container shown contains a variety of question cards, separated by colorful alphabetic index tabs. You can keep a variety of subject matter cards in such a container. Just be sure to include several KABOOM! cards in each collection.

You can modify the game with two different styles of KABOOM! cards. For a major KABOOM! card, players must return ALL their cards to the stack in the middle of the table, shuffling them in to disguise their location. For a minor KABOOM! card, players only need to return two cards (of their own choice) to the bottom of the stack.

You can also create a variation of this game by replacing your collection of question cards with trivia cards or other content. Activity 3-19 in this book, Riddles, contains over a dozen interesting questions and puzzles that are sure to challenge your students. Just be sure to include several KABOOM! cards in each deck you create.

6-16 THE VALUE OF AN EDUCATION

Learning is easy once you know the rules.

This index card activity is sure to engage your audience, as they attempt to figure out the secret. Let's start with twenty-six of the most familiar things in our world—the letters of the alphabet. The challenge is to place all twenty-six letter cards in the correct sequence after seeing that sequence for only ten seconds.

First, you'll need to create two collections of twenty-six block capital letters, A to Z. Place one set of index cards on a table near your audience, in the following sequence:

A E F H I K L M N T V W X Y Z
C O S
B D G J P Q R U

Next, invite a member of your audience to approach the table, view the above sequence (for just ten seconds), and then return to the other set of twenty-six index cards and place them in the same order. Chances are this first person will have difficulty placing each of the cards correctly.

Then illustrate the power of education to your audience by selecting a second member of the group. Walk with them as they approach the table with the sequenced cards and tell them that the letters are organized in three categories: all straight lines, all curved lines, a combination of straight and curved lines. After viewing the sequence for ten seconds, it is highly likely that this second person will be able to return and place all twenty-six duplicate cards in exactly the same sequence.

So, what is the difference in performance between the first and second volunteer? Education! Given exactly the same task, the person with even a small amount of education (additional information, insight, pattern recognition, call it what you will) can make a difficult task seem simple.

If you like this style of using puzzles to create teachable moments, see if you can determine the pattern in the following sequence:

A B D O P Q R
C E F G H I J K L M N S T U V W X Y Z

You can also illustrate the power of education using numbers instead of letters. What is the rule for memorizing the following sequence?

8 5 4 9 1 7 6 3 2 0

Teachable Moment: Education is important. With even a few seconds worth of education, you can perform amazing things.

The second sequence of letters is organized by those letters with an enclosed interior space (O) and those without (T). The sequence of numbers is placed in alphabetical order (Eight, Five, Four, Nine, One, Seven, Six, Three, Two, Zero).

6-17 THE WELCOME MAT

You are welcome here!

There is an interesting artifact in our culture that is a combination of utility and hospitality, known as a welcome mat. This simple and often disregarded item helps travelers wipe the dust from their shoes before entering a home. In addition to utility and function, a welcome mat also provides an invitation of welcome and inclusion.

You can use index cards to create your own style of welcome mats and these mats can provide valuable information to your participants (Meet us in Room 106), invitation (We are so glad you are here!), encouragement (Keep going, you are almost there), and direction (Turn left).

You can also create a sequential series of welcome mats that point your participants in the right direction, similar to the Burma-Shave signs of the 1930s. Keep on Going – Don't be Late – See You There – We Start at 8!

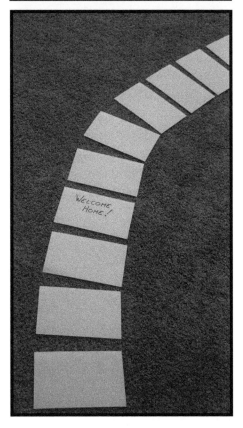

There are (at least) two different ways to use the welcome mat approach. You can create a path with hundreds of index cards (the yellow brick road approach) or you can individually place single index cards in key locations to help your audience find their way.

You can also use the welcome mat approach as a method for inspiring your audience, with positive slogans, quotes, sayings and directed messages (Happy Birthday Phil!).

If you choose to place your welcome mats on the floor, you might want to fasten these cards in place using blue painter's masking tape (which is easily removed) so that they do not blow away with the wind or become scattered as your participants walk over them. You can also laminate your cards (making them a bit more resilient to footprints).

What is most surprising about welcome mats is that most people look for information and directions on signs which are typically fastened to walls and vertical surfaces. The unique location of a welcome mat, especially one with a highly visible color, almost ensures that people will see it (and read it), even if they happen to walk over it at first.

In the 1864 science fiction novel *Journey to the Center of the Earth* by Jules Verne, cryptic messages are left by a 16th-century Icelandic alchemist, Arne Saknussemm. The initials A.S. occasionally appear along the path, helping the three explorers as they journey deeper and deeper into the earth. Which brings about a novel use for the welcome mat. If you happen to be interested in "escape rooms" you can use welcome mats to provide clues for the escape rooms you create. You can find a collection of escape room activities in the book *Teambuilding Puzzles* (ISBN 978-0-7575-7040-7) written by Mike Anderson, Jim Cain, Chris Cavert and Tom Heck, available from Kendall Hunt Publishers (www.kendallhunt.com). You can also download a PDF document on designing escape rooms at www.teamworkandteamplay.com.

6-18 A LITERARY SCAVENGER HUNT

Choosing the right book is the key!

For this book-based activity, you'll need an index score card and pen for each person and a collection of books. Invite each person to randomly choose one of the books available, ranging in content, illustrations, subject matter, size, weight, language and binding.

Then provide the following instructions, either verbally or written on a large flip chart or blackboard. Instruct each person to keep score of the points accumulated by the book they chose. Provide a prize (perhaps a book!) for the person with the highest score at the end of this activity.

1. One point for every number mentioned as a word on page 11. For example "three."
2. One point for every time the word "the" appears on the front, back or spine cover.
3. One point for every use of punctuation other than a period, on page 99.
4. Five points for every use of a woman's name on page 76.
5. Ten points for each time the letter z appears on page 27.
6. Ten points for each time the letter y appears in the table of contents.
7. Seven points for each illustration or photograph on pages 10, 11, 12, 13 and 14.
8. One point for every comma on page 17.
9. Twenty points for each word printed in *italics* on page 8.
10. One point for every chapter in the book.
11. Ten points if the book has an index of more than three pages.
12. One point for each word in the main title of the book.
13. Five points if the author's full name (no initials) is present on the inside title page.
14. Five points if the book has no ISBN number (978-0-4545-8761-2).
15. Ten points for a book published before 1959.
16. Twenty points for a book written in a foreign language.
17. Ten points to the heaviest book selected by a member of the group.
18. A bonus of 20 points for any book with a color illustration in the first chapter.
19. A bonus of 10 points for any book with a photograph on the front book cover.
20. A bonus of 5 points for any book with a dedication to a single person.

Simply acquainting people with a book may entice sufficient interest for them to take a closer look, or possibly even read it. This can be a brilliant way to encourage students to read.

I believe, without a doubt, that a library card is one of the most powerful things in the entire world. With one, you can open up a world of learning, entertainment, education, novelty, inspiration and more. Bookstores are great, too, but most libraries are free! Visit yours today!

6-19 CREATIVE GROUP FORMATION

Organizing large groups into smaller ones.

Here is a group formation activity in which you can not only organize a large audience into smaller, uniform size groups, but also impart a little learning or subject matter content in the process.

First decide what number of people you would like in each smaller group. Then organize a similar number of index cards for each group, and fill each card with unique information, so that when participants meet each other and share information, they will immediately know they belong together.

For example, if you want groups of four and you select Abraham Lincoln as one of your topics, you can include additional cards that describe key elements of his life. For example, the four cards could include Abraham Lincoln, 16th President of the United States, Gave the famous *Gettysburg Address*, Championed the Emancipation Proclamation. You might also include a photograph or illustration, a famous quotation, biographical information, etc.

Other potential collections of cards include elements to a recipe for chocolate chip cookies, lines from a familiar (or not so familiar) poem, historical dates of importance, lyrics from popular songs, multiple photographs from different perspectives of the same object, the opening lines of classic literature, historical figures and their contributions to society, illustrations of several works of art by the same artist, objects which are united by a unique theme (such as things made of plastic or action figures from a popular movie).

With this style of group formation, participants will have to think carefully when meeting others, and decide whether they are both part of a greater whole or not. Such investigation is a creative way to impart facts and knowledge on your audience, while at the same time creating the smaller groups you desire. You can, for example, include subject matter from your latest classroom lesson or from a lesson you are about to deliver (as a way of gauging the interest or knowledge of your audience before delivering your content).

There are any number of interesting books filled with completely useless information and trivia, where you can find dozens of suitable topics for this activity. Try searching for *Schott's Original Miscellany* (ISBN 978-1-5823-4349-7) by Ben Schott or *The Uncyclopedia* (ISBN 978-1-4013-0153-3) by Gideon Haigh. You can also find content in books of popular poetry, song lyrics, classic dialog from movies and TV shows, biographies of interesting people, historical information, mathematical formulas and equations, etc.

6-20 HEY BUDDY, CAN'T YOU READ THE SIGN?

Exploring diversity through language.

If you have ever traveled to a different part of the world, even the simplest instructions take on a whole new meaning when they are written in a language that is foreign to you. Some traffic signs carry universal pictograms which are helpful, but in many cases, words are typically written only in the local language.

Here are a few unique signs from around the world that I have collected over the years. See if you can figure out what each sign is trying to convey. I've also included a few signs that I have personally seen during my travels.

If you would like to share this activity with your next audience, I recommend typing in some standard sign language into www.translate.google.com and then translating it into another language. Prepare about a dozen signs by writing the translations onto index cards (with a hint on the back of each, such as where the sign might be seen). Then invite your audience to translate as many signs as possible. Bonus points if they find some humor in the translation and maximum points if they translate all the signs correctly.

One of my first conundrums in the language of signs happened when I traveled to Veracruz, Mexico, for the first time. After dinner one evening, I ventured to the rest rooms and discovered that they were only marked with a single letter each, M and H. I didn't want to make the mistake of entering the wrong room, so I waited for someone to come out. I learned later that the M stands for Mujeres (Women) and the H stands for Hombres (Men).

You can find dozens of interesting and unusual signs by searching the internet. For more amusing signs from around the world, see the book *Signspotting* by Doug Lansky (ISBN 978-1-74179-182-2).

CHAPTER SEVEN

BONUS ACTIVITIES

This seventh chapter is my last chance to share with you some rather unique card activities that didn't fit easily into one of the previous chapters. I hope you enjoy this eclectic collection of cool things to do with index and playing cards.

NO.	ACTIVITY NAME	TEACHABLE MOMENT	IDEAL GROUP SIZE
7-1	Monster Cookies	Tasty Cookie Recipes	Any!
7-2	Prayer Cards	A Community of Faith	6 or more
7-3	Things Are Not What They Appear	Fact versus Fiction	Any
7-4	Mind Reading Magic	Magic!	Any
7-5	Word Count	Linguistic Problem Solving	Any
7-6	Everyday Haiku	Poetic Forms	Any
7-7	Flat Dice	A Lesson in Probability	Any
7-8	Dance Cards	A Historical Perspective	20 or more people
7-9	Gratitude Cards	Reflecting on Gratitude	Any
7-10	He Can Do Little	Observation & Replication	Any
7-11	Redacted Poetry	Creative Expression	Any
7-12	The Box Maze	Trial and Error Solution	Any
7-13	Zoom	Communication Activity	20 or more people
7-14	Five Rooms Puzzle	Puzzle	Any
7-15	The Phonetic Alphabet	Communication	Any
7-16	First Flight	Creative Problem Solving	Any
7-17	Unblind Square	Leadership	Either or more
7-18	Honest Playing Cards	Learning to Play Cards	Tables of 4
7-19	Guess Who?	Icebreaker	10 or more people
7-20	The Gratitude Jar	Thankfulness	Any
7-21	21 Questions for Building Positive Relationships	Working Together	Partners or small groups

7-1 MONSTER COOKIES

Index cards as recipe cards.

One classic use for 3x5 index cards is recipe cards. Long before we had tablet computers in the kitchen (with downloaded recipes) all of our favorite things to make (and eat) were contained in these valuable metal boxes. Here are three of my favorite treats from around the world. Enjoy any of these variations of the classic oatmeal cookie recipe with a tall glass of cold milk.

MONSTER COOKIES (JANET BORTON, WOOSTER, OHIO, USA)

Double Batch		Full Batch		1/2 Batch		Ingredients
2	lb	1	lb	0.5	lb	Brown Sugar - Light
4	cup	2	cup	1	cup	White Sugar
8	tsp	4	tsp	2	tsp	Baking Soda
18	cup	9	cup	4.5	cup	Quick Oatmeal (1 box = 8 cups)
1	lb	0.5	lb	0.25	lb	Butterscotch Chips
1	lb	½	lb	¼	lb	Nuts – Pecans
1	lb	½	lb	¼	lb	Coconut Flakes
12		6		3		Eggs
1	tbsp	0.5	tbsp	0.25	tbsp	Corn Syrup
1	lb	0.5	lb	0.25	lb	Butter (not margarine)
3	lb	1.5	lb	0.75	lb	Peanut Butter - Crunchy
1	tbsp	0.5	tbsp	0.25	tbsp	Vanilla

Mix dry ingredients first, then add melted butter and peanut butter to vanilla, eggs and corn syrup and mix in a very large bowl. Place 8 cookies per sheet, flatten and bake at 350F degrees for 12-14 minutes.

When Janet's son Tim came to work with me as an intern one summer, he brought a large plastic container filled with his Mom's Monster Cookies (so named because they were monstrously large). Janet also had a house full of hungry boys, so she often made dozens of cookies at a time. One morning at breakfast, as Tim and I were planning our work for the day, I looked over at Tim and said in a solemn voice, "Tim, I'm just not sure this is working out. I thought we had an agreement, but obviously something has gone horribly wrong." I then showed Tim the nearly empty container of Monster Cookies, and his reply was swift. "I can fix this," he said, and a phone call and three days later we had a fresh batch of Monster Cookies, saving Tim's internship! Thanks Janet.

Flap Jacks (United Kingdom)

Melt and mix these three ingredients first: 2 tablespoons light corn syrup or golden syrup, ½ cup butter, ½ cup brown sugar. Then add 2 cups of rolled oats. Option: add ½ cup pecan pieces.

Bake 20-25 minutes at 350F degrees, middle shelf, on a greased pan. When cool, cut into bars.

I first discovered this delightful variation of oatmeal cookies in York, England. While golden syrup is common in the UK, you might have to look a little harder for it in North America or elsewhere in the world. Be careful not to add too much or too little syrup, or your Flap Jacks will turn out hard as bricks, or crumbly.

ANZAC Biscuits (Australia New Zealand Army Corps)

* 1 cup quick cooking oats
* 1 cup dry unsweetened shredded coconut
* 2 tsp ground ginger
* 2 tbsp boiling water
* 1 tbsp golden syrup

* 1 cup all-purpose flour
* 1 cup brown sugar
* 1 1/2 tsp baking soda
* 1/2 cup butter

1. Preheat oven to 350F degrees (175C degrees). Grease 2 baking sheets. Mix quick oats, flour, coconut, brown sugar, and ginger in a bowl. With your fingers, make a well in the center of the dry ingredients.
2. Dissolve the baking soda in boiling water. In a small saucepan, melt the butter, and stir in the golden syrup to combine. Pour in the dissolved baking soda, and pour the mixture into the well in the dry ingredients. Stir lightly until just combined; drop by rounded tablespoon about 2 inches apart onto the prepared baking sheets.
3. Bake in the preheated oven until the cookies are golden brown, 10 to 12 minutes.

I was invited to Australia a few years ago, and upon my arrival in Melbourne, I discovered some snacks had been laid out for me. Among the teas, jams and breads I discovered a package of delicious ANZAC Biscuits, named after the treats that families sent to enlisted personnel during the great wars. They're a little harder than a typical oatmeal cookie (so they survived the shipping to foreign lands), but yummy!

The index card file shown here and on the first page of recipes was my Mother's. Some of the best food of my childhood came from this tiny metal box. My favorite is elderberry pie, which my Mom baked for my birthday every year! Thanks, Mom.

7-2 PRAYER CARDS

Using index cards in prayer.

During my collection of activities for this book project, I compiled a large stack of ideas from friends, colleagues, facilitators, teachers, trainers and group leaders of all kinds. Some are obviously contributed by teachers, others by camp staff members, still others by corporate trainers. But of all the index card activities I have experienced, one of the most powerful is one that I used at a church retreat many years ago.

The college-age retreat participants had gathered after dinner for some social recreation and at the end of the evening I presented the group with a table full of index cards, some colorful pens and markers, and a roll of masking tape. Each person wrote down one specific thing that they were currently praying about and attached this to their back.

Then, as the group mingled, whenever someone honored the prayer request written on your back, they would simply place a hand on your shoulder as they prayed with you. This simple point of contact helped many in the group feel connected and empowered by the support they received from the community at large.

This can be a powerful activity to share with your camp staff, campers, retreat participants, families and religious communities of all kinds.

 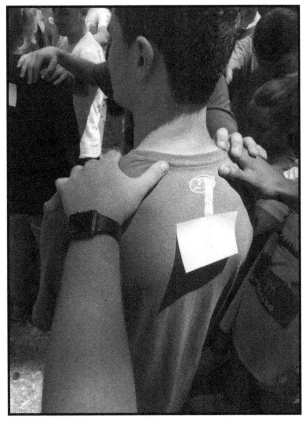

Soularium cards (ISBN 978-0-5733-4062-6) are a unique deck of photo cards with a Christian focus, available from www.CruPress.com. These cards and their images are designed to initiate discussions about faith and more.

7-3 THINGS ARE NOT WHAT THEY APPEAR

A collection of things that are different from their names.

It turns out that there are many things out there that are not exactly as they appear. I found more than a dozen in my daily life, and you can too! For example, a 2x4 piece of lumber is not actually 2 inches by 4 inches. It actually measures 1.50 inches by 3.50 inches!

Below you will find a collection of familiar things that are not what they appear. Prepare a collection of index cards for this activity, with the following things printed on the front side of a card, and the truth about that particular item on the back side of the card. Then see if your audience can separate fact from fiction when it comes to describing each of the following things.

After completing this activity, invite your audience to generate a list of additional "things that are not what they appear."

The item in question	**The truth about that item**
In the history of the United States, how many lakes in the northeastern part of the country have ever been given "great lakes" status?	Six: Erie, Huron, Ontario, Michigan, Superior and Lake Champlain (temporarily).
Catgut	Does not come from cats, it is made from the intestines of horses and sheep.
Where are Panama hats from?	Ecuador.
What is a camel's hair brush made of?	Squirrel fur.
Czechoslovakia	Is now divided into two countries: The Czech Republic and Slovakia.
Where is the lead in a lead pencil?	There is none, a pencil is made of graphite.
Guinea Pig	Is not a pig, it is a rodent.
Prairie Dog	Is not a dog, it too is a rodent.
Groundhogs	Are not hogs, they too are rodents.
The Cincinnati airport (location?)	It is located in Kentucky, not Ohio! The Cincinnati / Northern Kentucky Airport
Johnny Cake	Is not a cake, it is a type of bread.
Gingerbread	Is not bread at all, it is a type of cake.
Arabic Numbers	Are not from Arabic countries, they originally came from India.
The Hundred Years War	Actually lasted 116 years, from 1337 to 1453.
A Church Key	Used to open cans and bottles, not churches!

7-4 A MIND READING MAGIC TRICK

I can predict exactly what you are going to say.

I saved this great index card activity for the last chapter of this book. This magic trick is an easy way to get a quick laugh from your audience. There is nothing really profound here, just a fun way to entertain your audience. And best of all, you get to be the magician!

Start with a blank index card and a marker. Invite a member of your audience to pick a number between 1 and 1,000 (without sharing that number aloud). Then tell your volunteer that you can read their mind (as you write your prediction on the card) and you will write down exactly what they will say.

Then ask your volunteer, "Is the number 461?" At first they may look disappointed or confused as they say, "No." At this point, you produce the index card, with the word "NO" clearly printed on it in big block letters. Take a bow, magician. You are truly able to read minds!

You can find other impossible tricks to astound your friends in *Bet You Can't Do This!* by Sandy Ransford (ISBN 978-0-330-39772-9). Also check out the book, *The Compass in Your Nose and Other Astonishing Facts About Humans* by Marc McCutcheon (ISBN 978-0-8747-7544-2).

7-5 WORD COUNT

Making several words into many.

Here is a challenging word activity that you can play solo, with friends or in any size group. Begin with any collection of three words and write these at the top of an index card. For my personal example, I'll use the letters of my formal name, but you can use any three words you like.

Next, use any of these letters to form new words of five or more letters and write these on your index card. Bonus points for words consisting of ten or more letters and maximum points if you manage to form a single word using all the letters of the three words provided. Here are just a few of the words I can create from the fifteen letters in my name.

JAMES HALLIE CAIN

Miscellanea	Mescaline	Machines	Manacles	Chinese
Alliances	Jicama	Jasmin	Maniacs	Cinema
Lichens	Chains	Animals	Cleanse	Silence
Inhale	Chimes	Shaman	Chisel	Inches
Lance	Cleans	Enamel	Amnesia	Almanacs

You can probably generate an extensive list of words made from the letters of your own name. If you are having difficulties finding longer words made from those letters, there are a few websites that can be helpful: www.wordfinder.yourdictionary.com and www.word-grabber.com are both word generator websites that allow you to input letters and output various (English) words.

7-6 EVERYDAY HAIKU

And other poetic forms.

Index cards are the perfect size for expressing short messages, quotations, sayings and poetic forms of all kinds. After sharing the basic elements of these poetic structures, invite your audience to compose their own index card–sized masterpieces.

For example, a Haiku is a very simple Japanese poetic form with three lines consisting of five syllables in the first line, seven in the second line and five in the third line. The first poem on the left side is a little Haiku I wrote while formatting the content of this page. The second Haiku is a funny one, that probably only makes sense to poets and people who know what a Haiku is!

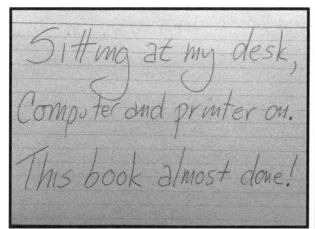

But Haiku is not the only poetic form worth exploring. Indeed, there are more than a dozen different and unique forms. For example, Dr. Seuss often wrote in iambic pentameter, with five "feet" per line. Music has a beat. Poems have feet. Shakespeare wrote sonnets. Shel Silverstein wrote in rhyme in his books *Where the Sidewalk Ends, A Light in the Attic* and *Falling Up.* But one of my all-time favorite poets is Brian Andreas who writes in free verse. He created the very unique, often humorous and occasionally poignant *Story People* (ISBN 978-0-9642-6604-0).

Other poetic forms include the limerick (a humorous five-line poem), concrete poems (which take the shape of the object they discuss, such as a stop sign octagon) and the quatrain (a four-line poem that usually rhymes).

The next time you want to add some artistry to the reviewing and debriefing component of your teambuilding program, consider inviting your audience to present their final comments for the day in one of these poetic forms. No doubt some of these gems will be worth sharing and saving!

You can find poetic forms in many places. Ernest Clive recently bought the quatrain into focus in his book *Ready Player One* (ISBN 978-0-307-88744-3). James Rogauskas is fairly irreverent with his presentation of *Office Haiku* (ISBN 978-0-312-35248-4). For even more historical and occasionally hysterical poetry, search the internet for your particular poetic form of choice.

7-7 FLAT DICE

Mathematical probabilities.

You probably know, if you have ever played with dice, that the probability of seven is higher than any other combination when throwing a pair of dice. But what if you wanted to create a collection of dice with an even possibility of throwing any number. Is it possible? Not surprisingly, the answer is yes!

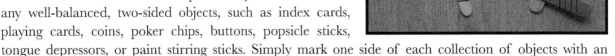

You can make a set of even probability dice from almost any well-balanced, two-sided objects, such as index cards, playing cards, coins, poker chips, buttons, popsicle sticks, tongue depressors, or paint stirring sticks. Simply mark one side of each collection of objects with an increasing range of the numbers 1, 2, 4, 8, etc. and leave the other side blank.

With the collection of four sticks shown here, your two-sided dice can have a range of zero to fifteen, and every one of those numbers has an even probability of occurring. You can verify this by throwing your dice 100 times and recording the outcomes. If you happen to notice some irregularity in the distribution of totals, one or more of your objects may be unbalanced or have the tendency to drop the same way no matter how it is thrown. If you do get a flat distribution for your choice of dice, then you have created something mathematically random (which is no small task).

Unlike regular dice, the four even-probability (EP) dice mentioned here include zero and one as potential totals, as well as 13, 14, and 15.

If you have a single EP stick (die), you have a range of zero or one. Add a second stick and your range increases from zero to three. Add a third stick and now your range is zero to seven. A fourth stick (like the example shown) has a range of zero to fifteen, and a fifth stick increases the range from zero to thirty-one.

Once you have created your own set of even probability dice, your next adventure will be to substitute these new dice for standard dice in any of your favorite board games. Enjoy!

Let's compare the probabilities (%) of each of the following totals, for a pair of standard (fair) dice and the four even-probability (EP) flat dice mentioned here.

Total Value	0	1	2	3	4	5	6	7	8	9	10	11	12	13	14	15
Std. Dice	0	0	2.8	5.6	8.3	11.1	13.9	16.7	13.9	11.1	8.3	5.6	2.8	0	0	0
EP Dice	6.25	6.25	6.25	6.25	6.25	6.25	6.25	6.25	6.25	6.25	6.25	6.25	6.25	6.25	6.25	6.25

As you can see, if you create a collection of well-balanced even-probability dice, you'll always have the same possibility of throwing any of the numbers within the range available. That should make some of your favorite board games interesting!

7-8 DANCE CARDS

Is your dance card full?

It might seem that index cards and dancing are an odd combination, but dance cards were quite fashionable a century ago. In fact, thanks to Karen Canning and Jim Kimball of Geneseo, New York, the authentic dance card featuring the Brockport (where I now live!) Orchestra from 1877 is shown here.

Dance cards presented not only a program for the event, but also the opportunity to meet and dance with others, capture their names and have a memento to take home after the event.

While not from the same time period, the dance known as Polster Tanc (or the pillow dance) combines dancing with index cards! The dance begins with one dancer standing in the center of the room, holding a single large index card. During the music for the first part of the song (a waltz), this dancer mimics a leaf blowing in the wind as they twirl around the center of the room, while also looking for the person that will be their next partner. In the second part of the music, the single dancer places the index card at the feet of their chosen partner and both dancers kneel (in ballroom position) dancing slowly to the music of the second part of the song. In the third (and slightly more upbeat) part of the music, both dancers stand and dance together (polka) around the room. At the completion of this third part of the dance, the index card is torn in half, with each dancer receiving one piece. The three dance movements are repeated the second time through the dance (waltz, slow dance, polka) and the index cards are again torn in half.

The number of dancers increases as the song continues (1, 2, 4, 8, 16, 32, 64...) and the size of the index card decreases proportionally as well.

I first learned Polster Tanc at the Buckeye Leadership Workshop (www.buckeyeleadership.com) held annually at the Recreation Unlimited Conference Center in Ashley, Ohio in the spring of each year. This is one of my favorite places on earth to learn all kinds of recreational activities, including teambuilding, quilting, games leadership, social dancing, icebreakers, crafts, storytelling, song leading and many, many more. The version of Polster Tanc that I enjoy was recorded by the Duquesne University Tamburitzans for Folk Dancer Record Service, copyright 1950. Michael Herman Folk Dance Series MH 45-3034 B.

7-9 GRATITUDE CARDS

Gratitude—the quality of being thankful.

While the Thank You Cards activity in this book focused on thanking others, the Gratitude Cards generated here are for the benefit of the writers themselves.

In the book *59 Seconds*, Richard Wiseman reveals that having people list three things that they are grateful for in their life or to reflect on three events that have gone especially well recently can significantly increase their level of happiness for about a month. This, in turn, can cause them to be more optimistic about the future and can improve their physical health.

Making a Gratitude Card is a reminder that each of us indeed has things in our lives for which to be grateful: good health, family, friends, pets, adventures and more.

Invite your audience to take an index card and write down three things for which they are grateful and then share these three things with others in groups of three to five people. At the completion of this activity, encourage participants to take these Gratitude Cards and post them (on their refrigerator, in their office, on the dashboard of their car, or in some other convenient and visible space that they are likely to see every day).

If you happen to have a creative or artistic audience, visit Pinterest.com for some truly amazing and artistic ways to express thankfulness and gratitude, including many versions with index cards.

I have had the opportunity to visit more than thirty countries so far and one of the first things I try to learn when I visit a new country is how to say hello and thank you in the local dialect. With only these two phrases, you'd be surprised how easy it is to connect with people around the world. Next time you travel to a foreign country, try learning these two phrases before you arrive.

You can find this and many other great activities in the book, *100 Activities That Build Unity, Community & Connection* (ISBN 978-1-60679-374-9) by Jim Cain, available from www.healthylearning.com and www. training-wheels.com.

7-10 HE CAN DO LITTLE

Entertainment fun around the table.

This classic entertainment has been around for over 100 years. While seated around a table (perhaps after a dinner party or a meal at summer camp), one person grabs an index card and taps the table multiple times while saying, "He can do little that cannot do this!" and then passes the card to the next person. The challenge is for members of the audience to replicate exactly what the first person has done (card tapping and the phrase "He can do little that cannot do this!"). Any dinner guest who correctly replicates the task is commended. If incorrect, the guest passes the card on to the next person at the table. The secret of the task is that the card must be tapped using the right hand but passed to the next person using the left hand.

7-11 REDACTED POETRY

Creative expression.

I saw the angel in the marble and carved until I set him free.
—Michelangelo

Italian painter, sculptor, architect and poet Michelangelo di Lodovico Buonarroti Simoni once replied, "Every block of stone has a statue inside it and it is the task of the sculptor to discover it." So too, is the art of redacted poetry. Redacted, or blackout poetry, begins with a page from a newspaper, magazine or book and the artist removes all the words that do not contribute to the final message they wish to convey. Austin Kleon popularized this form of poetry with his book, *Newspaper Blackout* (ISBN 978-0-0617-3297-3).

One of the ideal resources for this unique style of poetry are those old *Reader's Digest* condensed books found in garage sales, library sales and secondhand stores, usually quite cheaply. These books tend to be excellent choices because they seldom include language or text that is sensational or profane. Rather, they provide a single page of text that lends itself to the creation of a redacted poem, after first inviting the artist to read the content and decide for themselves what is worth keeping and what can be discarded.

7-12 THE BOX MAZE

If at first you don't succeed, try, try again.

Sure, there are thousands of mazes out there, but this simple maze is one of the most challenging that I know. You can transfer the grid provided to a large index card or print it on an index card using the instructions found in the reference section of this book.

Think of each square in this grid as a room in a maze. Beginning with the room marked with an X, reach the exit by passing through all of the other rooms, by going in and out of each of the other rooms only once.

EXIT

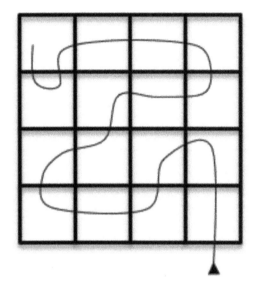

The solution to this maze puzzle can be found in the subtle way the original challenge was written. Pass in and out of each of the <u>other rooms</u> just once. Leaving some creative wiggling room for the solution shown here.

7-13 ZOOM

Make a book into a deck of cards.

An interesting communication activity can be created by trimming the binding from the book *Zoom* by Istvan Banyai and turning the pages into a series of cards. Then shuffle these card pages, distribute them to your audience (one page per person) and see if they can place the pages in the correct order by communicating the content of each page verbally (without showing the actual page).

Zoom and *Re-Zoom* by Istvan Banyai are wordless picture books that follow a unique theme: that of a zoom lens as it progresses through a series of thirty pages, from close-up to a panoramic view. The sequence in *Zoom* is a bit easier to follow, especially for younger audiences. In the book *Re-Zoom*, the distance between illustrations is larger and placing the cards in order is more challenging.

7-14 FIVE ROOMS PUZZLE

Can you cross all the walls just once, with one continuous line?

Five Rooms is a classic puzzle in topology (the study of geometrical properties and spatial relationships). But don't let those big words scare you, this puzzle is challenging and fun! Best of all, you won't even need a pencil to do this puzzle. You can use a piece of string instead.

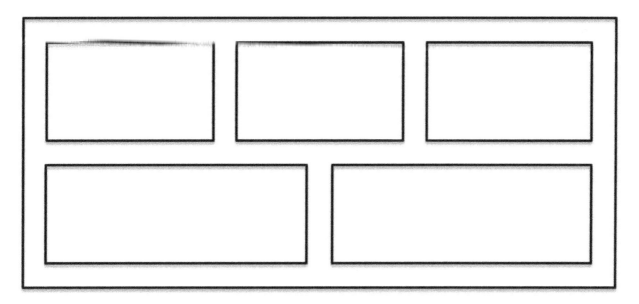

The challenge is to see if you can construct a continuous line that passes through each of the sixteen walls exactly once each. The smaller illustration below has disconnected each wall segment so that you can clearly see each of the sixteen individual wall segments.

Draw the outline of the five-room puzzle on a large index card. Then use a piece of string to trace your path (instead of drawing with a pencil) until you find a solution. One possible (rule bending, but not breaking) solution is shown below. You can also print this five-room drawing on a large index card. See the reference chapter of this book for more information about printing on index cards.

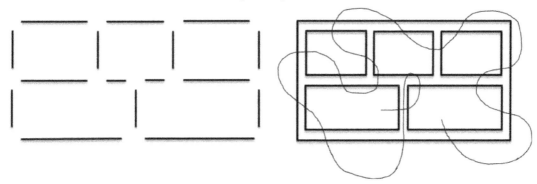

You can find this puzzle and ninety-nine more in *Teambuilding Puzzles* (ISBN 978-0-7575-7040-7) by Mike Anderson, Jim Cain, Chris Cavert and Tom Heck, available from Kendall Hunt Publishers (www.kendallhunt.com).

7-15 THE PHONETIC ALPHABET

Using symbols to convey sounds

One of the clearest methods of conveying phonetic sounds using symbols is the phonetic alphabet. To create the cards for this activity, you can begin with blank index cards (on which you write the capital letters of the alphabet on one side and the phonetic alphabet on the other) or purchase a deck of alphabet cards from your local educational store and write the phonetic alphabet on the back side of each alphabetic character card. Here is the official phonetic alphabet:

A	Alpha	H	Hotel	O	Oscar	V	Victor
B	Bravo	I	India	P	Papa	W	Whiskey
C	Charlie	J	Juliet	Q	Quebec	X	X-Ray
D	Delta	K	Kilo	R	Romeo	Y	Yankee
E	Echo	L	Lima	S	Sierra	Z	Zulu
F	Foxtrot	M	Mike	T	Tango		
G	Golf	N	November	U	Uniform		

The Phonetic Alphabet is officially denoted as the International Radiotelephony Spelling Alphabet and is largely used by the military for representing sounds with symbols.

After creating cards for each letter of the phonetic alphabet, invite your audience to spell their full name phonetically using these cards.

7-16 FIRST FLIGHT

Keeping an index card up in the air.

On December 17, 1903, at 10:35 a.m., Orville and Wilbur Wright demonstrated heavier-than-air flight was possible as they flew their airplane for twelve seconds, covering a distance of 120 feet.

Now, more than 100 years later, you too can attempt to perform a similar task, by keeping a heavier-than-air index card aloft for twelve or more seconds.

For this challenge, you can fold the paper in any manner you like but you cannot add anything to it (such as adhesives or additional weight). Once released, you cannot physically touch the card until it reaches the ground.

Some of the more creative (and successful) techniques used in this activity include placing the index card on a wall and having a team of four or more people blow air against the card for the duration of twelve seconds (not an easy task). Another method is to drop the index card from a great height, especially if there is wind. Folding the index card into a paper airplane, helicopter or spinning wheel typically prolongs the flight time.

If you'd like to read more about the history of flight, try reading *The Wright Way—7 Problem-Solving Principles from the Wright Brothers That Can Make Your Business Soar* by Mark Eppler (ISBN 978-0-8144-0797-8) and *To Conquer the Air—The Wright Brothers and The Great Race for Flight* by James Tobin (ISBN 978-0-7432-5536-4).

7-17 UNBLIND SQUARE

Using a rope to explore leadership.

Many facilitators know a version of the activity Blind Square where blindfolded participants find a rope and then attempt to create a perfect square with it. No blindfolds are needed for this sighted but still challenging version of creating shapes with rope. You'll need about 2 feet of rope for each participant (eight to fifty people) for this activity. For twenty-five participants, 50 feet (15 meters) of rope is ideal. Then sketch the four shapes featured here onto four large index cards, one shape per card.

Begin by inviting each of your participants to grasp the rope. Then ask a participant standing near the ends of the rope to tie these ends together with a knot. Throughout this activity group members may slide their hands along the rope, but they cannot let go or move past any other participant.

Show one participant in the group the first illustration of a perfect square. Instruct this person to lead the group (without letting go) in creating this shape with the rope. Provide feedback on their leadership performance. Did the leader, for example, just give instructions (telling) or rather communicate the exact shape to the group (shared vision)?

Next, show a different participant the second illustration (the hourglass shape) and ask them to lead the group in creating this shape with the rope. Again, discuss the leadership required to successfully complete the task.

Then show the entire group the third illustration (the three-triangle hazard symbol) and invite them to create this more challenging shape. This trial begins with everyone in the group knowing the shape required and typically creates a sense of shared leadership.

Conclude by showing the group the star image and ask them to create this shape with the rope. The star is a very challenging shape, especially with a rope that has been tied into a circle. But who tied that knot? The facilitator? No, the participants themselves! Once a group comes to this conclusion, they typically untie the knot to complete the task. Debrief this activity based upon the leadership, communication, problem-solving and teamwork capabilities of the group.

If you want to additionally challenge your participants, consider having them construct a three-dimensional rope shape, rather than the two-dimensional shapes shown. Or have them begin with their rope circle on the ground and time them through multiple attempts to create a challenging rope shape in the least amount of time possible. You can also challenge a large group by using a rather small length of rope. This will bring them much closer together. A greater variety of rope shapes, letters, words, and numbers are possible if you use an unknotted rope (with two ends) rather than one that has been knotted into a rope circle.

You can find this activity and many more in the book *Rope Games* (ISBN 978-0-9882046-1-4) by Jim Cain. You can also find equipment for this activity in the *Rope Games Kit*. Both are available from Training Wheels, Inc. at 1-888-553-0147 or www.training-wheels.com.

7-18 HONEST PLAYING CARDS

An honorable way to play cards.

If you have ever struggled to teach a child how to play a new card game, here is an easy solution—Honest Playing Cards! The original thought I had was to create transparent playing cards, so that players could see each of the cards in other people's hands. All I had to do was replace standard copier paper in my printer with overhead transparency stock and print out a whole deck of cards. But then I thought of an easier way, simply glue two identical cards together, so that the card can be seen from both directions. But even that solution has its drawbacks. Double cards are not easy to shuffle! So after a bit of experimentation, I stumbled onto the easiest and least expensive solution of all, create your own playing cards using index cards and draw the suit and value on each side of the card. You can actually create some artistically unique cards in the process.

No more waiting to find out what your cards are during a deal or wondering if your neighbor has an ace. No more explaining the rules over and over. No more wondering what the next card in the pickup pile might be. Now each player can clearly see the whole range of cards on the table and in other player's hands.

A few of the more artistic cards I've seen include the Fine Line deck of playing cards from Dear Adam (www.dearadamobjects.com) and a "homemade" card deck that I found one Christmas at Bed, Bath and Beyond.

If you choose to create your own cards, index cards do work, but a better choice might be to visit your local teacher's supply store and purchase card stock or flash cards. These have rounded corners, just like regular playing cards.

7-19 GUESS WHO?

Getting to know others.

For your next gathering, try this simple icebreaker. Invite everyone attending to write three interesting things about themselves on a small index card. Bonus points for things that are unusual or unknown to others in the room.

Next, decide which version of the game you prefer. You can either shuffle the deck of cards, deal one card to each person present, and invite everyone to search for the owner of the card they hold. Or, you can post all cards to a bulletin board or wall so that during breaks, members of your audience can read each card and write on each card who they believe owns that card.

7-20 THE GRATITUDE JAR

A full year of thankfulness.

A few years ago, I visited my friend Shawn Moriarty and his wife Jen. Shawn is a talented outdoor educator and creator of the ecological Sudoku-like activity found in Chapter 6 of this book.

One night, while we were having dinner together, I noticed a unique glass jar on a shelf next to the dining room table. When I asked Shawn what it was, he told me the story of their gratitude jar.

Shawn and Jen decided that they would use the jar to keep track of all the wonderful moments they experienced throughout the year. Every time something wonderful happened to them, they would take an index card and write down a brief note describing the event and place it into the jar. Then, on New Year's Eve, they would pour out the contents of the jar and read all the index cards, reflecting with gratitude for the wonderful things that they had experienced throughout the year.

I thought it was such a wonderful idea that I made my own version of the jar when I returned

home, and even made duplicates for my entire family as Christmas presents that year. It is an outstanding way to remember all the wonderful things, big and small, that happen to us each year.

During my first visit to China, at the end of a conference, I was presented with a "fun box'" of inspirational words, thank you notes and expressions of gratitude from the participants in my workshop. This box reminded me of the gratitude jar concept and remains a treasured keepsake of my first visit to Beijing, China.

7-21 21 QUESTIONS FOR BUILDING POSITIVE RELATIONSHIPS

Working together successfully

For me, there are three essential elements necessary to create a high-performance organization—a worthy task; a chance to continuously grow, improve and learn new things; and the opportunity to build and maintain positive working relationships.

The relationship component is one of the most challenging and least supported of these three essential elements, so I have compiled the following twenty-one questions specifically designed to help new teams create a positive working relationship. I recommend that you share these questions with partners and small groups (of up to six people) at the very beginning of their time together and ask them to explore these questions as a way of getting to know each other, establishing trust, honesty, and open communication.

My favorite way to conduct this activity is to invite two people that need to work successfully together in the future to share these twenty-one questions over a long meal together. In many ways, this single event can be the most productive way to spend an hour or two at the very beginning of a new assignment or project.

On the following page you'll find a collection of twenty-one questions. To make your own set of cards, transfer these questions and their associated number onto twenty-one index cards. These questions are designed to be explored in order, building trust as the questions progress. You'll need one deck of twenty-one cards for each group participating in this activity.

The first seven questions are simple, general questions that most people will find easy to discuss. The second seven questions go deeper and require a higher level of honesty and disclosure. The final seven questions get to the heart of working together successfully. These twenty-one index cards filled with twenty-one questions of increasing honesty and disclosure are designed to unite your partners, teams and their organizations and identify attributes that may need improvement before this group can function at their highest ability. These questions work best with partners or small work groups of up to six people. Because of the intimate nature of the conversation generated by these questions, groups larger than six people are not recommended.

The twenty-one questions in this relationship-building activity were specifically chosen for occupational (work) relationships, not romantic (couple) or family relationships, which operate best with a slightly different set of rules and boundaries. But suffice to say that all relationships can benefit from open and honest conversation and communication.

Ed Daugherty, director of the outdoor program at Davidson College, shared with me that two trip leaders are chosen for each section of the multiday trek program they call the Odyssey. The cohesiveness of the leaders in working together was an essential part of the success or failure of this wilderness program. In an effort to improve that partnership, trip leaders often explore a collection of relationship questions before joining forces on an expedition. Open and honest conversation at the very beginning of their time together greatly improved the quality of the trip leaders' teamwork.

Coming together is a beginning.
Keeping together is progress.
Working together is success.
—Henry Ford

7-21 21 QUESTIONS FOR BUILDING POSITIVE RELATIONSHIPS

1. Tell me the story of your name.
2. Find three things you have in common.
3. Outside of work, what matters most to you?
4. What are you grateful for?
5. What are your pet peeves? What annoys you?
6. What inspires you?
7. What have you done big or small that makes the world a better place?

8. What skills do you bring to this task?
9. Discuss five events in your life that have brought you here today.
10. What do you need in order to do your best?
11. Do you prefer independent decisions or group decisions?
12. How do you define success?
13. Finish this sentence: The job is done when...
14. What can I do that would help you?

15. What excites you about this assignment?
16. What concerns do you have about this assignment?
17. What do you do when you are: hungry, angry, tired or frustrated?
18. What do you like most about us working together?
19. What do you find most challenging about working together?
20. How can our work styles complement each other?
21. How can we keep our working relationships positive and productive?

RECOMMENDATIONS, TIPS, IDEAS, AND SUGGESTIONS FOR CREATING AND STORING YOUR OWN COLLECTION OF INDEX CARD GAMES AND ACTIVITIES

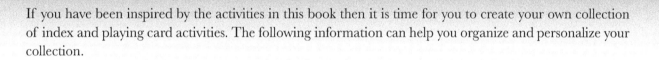

If you have been inspired by the activities in this book then it is time for you to create your own collection of index and playing card activities. The following information can help you organize and personalize your collection.

ABOUT INDEX CARDS

Let's begin with some basic information about index cards. In North America, index cards come in three common sizes (3x5, 4x6 and 5x8 inches) packaged with 100 cards per deck. Some office supply stores carry half-size index cards (3x2.5 inches). In other parts of the world (Spain, for example) you can also find smaller index cards (No. 1 cards are 65x95 mm or roughly 2.5x3.75 inches) and larger ones (No. 5 cards are 160x220 mm or approximately 6.25x8.5 inches). Other cards are also available, such as business cards (2x3.5 inches), calling cards and note cards of various sizes, shapes, patterns (plain, lined, grid) and colors. For large projects, you can purchase index weight paper (8.5x11 inches) such as Wausau Exact Index.

Index stock is fairly uniform around the world, but recently "heavyweight" index cards (about 50 percent thicker than regular index cards) have become available. For most of the projects in this book, the common weight of index card stock is acceptable. If you plan to use your cards often, you might consider laminating these cards.

Office supply stores carry both white and colored index cards (including bright neon colors). For truly unique index stock, visit a paper or craft store where you can typically find a complete pallet of colors and textures on card stock.

THE HISTORY OF INDEX CARDS

Index cards and the index card filing system were invented by Carl Linnaeus in the late 1700's and popularized in libraries a century later by Melvil Dewey. While computerized records have largely replaced index card filing systems, the cards themselves are still widely used for craft, office, home and personal use.

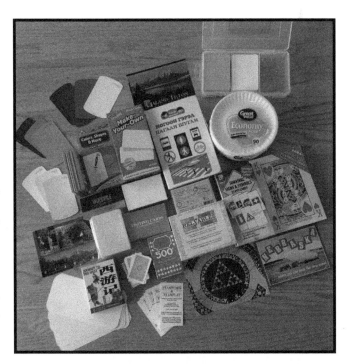

ALTERNATIVES TO INDEX CARDS

If you happen to be in a location where index cards are unavailable, you can often substitute small paper plates for about the same price. You can also repurpose old playing cards, educational flash cards, business cards and other cardlike objects to create your collection of index card games and activities.

STORING INDEX CARDS

Once you create the cards necessary for an activity in this book, you will need a place to organize and store these cards. In the photograph shown here, you'll find my creative collection of index card–sized storage containers, boxes, files and envelopes. My favorite is the zippered clear window envelopes available at Walmart.com for less than a dollar each. You can easily use different colored envelopes for each activity or write the name of each activity in permanent marker on the back of each envelope. You can also find index cards and index cards on perforated sheets that you can run through your printer at Walmart.com.

There are two other storage devices that are worth mentioning here, especially if you create multiple sets of activity cards. The first is a simple photo album, with multiple clear plastic pages for storing 3x5 activity cards. The second is a multipocket coupon holder, available in office supply stores. This particular file system will keep a dozen or more different activity cards well organized and at your fingertips.

One of the more interesting repurposing storage containers I discovered for holding my activity cards is old video cassette (VHS) storage boxes. These plastic boxes have snap closures and you can easily put 100 or more cards into each container.

PRINTING ON INDEX CARDS

For many of the activities in this book, printing text or illustrations on multiple index cards can be a time-saving alternative to hand drawing all the information you need. One of the simplest ways to print index cards is to purchase index card stock (heavy weight paper, such as Wausau Exact Index 110#), print on it as you would any 8.5x11 inch paper, and then cut out 3x4 (or 4x6, or 5x8) index card pieces after printing. Avery (the home office supply company) makes printable 3x5 cards suitable for inkjet or laser printers (Avery #5388) and each pack comes with free templates, perfect for many of the activities in this book. With most computer word processors, you just identify which Avery product code you are using and the templates automatically are presented. Another alternative is to print on large labels and then attach these labels to index cards.

You can also print directly onto index cards using some printers, typically the biggest cards work best. You can find techniques for printing flashcards, index cards and even playing cards at such websites as www. instructables.com.

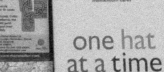

RESOURCES AND REFERENCES

"There are two things that will make you the person you are going to be in the next ten years; the books you read and the friends you keep."

While researching activities for this book, I read dozens of publications new and old, filled with interesting ideas. What follows here are my favorite books and the ones I found most valuable. I hope you will seek out these books and enjoy them as much as I have.

BOOKS WITH CARD ACTIVITIES

Fun with Pencil and Paper by Joseph Leeming, 1955, ISBN 978-0-3973-0300-9. You can turn almost every activity in this book into an index card activity.

Games and Fun with Playing Cards by Joseph Leeming, 1949, ISBN 978-0-4862-3977-2. One of my favorite books for creative ways to play with cards.

Deal Me In! The Use of Playing Cards in Teaching and Learning by Margie Golick, 1988, ISBN 978-0-8843-2253-X.

Playing with a Full Deck by Michelle Cummings, 2007, ISBN 978-0-7575-4094-3. Fifty-two team activities using a deck of cards.

The Teamwork & Teamplay Training Cards by Jim Cain, 2014, ISBN 978-0-9882-0462-1. Seventeen teambuilding activities using a very unique deck of large-format cards, with instructions.

Teambuilding with Index Cards by Jim Cain, 2018, ISBN 978-1-5249-6498-6. One hundred eighty activities for teachers, trainers, facilitators, and group leaders of all kinds that turn ordinary index and playing cards into extraordinary teaching tools.

Team Building A La Card: Affordable Adaptations of Team Activities by Jon Grizzle, 2018, ISBN 978-1-5448-5349-9. Familiar team activities modified to be facilitated with playing cards.

The Chiji Guidebook—A Collection of Experiential Activities and Ideas for Using Chiji Cards by Chris Cavert and Steven Simpson, 2010, ISBN 978-1-8854-7384-4. The book that goes along with one of the first decks of pictorial debriefing cards ever made.

When you are searching for books, you can obviously find many of the above titles at www.amazon.com but did you know that if you go to www.smile.amazon.com (same site, same prices, same service) Amazon will donate a portion of your payment to the charity of your choice?

Another valuable resource for used books and occasionally out-of-print books is the website www.allbookstores.com, which will show you a list of bookstores that currently carry the title of your choice, what they cost (including shipping) and where to find them.

ADDITIONAL BOOKS BY JIM CAIN

Teamwork & Teamplay by Jim Cain and Barry Jolliff, ISBN 978-0-7872-4532-0. 417 award-winning pages that are considered by many to be the "essential" teambuilding text.

Essential Staff Training Activities by Jim Cain, Clare Marie Hannon and David Knobbe, ISBN 978-0-7575-6167-2. Make your next staff training active, engaging, memorable, effective and fun!

A Teachable Moment—A Facilitator's Guide to Activities for Processing, Debriefing, Reviewing and Reflection by Jim Cain, Michelle Cummings and Jennifer Stanchfield, ISBN 978-0-7575-1782-2. One hundred thirty of the best debriefing techniques ever assembled.

The Revised and Expanded Book of Raccoon Circles by Jim Cain and Tom Smith, ISBN 978-0-7575-3265-8. Over 100 team activities with a single piece of tubular webbing. This publication is also available in Japanese and Chinese.

Teambuilding Puzzles by Jim Cain, Chris Cavert, Mike Anderson and Tom Heck, ISBN 978-0-7575-7040-7. One hundred puzzles for teams that build valuable life skills. Useful for escape rooms and other teambuilding challenges.

The Big Book of Low Cost Training Games by Jim Cain and Mary Scannell, ISBN 978-0-07-177437-6. Effective activities to reinforce training topics. Also available with a translation in Polish.

Find Something To Do! by Jim Cain, ISBN 978-0-9882046-0-7. Over 130 powerful activities that require no equipment at all.

Rope Games by Jim Cain, ISBN 978-0-9882046-1-4. Facilitate an infinite variety of team challenges with a finite collection of ropes.

The Teamwork & Teamplay International Edition by Jim Cain, ISBN 978-0-9882046-3-8. Fifty-one team activities, sixteen languages, one world!

100 Activities That Build Unity, Community & Connection by Jim Cain, ISBN 978-1-60679-374-9. The world's best icebreakers and so much more!

Team Activities That Promote Learning and *More Team Activities That Promote Learning* by Jim Cain, Chinese and English in one volume.

Teambuilding with Index Cards by Jim Cain, ISBN 978-1-5249-6498-6. One hundred eighty activities for teachers, trainers, facilitators and group leaders of all kinds that turn ordinary index and playing cards into extraordinary teaching tools.

You can find even more teambuilding activities and free downloadable PDF files from Jim Cain on the Teamwork & Teamplay website, at www.teamworkandteamplay.com.

RECOMMENDED DECKS OF CARDS

As I write the pages of this book, I stare up at a bookcase in my office filled with card-related books, articles, activities and more. One entire shelf is filled with a wide variety of cards from around the world. Here are some of my favorites that I am happy to recommend:

Happy Salmon—The High-Fivin', Fin-Flapping Card Game, by Ken Gruhl and Quentin Weir, from North Star Games (www.NorthStarGames.com).

Zoom (ISBN 978-0-1405-5774-9) and *Re-Zoom* (ISBN 978-0-1405-5694-0) books by Istvan Banyai. Just cut the binding off these inexpensive books and you have illustrations that form a continuous collection of zoomed images. These make for an interesting communication activity.

Reality Check—Zoom Between Worlds, sixteen large-format picture cards from Metalog Training Tools (www. metalogtools.com).

Exploding Kittens, a card game for people who are into kittens and explosions, and laser beams and sometimes goats, by the creative minds of Elan Lee, Matthew Inman and Shane Small (www.explodingkittens.com).

52 Fathoms, playing cards for the adventurous at heart. A collection of Kerfuffle-like actions printed on playing cards, from High 5 Adventure Learning Center (www.high5adventure.org).

Ubuntu – There exists a common bond between us all... from High 5 Adventure Learning Center (www. high5adventure.org). Dozens of fun games with these creative picture cards.

Epic Cards (Experience, Passion, Integrity and Creativity), tools for teaching and promoting creativity, by Daniel Cape (www.experiencetocreativity.com).

Training Cards from Teamwork & Teamplay by Jim Cain, offers fifty-two large-format cards in full color, plus instructions for playing seventeen of the best activities from this book. Available from www.training-wheels.com, www.trainerswarehouse.com and www.healthylearning.com. Also available in a dual-language Chinese/English version (see www.teamworkandteamplay.com for more information).

Five Crowns, the game isn't over 'til the kings go wild! One of my favorite card games for two to seven players, from Set Enterprises (www.setgame.com).

One Night Ultimate Werewolf, by Ted Alspach and Akihisa Okui, from Bézier Games. A quick game for three to ten players, complete with a downloadable app that instructs the play.

Chiji Cards by Steve Simpson, are one of the first (and best) picture style debriefing cards ever. Now with a full book of ideas for their use (www.chiji.com).

Some ee Cards, a creatively quirky collection of electronic greeting cards that can be found online at www.someeecards.com.

Fine Line, playing cards in pictures and words. A truly unique deck of playing cards available from www.dearadamobjects.com.

Action Pak Debriefing Cards, 100 large-format cards that span the full range of human emotion (both positive and negative attributes) with illustrations and words. Designed by Craig Rider and available from Teamwork & Teamplay. Email Jim Cain (jimcain@teamworkandteamplay.com) for more information.

Soularium Cards, a dialog in pictures; fifty images and questions with a Christian focus, from www.CruPress.com.

Feelings Marketplace Cards and *Feeling Marketplace Games for Kids* from Action for Excellence Int'l (info@AEIAction.com). Large-format cards with illustrations and words for exploring feelings.

EmotiCARDS from the creative minds of Ryan Eller and Jerrod Murr. Emoji images in color on high-quality cards. There is also an activity guide available at www.myparadignshift.org.

Images of Organizations, Visual Metaphor Cards from RSVP Design. Available at www.shop.rsvpdesign.co.uk. The best visual debriefing cards I know of, in the entire world!

Workstations, a challenging team problem-solving game, also from RSVP Design. Similar to the activity *13 Clues* in this book (www.shop.rsvpdesign.co.uk).

Climer Cards, reflection cards based on watercolor painting by creativity expert and facilitator Amy Climer (www.climerconsulting.com).

Family Talk, 100 question cards to get the whole family talking. Perfect for the activity The Question Box, in this book (www.aroundthetablegames.com).

Shiruranai Cards, abstract line-art reviewing cards from Project Adventure Japan (www.pajapan.com).

Strength Cards and *Choosing Strengths*, colorful cards that spark life-changing conversations about strengths, from St. Luke's Innovative Resources (www.innovativeresources.org).

Picture This, color photographs for conversation and reflection (www.innovativeresources.org).

One Hat at a Time, Momentum Cards, for people with more hats than heads, more roles than time! Created by Christie Latona and Laura Lind-Blum (www.onehatatatime.com).

Water Works, Leaky Pipe Card Game. Still a classic, and you can find copies at Amazon.com.

Agile in A Flash, Speed-Learning Agile Software Development, Agile Cards for Agile Teams. Yes, you can even use cards for learning how to program software! Jeff Langr and Tim Ottinger have created a deck of learning cards for Agile Project Management, ISBN 978-1-8343-5671-5.

MY FAVORITE ACTIVITIES IN THIS BOOK

I chose the 180 activities in this book from an original collection of over 300 possibilities that I had researched, invented and collected over the years. Many of these activities have produced amazing results with groups. Some of my favorite card activities in this book include:

The Big Question – The best icebreaker I know!
First Impressions – A guessing game/icebreaker, so much fun.
The Dice Game – A fun way to play together.
Match Cards – A wonderful way to explore character with teams.
The Big Answer – A unique way to solicit help from your friends and colleagues.
Word Circles – One of the best linguistic team challenges ever.
Kerfuffle – Creating three minutes of pure chaos.
Thumbprints – A visual debriefing technique.
The Gratitude Jar – Reflecting on gratitude can make you happier and healthier!
Monster Cookie Recipe – The best cookie recipe I know!
Quotes in Order – A unique way to memorize a significant quotation.
Expressionist Teambuilding – A fast-paced, artistic teambuilding activity.
Thirteen Clues – Logical puzzles come to life in this thirteen-part mystery.
KABOOM! – An explosively fun way to learn.
Numerical Logic Puzzles – Introducing Suguru, you'll love it.
21 Questions for Building Positive Relationships – Open communication.

A FINAL THOUGHT ABOUT THE VALUE OF CARDS

A noteworthy quote (about cards), from the 1914–1917 Imperial Trans-Antarctic Expedition of Sir Ernest Shackleton and the crew of the Endurance. *Two British pounds per card in 1916 would be worth about $10,000 U.S. dollars for a full deck of cards today!

> *"At this period, the monotony had become terrible. Fortunately, before the Endurance sank I had retrieved three packs of cards. One of these was Shackleton's own, but this did not prevent me presenting it to him with lordly generosity, for which he thanked me very much. Another I gave to the men, and the third I kept for my own tent. These cards proved a godsend. I once worked out that they were worth two pounds* a card to us!"*

—Frank Worsley
Ship's Captain of the *Endurance*
While stranded on the ice at Patience Camp in Antartica
1916

ABOUT JIM CAIN AND TEAMWORK & TEAMPLAY

Dr. Jim Cain is the author of seventeen texts filled with powerful team and community-building activities from around the world, including *Teamwork & Teamplay* (which won the Karl Rohnke Creativity Award presented by the Association for Experiential Education [AEE]), *A Teachable Moment, Teambuilding Puzzles, The Book of Raccoon Circles* (now available in Japanese and Chinese), *Essential Staff Training Activities, The Big Book of Low Cost Training Games, Find Something To Do, Rope Games, Teamwork & Teamplay Training Cards* (now available in a Chinese/English version), *The Teamwork & Teamplay International Edition* (featuring fifty-one activities translated into sixteen different languages in the same book!), *100 Activities That Build Unity, Community & Connection, Team Activities That Promote Learning, More Team Activities That Promote Learning* and this book, *Teambuilding with Index Cards*. His train-the-trainer workshops are legendary in the adventure-based learning world and have taken him to all fifty states and thirty-two countries (so far). He is the innovator of over 100 teambuilding activities used by corporations, colleges, camps, conferences and communities. But mostly, Jim likes to share his unique collection of team challenges, games, puzzles, training techniques and community-building activities with audiences of all kinds, all over the world.

Jim is also the creative mind behind his active training company Teamwork & Teamplay, which provides staff trainings, facilitation, teambuilding equipment, debriefing tools, curriculum development, reference books, conference workshops, keynote and playnote presentations, and teambuilding consulting services.

For more information or to invite Dr. Jim Cain to your next event, visit the Teamwork & Teamplay website at www.teamworkandteamplay.com or contact Jim Cain at (585) 637-0328.

Jim Cain, Ph.D.
Teamwork & Teamplay
468 Salmon Creek Road
Brockport, New York 14420 USA
Phone (585) 637-0328
jimcain@teamworkandteamplay.com
www.teamworkandteamplay.com

THE TEAMWORK & TEAMPLAY TRAINING CARDS

For those that prefer a professionally formatted and printed collection of index card activities, I created a unique deck of large-format playing cards as a companion deck for this book. I chose seventeen of the most unique and powerful activities from this book, along with instructions and had a commercial publisher print them in color onto sixty-five large-format (5x8) heavy card stock.

The Teamwork & Teamplay Training Cards pictured here include painless icebreakers, inspirational thoughts for the day, four unique and challenging mysteries to solve, puzzles, character building activities, team challenges, tongue twisters, linguistic challenges, playful card games, powerful debriefing ideas, creative problem-solving activities, card tricks and many more activities that create wonderful teachable moments. Specific activities (by name) include The Big Question, Thirteen Clues, The Match Game (with words of character), R U More Like Questions, Hieroglyphics, Card Tricks, Acronyms, the Personal Pyramid, Tongue Twisters, the 15th Object, Pass the Deck, Watch 4 It, the debriefing activity Thumbprints, and many more. The deck also includes a complete collection of playing cards (fifty-two) and thirteen instruction/debriefing cards.

These cards (along with many of my other books are available from Training Wheels, Inc. (www.training-wheels.com), Trainer's Warehouse (www.trainerswarehouse.com) and the Healthy Learning (American Camp Association) Bookstore (www.healthylearning.com).

In 2018, I also created a version of these cards with both English and Chinese text on them, available from FangMa International Education and Culture Company, LTD of Beijing, China. For more information about these cards, visit the T&T website at www.teamworkandteamplay.com.

THE TEAMBUILDING WITH INDEX CARDS PLAYLIST

Here is a list of every activity in this book. Use this list the next time you are planning an event.

ICEBREAKERS AND OPENING ACTIVITIES

The Big Question • Autographs • First Impressions • Who Belongs to This Card? • Doodles • Thought for the Day
Have You Ever? • Personal Pyramid • Are You More Like? • Statistical Treasure Hunt • Draw Me a Story
Best, Worst, First • X Marks the Spot • Story Cards • Crossword Names • The Question Box • Believe It or Knot
Broken Token • The To Do List • The Soap Box • Links of Chain

TEAM CHALLENGES

Quotes in Order • Match Cards • Word Circles • The Lighthouse • Where Do You Stand? • Blind Find • Three Chairs
Sabotage • The 15th Object • Snowflakes & Butterflies • Acronyms & Abbreviations • Back Writing • Back Writing 2.0
Hieroglyphics • Reach for Your Dreams • Thirteen Clues • Einstein's Riddle • Alphabet Soup • Next • Changing Places
Tangrams • Interference • Stepping Stones • The Proper Sequence • The Transportation Card • Build It • Card Tossing
Paper Pushers • Pass / Fail • A Perfect Match • Part of the Rainbow • It's Your Choice • Everything on the Tray
The Beast • Expressionist Teambuilding • Connections • Four in a Row

PUZZLES AND GAMES

Kerfuffle • The Dice Game • Mrs. Right • The Story Game • Tora, Tora • Birthday Cards • Math Magic • Slam Poetry
Just One Word • Tangram Quilt • The Arrowhead Puzzle • Seven Folds • Conundrum Cards • House & Utilities
Drawing in the Dark • Alphabetically • Tongue Twisters • Riddle Cards • Close all the Doors • Ultimate Tic-Tac-Toe
Triplets • Card Tricks • Speed Spelling • The Walkabout Challenge • Making Stuff Up • Directionally Challenged
What are we Yelling? • Sherlock Holmes • The Internet Shopping Network • Verbose Verbiage • The Whole Story
Seven Dots • Refrigerator Art • Board Games • Why? Because! • Jigsaw Hunt • Numerical Logic Puzzles
Team Origami • Squiggles • Nursery Rhyme Headlines • Nursery Rhyme Mysteries • Obscured • Snap Words
The Secret Word • Pirate's Treasure

Reviewing, Reflection, and Closing Activities

Thumbprints • Fortune Cookies • Pillow Talk • The Free Pass • End of the Day Questions • Watch 4 It
DIY-Debriefing Questions • Worms • The One Ball That Does It All • Message in a Bottle • Post Card Debrief
One for the Road • Consensus Cards • Session Evaluation Cards • Thank You Cards • 5 F's • Share Something
Action Pak Debriefing Cards • The Final Word • Debriefing Bingo Cards • The Toss of a Coin

Creative Things to Do with Playing Cards

Search & Rescue • Pass the Deck • I Doubt It • Press Ten • The Four Card Challenge • The 4x4 Puzzle
The Ten Card Square Puzzle • The 12 Card Racetrack Puzzle • Stack the Deck • Playing Card Icebreaker
Never! • The Hunt • The Poison King • The Extra Card • Four of a Kind • Action / Reaction

Activities for Teachers, Trainers, and Facilitators

The Match Game • Six Word Stories • Environmental Sudoku • The Sudoku Square Technique • One Long Line
Passing Through • The Top Ten • The Creativity Slam • Goal Setting • Searching for the Answers
Almost Lost in Translation • Unique Debriefing Cards • Camouflage • Line Up • Scenarios & Simulations
The Big Answer • KABOOM! • The Value of an Education • The Welcome Mat • A Literary Scavenger Hunt
Creative Group Formation • Hey Buddy, Can't You Read the Sign?

Bonus Activities

Monster Cookies • Prayer Cards • Things Are Not What They Appear • Mind Reading Magic • Word Count
Everyday Haiku • Flat Dice • Dance Cards • Gratitude Cards • He Can Do Little • Redacted Poetry • The Box Maze
Zoom • Five Rooms • The Phonetic Alphabet • First Flight • Unblind Square • Honest Playing Cards • Guess Who?
Gratitude Jars • 21 Questions About Relationships

WHAT PEOPLE ARE SAYING ABOUT JIM CAIN'S NEW BOOK *TEAMBUILDING WITH INDEX CARDS*

I enrolled in a leadership program in my community. At our first meeting, the program facilitator pulled out a stack of index cards and started passing them around. After several high-powered activities, I was truly impressed with the quality of the event and the outstanding teachable moments generated by such simple resources. At the end of the first program, our facilitator offered to loan us our choice of leadership books to read before our next meeting. I chose the book containing all the index card activities!

It seems like our school district is always reducing our training budget dollars. When our most recent budget allocated less than $50 dollars for training resources, I was worried that we would have to cancel our staff teambuilding workshop this year. Luckily a friend shared with me your Teambuilding with Index Cards book and I created all the resources I needed for almost no money at all. Now my boss thinks I am a teambuilding genius!

When my training department supervisor asked me for my equipment budget request for the year, I told her I only needed ten packs of index cards. Then I showed her a copy of the book Teambuilding with Index Cards. Now everyone in our department has a copy.

Our school may not have all the resources that bigger schools have, but we do have office supplies! That resource and the book Teambuilding with Index Cards enabled me to teach some powerful lessons this past year.

I was pressed for time preparing for a last-minute teambuilding workshop. With no time to purchase teambuilding props, this book was a lifesaver. I just opened the pages, grabbed some markers and index cards and created everything I needed to keep a group of 23 participants engaged for two whole hours. Thanks Jim!

An entire teambuilding program in a deck of cards. Wonderful!

Once again Jim Cain has made the complicated and occasionally difficult challenge of facilitating teambuilding programs very simple indeed.

I spent an hour with your book today and created enough index card training activities to last an entire semester!

I was skeptical that index cards alone could be a valuable teambuilding resource, until I tried a few of the activities from your book. Not only are the props for these activities inexpensive and lightweight, but the activities themselves produce outstanding results with my audiences and workshop participants. I have become a true believer!

250